Beyond Loyalty

Contents

Translator's Note

The issei, or "first generation" of Japanese Americans, immigrated to the United States from Japan in the late 1800s and early 1900s. Their children who were born in this country are known as nisei, meaning "the second generation." Some of these nisei children were sent back to relatives in Japan to attend school for a few years, to absorb their parents' native language and culture. When these young people returned to the United States, the Japanese American community called them "kibei nisei" (meaning nisei who have returned to America), or "kibei" for short. Minoru Kiyota was born in Seattle and grew up in San Francisco, California, and Hiratsuka, Japan, where he lived for four years with his grandparents and attended Japanese schools. He is a kibei.

During World War II, all West Coast residents of Japanese descent—issei, nisei, and kibei alike—were forced from their homes and incarcerated in makeshift concentration camps located in desolate areas of the United States. A high school student at the time, Kiyota was dismayed by this disruption of his life and education and humiliated by the treatment he received. In anger and frustration, he refused to affirm the loyalty statement required of all Japanese Americans in the camps and, under duress, even renounced his American citizenship.

Because of the severe mental anguish Kiyota experienced over these issues, he desperately desired to create a life where questions of political loyalty and disloyalty could no longer tear him apart. This narrative relates his struggle to cope with a situation full of ironies caused by a war between the country of his birth and the country of his ancestry and to deal with the complexities of the reality he faced without compromising his own integrity.

Released from the Tule Lake Segregation Center in March 1946—more than half a year after the war had ended—Kiyota accepted a scholarship to the College of the Ozarks in Arkansas and later completed his bachelor's degree at the University of California, Berkeley. He worked for U.S. Air Force Intelligence during the Korean War, volunteering to be sent north of the 38th parallel. Then, caught in a tangle of legal difficulties concerning his citizenship, his U.S. passport literally yanked from his hands, Kiyota remained in the Far East to continue his studies in Japan, earning both master's and doctoral degrees in Indian philosophy from Tokyo University.

Given these experiences of his early years, Minoru Kiyota is an American who lives and moves between two cultures and who passionately devotes his life to creating a better understanding between them. For more than three decades he has taught Buddhist thought to University of Wisconsin graduate and undergraduate students, supervising twenty-eight Ph.D. students who now teach at colleges and universities around the world—in Japan, Korea, Taiwan, Vietnam, and the United States. In grateful recognition of his personal and scholarly influence on their lives, a number of these former students in 1990 published the volume *Buddha Nature: A Festschrift in Honor of Minoru Kiyota*. Kiyota himself has published and lectured widely on Buddhism and on the martial arts in both Japan and the United States and has organized bilingual conferences to encourage direct dialogue between Japanese and American scholars.

When not teaching Buddhist studies, Kiyota may be found in the University of Wisconsin gym, where he instructs students in the philosophy and practice of *kendō* as a means to integrate the martial and the liberal arts. Here *kendō* is taught as an academic subject, not just as a sport. Enrollment in Kiyota's *kendō* course invariably fills up as soon as registration begins.

Minoru Kiyota originally wrote this book in Japanese while on research leave in Japan, publishing it in that country in 1990 under the title *Nikkei hangyakuji*. With the author's permission, I have translated the book into English, for I believe that Americans need to hear his story. When he wrote the Japanese version, Kiyota cast his narrative as a novel in the third person with a young man named Keiichi as the protagonist. According to the author, the more impersonal form allowed him a needed sense of detachment to describe events that he still found extremely painful to discuss. But *Beyond Loyalty* is not fiction. It is the autobiography of Minoru Kiyota—a feisty kibei who defied the forces working to victimize Japanese Americans during World War II and who ultimately succeeded in overcoming his own bitterness to make a positive contribution to society.

In commenting on the historical context of events in which he participated, Kiyota at times expresses strong feelings—indeed, he clearly voices in these pages his personal judgment on events and people connected to the internment of Japanese Americans. Others have published their own accounts of the same years, and the reader is encouraged to compare these—while keeping in mind that the internment, the loyalty statement, and the Renunciation Act have all since been repudiated by the president, Congress, the courts, and those Americans who sincerely value liberty and justice for all.

The author and I consulted extensively while I worked on the English version of the book. Basically, the original text remains intact, although it has been transposed into first person and a few clarifications were added, repetitious passages deleted, and sections rearranged to contextualize events. All revisions were made with the full participation and approval of the author. He has rewritten the section entitled "Reflections" for the English edition and has added an appendix. Illustrations are from the author's private collection.

Japanese names mentioned in the text are rendered in traditional Japanese manner with family name preceding personal name. The author and other Japanese Americans use the Western order, with surname last. The author is called "Min," a nickname for

Minoru, by English speakers in this country. Forms of address in the Japanese language tend to be more complex than in English and reveal the personal relationship between two individuals and sometimes the social relationship between their families. Thus when addressed in Japanese, young Kiyota is variously called "Botchan" (something like "young master," usually said with affection of a young male belonging to a family of respected social status), "Minoru-kun" (informal and familiar, used by peers or older males), and "Minoru-san" (more formal). These different forms of address have been retained in the English edition, in part to indicate that certain conversations (even in America) are taking place in Japanese and in part to convey the flavor of Japanese culture.

Beyond
Loyalty

1 *Pearl Harbor Day*

December 7, 1941. San Francisco's blue sky was cloudless that Sunday morning, although the heavy, mournful horn echoing over the peaceful port city suggested that fog still shrouded the harbor entrance.

I put on a new white shirt and tie with my good suit and set out at a leisurely pace toward the Presbyterian church on the northeast side of Japan Town. On my way I passed two black men staggering along the sidewalk, apparently still feeling the effects of their Saturday night drinking bout. The Japanese-run stores on Post Street were not yet open, but at the shoeshine stand next to the drugstore a black man was hard at work polishing the shoes of a white man, briskly moving his cloth to the rhythm of a jazz tune he whistled.

I followed Post Street up to Octavia, where the church stood on the north side of the intersection. Some other young churchgoers were already gathered in front, joking among themselves. I cast a shy but appreciative glance toward the young girls in the group, all dressed up for Sunday morning.

This church was originally founded by the missionary Dr. Ernest A. Sturge to serve a small group of first-generation Japanese immigrants—the issei. Dr. Sturge's sermons, later collected in a book entitled *Arrows from My Quiver*, often highlighted the qualities of discipline and austerity that he saw as characterizing both traditional Protestant Christianity and *bushidō*, the code of the

Japanese warrior. This American minister felt at home with the issei, models of that Japanese tradition of stern discipline. And those upright members of the first generation of Japanese immigrants regarded him in turn with great affection. Though Dr. Sturge had passed on years ago, the issei in the congregation still recalled with nostalgia his fatherly presence among them.

The service for the older members of this church was conducted by an issei minister in Japanese and was always the first service on Sunday morning, held from 9:00 to 10:30. Then a Caucasian minister conducted an English service for the American-born second generation—the nisei—from 11:00 to 12:30.

Never very musical, I sang the hymns that Sunday morning in my usual lackluster manner. I listened more or less attentively to the tedious sermon, then bowed my head mechanically for the offering and the prayers. Church for me was pretty much just something to do on a Sunday morning.

After the benediction I hurried home, grabbed some lunch, and immediately headed to the matinee at a nearby movie theater. The action-packed western soon enveloped me in its familiar fantasy realm of good guys and bad. That world of black and white was all I knew then—I was still innocent of the world of gray that resides in the interval between good and evil, between right and wrong.

The movie ended just before four o'clock. I walked out of the theater and onto the street and immediately sensed something ominous. The people walking past—both blacks and whites—were looking tense, apprehensive. Then the shrill cry of a newsboy on the street corner banished my movie-theater daze and thrust me rudely into the real world.

He was yelling at the top of his lungs, "Extra! Extra! Japs attack Pearl Harbor!"

That newsboy's angry cry and the paper's bold, black headlines seemed to accuse me personally of some terrible wrongdoing. Trembling and breathless, I ran for home as fast as I could.

I am an American. But I am also Japanese.

2 A Child of Two Homelands

My father grew up in a farming community in Kanagawa Prefecture southwest of Tokyo. While a young man, he was drafted into the Japanese Army to fight as a private in the Russo-Japanese War of 1904–1905. A few years after Japan's victory he emigrated to the United States. Although not at all a robust man, the only job he could find in this country was lumbering in the mountain forests of the Northwest near the Canadian border. He worked there for over a decade before finally saving enough money to return to Japan to find a bride. By this time he was in his late thirties, and the young woman he married was more than ten years his junior.

When my father returned with his new wife to the United States, he opened a small dry-cleaning establishment on a street corner in Seattle. World War I had ended and business was pretty good for a few years. Then came the worldwide crash of 1929, and the dry-cleaning business failed. My first memories are of the period after the crash, when our family had moved south to San Francisco.

The four-story Kashū Hotel stood on a corner in San Francisco's Japan Town. Its owner was a man from Fukuoka in southern Japan. The glass front door was heavy for a child to push open, but once inside five or six easy steps led to the front desk. Across from the desk extended an elegant lobby with a plush carpet. There, however, the elegance ended. Just beyond the lobby a corridor branched into three separate stairwells, each leading to a different floor above. Every floor of the hotel had a high ceiling, so these stairs were extremely long and dark. Sometimes I saw the bigger children playing on the dirty, tattered carpet covering the steps.

Nearly all the guests in this hotel were Japanese. Most were long-term residents, so the majority of accommodations were equipped with kitchens and partitioned into more than one room. The building itself was rectangular with a small inner courtyard where reeking garbage cans made it impossible for people living in the inside rooms to open their windows. Those inner apartments, moreover, were so dark that their occupants had to keep their lights burning even in the daytime.

For all its elegant lobby, the hotel was a dismal place to live.

My parents rented two rooms in the front of the hotel facing Sutter Street. I passed many an hour gazing out the window at the street cars clattering up and down the hill every ten minutes or so. Across the street was a big redbrick car repair shop that must have been built during the years when Fords were being produced in large quantities. These were Depression days, however, and there were few cars to repair now. On the whole, the neighborhood around the hotel was a quiet one.

I often went with Mother to call on another hotel resident, an elderly lady named Mrs. Yoshida, who came from Wakayama Prefecture in Japan. She lived in one of the dimly lit inside rooms. We would find her shelling beans or knitting, her kitten frisking about her feet in pursuit of the ball of yarn. Mrs. Yoshida was a widow with no children, who earned her living as a cleaning lady in the homes of white families.

Sometimes she would confide in me hopefully, "You know, I'm going to hurry up and save my money so I can go back to Japan pretty soon."

At other times she was not so optimistic.

"*You'll* burn a stick of incense for me when I die, won't you?" she would plead.

An old bachelor in his seventies stopped by frequently to visit my parents. He came to this country from Fukui Prefecture in Japan. This man entertained us with tales of a time when the neighborhood around the hotel was all open space, just a few decades before. In those days, he told us, there were big horse barns and rowdy men swaggering about with six-shooters. Some of the houses and sheds in the neighborhood did still look as though they might be converted horse barns. The old man loved to reminisce about those good old days and to boast that he, too, had carried a pistol. But now he was old, and he went faithfully every Sunday to services at the new Honganji Buddhist church on the corner of Pine and Octavia. Faced with old age and death, he had turned to the faith of his ancestors, the Buddhist Shinshū sect, which had deep roots in his home prefecture in Japan.

His friend Mr. Ōta, a man in his fifties, came from Shizuoka Prefecture. He was also reputed to have packed a pistol and to have frequented the local gambling establishments in his youth. Now, though, Mr. Ōta lived a quiet life running a barbershop on Geary Street. On chilly winter days the gas heater in his shop burned from morning to night, a ring of middle-aged men huddling close to its warmth. Ōta had a wife in Japan and clearly longed to go home, but he showed no sign of doing so.

Unlike his elderly friend, Mr. Ōta was not the least bit religious. After he closed up shop at night he would go out, get drunk on whiskey, and then come back to the hotel and crawl into bed with all his clothes on. Still, he was a kind man. Knowing how poor my family was, he gave me a haircut once a month at no charge to my parents. On Sundays he occasionally took me to Ocean Beach, an amusement park by the sea in San Francisco. He loved to show off his skill at the shooting gallery there. Whenever he hit all the targets he would treat me to a hot dog and a Coke—a real feast, I thought!

I loved this irreligious fellow—and not just because he gave me free haircuts or took me to the amusement park. Although I didn't understand such things at the time, I think it was more a matter of the spirit. Ōta never troubled anyone else with his loneliness; he contented himself with his barber trade and refused to indulge in self-pity. Most likely it was pride that kept him from going home to Japan. Like all the other issei, he had come to America full of youthful hopes and dreams, but as he encountered the real hardships of life in a strange land, his hopes had evaporated one by one. For solace, he turned to his whiskey and refused to think about past or future. He did not try to conceal his human failings, though. At least he made the effort to remain true to himself.

Years later Mr. Ōta did at last return to Japan, just before war broke out in the Pacific.

After supper one chilly winter's evening shortly before Christmas, I went into the living room of our hotel apartment to sit by the gas heater. As I basked in its warmth, idly fingering the curtain that served as a room divider, I became drowsy and without thinking pulled the curtain a little too close to the heater. Flame instantly leapt from heater to curtain and a pillar of fire mounted to the ceiling. My screams brought Mother rushing from the kitchen where she had been cleaning up the evening meal. She quickly pulled a quilt off the bed and threw it on the fire to smother the flames, barely averting a much greater disaster. But now the ceiling and walls around the curtain were charred and ugly.

All night Mother agonized over what to do. Early the next morning she hurried down to find the hotel manager. When she explained to him what had happened, apologizing abjectly, the young man took pity and assured her that he would not inform the hotel owner. He told her that if our family could find another place to live right away, then he himself would repair the walls and the ceiling. A friend helped my parents locate a new place to rent—the second-floor apartment of an old three-story house near the corner of Webster and Geary—and we moved our few belongings that very day.

Our new home was at the edge of Japan Town, in a neighborhood with a mixed population of blacks and Japanese. The place was run-down, but the rent was cheap. It had a large kitchen and five big rooms. All the houses in Japan Town were pretty old. In the fire that followed the great San Francisco earthquake of 1906, the area of the city east of Van Ness Avenue had burned completely and was subsequently rebuilt. The west side, where Japan Town was located, however, had escaped the fire and was full of aging dwellings that pre-dated the quake.

Since most Japanese immigrants had received only a grammar school education in Japan, they brought little in the way of mar-ketable skills when they came to this country. About their only option when they settled in cities, as my parents did, was to work as servants in the homes of white families. After the failure of my father's Seattle dry-cleaning business and our subsequent move to San Francisco, he never again seemed to have the ambition to try anything on his own. He was a hard worker but a nervous sort, stub-born and inflexible. He had one talent, though, and that was to per-form faithfully any task assigned to him. In that sense he was well suited to work for other people. He found a job as a live-in servant in a Caucasian household and resigned himself to that undistin-guished existence.

The head of the large three-generation family for whom my father worked was an entrepreneur of French descent. The house-hold already had a cook, a butler, and a maid, but it was such a big family that there was always plenty of work. My father used the skills he had acquired in his business in Seattle, doing laundry and iron-ing all day long. Then he would help wash the pots and pans after dinner.

I remember my father liked to boast that he was "a gentle-man's gentleman." Indeed, he always dressed in suit and tie when he went out, his black shoes polished to a luster. But his own dreams had long since died. On his weekly day off he would visit us, appar-ently for lack of any other outside interests. It seemed as though he was there just to kill the time. If Mother was out working, he would fix dinner for the two of us—usually bread and sausage—but he never had much to say to his son, so we ate our meals in silence.

Sometimes my father spent the night at home before return-ing to work. On those occasions he arose at five o'clock the next morning, put on his suit and tie and shiny black shoes, and stealth-ily slipped out the front door. Soon afterwards, Mother got up and prepared to leave for her job. Warm in my bed, I listened to the sounds of her departure. For a long time after she left I would gaze at the spider's web in one corner of the aging ceiling, eyes filled with tears of thankfulness for my mother. I did not, however, see much to appreciate about my father.

Early one Sunday morning, the landlord came pounding on our front door without bothering to ring the doorbell. I shuddered when I heard him. My father, who was sleeping later than usual in the bed beside me, drew the quilt over his head and let Mother go to the door. She pulled the string to release the lock at the bottom of the stairs, and the landlord, a huge man, came bounding up the steps with terrifying force, loudly demanding his rent. When Mother told him she did not have the rent money ready for him because it was a Sunday, he raised his hand threateningly.

"You dirty Japs!"

He spat out each individual word.

"Well, you'd better have it by tomorrow!" he blustered, and crashed back down the stairway, slamming the door as he left.

After that incident my father came home less and less frequently. Although my parents were still technically married, they now began to live virtually separate lives. My father made no contribution to the support of his family—he was squirreling away every bit of his small earnings for his own future security.

My mother was a woman of independent spirit, but when I was small she was often so ill that she had to spend the day in bed. After my father moved out, however, she forced herself to go to work several hours each day despite her poor health.

Mother worked as a cleaning woman in the homes of white families. Sometimes she took me along with her. One of the families she worked for lived in a luxurious apartment house with a dozen or more expensive automobiles parked outside. The building had several large, silently gliding elevators, but as a domestic employee Mother was not allowed to use these. Instead, she walked down a long corridor and climbed a steep stairway.

Even during the daytime the lights in the hallway and over the stairs shone softly on the thick carpeting in the apartment building. And on San Francisco's chilly spring mornings, it was always comfortable and warm inside this luxurious place. The hearts of the people who lived there, however, seemed as cold and hard as the concrete building itself—and were probably as lonely as its silent corridors.

"You just sit in that chair now, and don't you budge," Mother cautioned me. "The lady who lives here is scary—she'll give you a scolding if you move."

Thus admonished, I would sit absolutely still on my chair for two or three hours at a time, barely breathing. One day as I sat there, I heard a woman screaming hysterically. A few moments later my mother burst into the small room where I waited, a handkerchief held to her tear-stained face. I had no idea what was happening, but the sight of my mother crying upset me terribly. She grabbed me with one hand, her purse with the other, and raced down the steep staircase, through the long hallway, and out the door. Only then did I dare take a deep breath.

"Mama, what happened?" I asked, gazing up at her.

"It was nothing, Minoru. Let's go home now, shall we?" she said, regaining her composure.

Later I learned that Mother had accidentally broken a plate, and her employer had started screaming at her that she was fired. The lady's arrogant tirade was so unbearable that Mother rushed out of her house without getting paid for the day's work—a real shame, since that heartless woman ended up getting her house cleaned for free that day. Young as I was, I felt terribly sorry for my mother, having to work as someone else's servant like that. And I was furious at that mean white lady.

Nevertheless, Mother seemed to have forgotten this incident by the following morning. She quickly located a new job through a Japanese employment agency and went to work for another family. Indeed, she was amazingly cheerful about it all—for now she was going to make better money than before. I was surprised and reassured at the way she bounced back after that terrifying experience. I understand now, though, what was happening then—my mother was developing the instinct for survival that all socially oppressed people must learn if they are to make their way in this world. Luckily, her health began to improve as well.

Another time I went with Mother early in the morning to her job at a large mansion belonging to a different white family. She must have had more work than usual that day, for by lunchtime she still had not come back to the room where I waited for her. I had sat there quietly for hours, but I was a small boy and I badly needed to go to the bathroom. Finally, I could wait no longer and made a large wet circle on the beautiful carpet. Mother didn't scold me, but after that I was no longer allowed to come into that house with her. Instead, I had to sit all day long on a bench in the park across the street, holding a piece of bread with jam, waiting for Mother to finish her work and take me home. I couldn't help but envy the other children my age playing happily in the park with their mothers watching over them. They were all white children.

This park where I spent the days waiting for Mother was a little north of Japan Town, atop a steep hill. It was a large park, bounded on the north by Washington Street and on the south by Sacramento; Gough and Laguna formed its eastern and western boundaries. Officially, it was named Lafayette Park, but as Japanese residents found that difficult to pronounce they usually called it Sacramento Park. There were a number of such parks throughout the city of San Francisco—a bit of city planning inspired by the tragic fire that followed the 1906 earthquake. In case of a similar disaster in the future these green belts were to serve both as firebreaks and places of refuge.

The groundskeepers in the park at first looked askance at the small boy sitting all alone on a bench hour after hour, but soon they began to smile and say, "Hello there, son." After that, they became my silent guardians as they went about their work in the park.

The house where Mother worked was an impressive three-story white mansion across Washington Street on the north side of the park, the home of the president of a large dairy products corporation. Its spacious front yard was crossed by a semicircular drive along which the cars would sweep up to the front entrance and then out again. Beautiful flowers bordered the drive, and trimly mani-cured shrubbery surrounded the house, sternly protecting its pri-vacy. Charming cable cars ran leisurely up and down the street. It was a lovely, peaceful neighborhood.

I always stayed within sight of the mansion, but at times my gaze was drawn to the beautiful scene of San Francisco Bay in the distance below the hilltop park. Now and then the heavy sound of a ship's horn would break the silence. One morning, I spotted a large, handsome vessel with a Japanese Rising Sun flag that fluttered in the morning breeze. It was one of the ships on the regular run of the Japan Mail Line. Although I had never been to Japan, I recognized the flag. I jumped off the park bench and shouted excitedly.

"That's a Japanese ship! It's a Japanese ship!"

I chased after the great ship, watching its progress as it sailed slowly toward the mail piers along the east side of the bay, sounding its horn intermittently as it traveled. Finally it moved out of view.

Someday I'm going to Japan on that ship! I vowed to myself.

After that I always watched eagerly for more Japanese ships when I was in the park.

Soon I was old enough to begin attending public school. I was self-conscious at first among so many Caucasian children, but they included me in their play without a second thought. I adored my young teacher, Miss Tuft. Every morning she would greet us in her clear, gentle voice.

"Good morning! How are you this morning?"

I would grin with delight, quite sure that her words were meant for me alone. Our class began each day with teacher and pupils all sitting together in a circle. In this atmosphere, I soon felt confi-dent that both the Japanese and the Caucasian children in the class were my friends. Racism did not exist in this realm of small children.

There were differences among us, however. The school served a healthy snack to the pupils at ten o'clock each morning, but since my family could not afford the cost of the snack, I remained in the classroom every day while other children went to get their milk and cookies. On the days when a child was absent, Miss Tuft always gently urged me to go and take the extra snack. I squirmed in embarrassment every time this happened, but in the end I accepted her kindness. Perhaps if I had been a Caucasian child, I might have taken the milk and cookies with less embarrassment. Logically, if a child were absent and no one drank the milk, it would just go to waste—there really was no particular reason to be grateful to the teacher. Despite my family's poverty, however, I had absorbed an Asian sense of shame, and I had learned the meaning of gratitude. I don't think it was just a matter of culturally different value systems, though. Even as a small child, I somehow intuited that such apparently trifling matters *do* express something significant about the relationship between two human beings.

Miss Tuft was skilled at drawing out the special talents of each child in her class. Dewey's philosophy of pragmatic education was then in its heyday, and Miss Tuft exemplified the very best of this approach. One day, for instance, she asked all the pupils who had dogs at home to bring them to school. She assembled the children and the dozen or so dogs on the roof of the school and proceeded to explain in detail the distinctive characteristics of each breed, allowing us plenty of time to get acquainted with the dogs. Through this process, Miss Tuft managed to take advantage of the natural affection between children and animals to foster friendship among the children themselves.

I thrived in the warm environment of Miss Tuft's classroom, excelling especially in arithmetic and spelling. Miss Tuft was always generous with her praise, and in response I studied even harder. The pupils' record chart was posted on the classroom wall, and those who did well received stars by their names. The Japanese names invariably had many stars after them. From an early age the Japanese children would quietly but persistently strive to do their best in school, whatever their family's economic circumstances.

At the end of each school year, my mother entrusted me with a costly and beautifully wrapped Japanese gift to take to my Caucasian teacher. The parents of other Japanese American pupils did likewise, even though almost all our families were poor. Long inured as they were to adversity and oppression, our parents were deeply grateful to the teachers for their efforts to give us children new opportunities through education.

When I was in the fourth grade, Mother told me that I must learn some Japanese. She read to me from children's picture books every evening after she came home from work so that I would begin to associate the written symbols with their sounds. She also read to me from a book of moral precepts that she herself had studied in school in Japan as a young girl. The contents of this book were quite simple— it was a collection of old adages. Proverbs like "Those who study will succeed; the lazy will be beggars" were presented so vividly in the text and illustrations that even a young child could grasp their meaning. That saying in particular impressed upon me the idea that even the oppressed could succeed if only they applied themselves to their studies. It was old-fashioned advice, but I knew that it spoke to my own situation. I looked into my mother's eyes and promised her that I would indeed study hard.

Soon after that I began attending after-school classes at Golden Gate Institute, the largest Japanese language school in San Francisco. From the Japanese teachers there, I learned the rudiments of the language and after a few months began to memorize some of the Chinese characters in which it is written. I did not very much like studying at this Japanese language school, however. I got tired of mechanically memorizing all those characters and chanting aloud from the insipid textbooks they gave us. The Japanese instructors in that school could have learned a great deal about effective teaching methods from my Caucasian public school teachers.

Besides, I wanted to play after school like the white children. Even my nisei friend Joe didn't have to go to Japanese language school, and I envied his more permissive home life. So, despite my earnest vow to my mother and unbeknownst to her, I began to skip Japanese classes to play touch football in Sacramento Park with Joe and other friends. One day, though, when Mother left work early because she was not feeling well, she found me playing ball with my friends in the park. She did not say a word, just looked at me and hurried on toward home. Chagrined at being caught, I followed silently after her. When we got home, she turned to me.

"Minoru, I would gladly work my fingers to the bone for your education, but I am *not* prepared to work so that you can amuse yourself in the park," she said quietly but firmly.

I had nothing to say to that.

"Next year you will go to Japan and you will be attending school there. You had better study Japanese now so your Japanese classmates won't laugh at you," she told me.

Japan! A land I had seen only in pictures, the place I had longed to go ever since I was a small boy. I hung my head with contrition. Now I was genuinely sorry for skipping Japanese classes, but I found myself unable to apologize in words to my mother. I told myself sternly, though, that if I were going to Japan, then I had better attend Japanese classes every day and study as hard as I could.

Not long after that, I began attending jūdō classes three evenings a week in an old basement room on Sutter Street. Wisely foreseeing one of the problems I would encounter in school when I got to Japan, Mother insisted that it made more sense for me to learn jūdō rather than football.

"You must prepare yourself so the children in Japan will not make fun of you," she warned me.

The jūdō lessons involved two hours of fierce training. There were two or three young instructors, but it was a sixty-year-old white-haired man who paid special attention to me. He had studied jūdō in Japan as a young man, before coming to the States. He spoke little English and during the day worked as a custodian in an apartment building in San Francisco. At every lesson, after giving instructions on safe ways to fall, he would add basic lessons in footwork and throws. He took particular care to teach me—like him, small in stature—the sort of throws that are most effective when fighting a larger opponent. But he gave me a stern warning.

"You are never to use jūdō in a fight. Jūdō is training for your own personal development. If you ever use it to fight, you are not to come back to this gym again."

This whole endeavor was a new experience for me. Through jūdō I began to discover a world of inner strength that I never before imagined I possessed. It was a kind of strength that even gave me confidence to restrain myself in circumstances where that seemed the wiser course.

One such situation occurred after school one day, when a big Caucasian schoolmate started bullying me. He grabbed me, pushed me down, and lay on top of me, pummeling my face. He was probably trying to impress the girls who were standing around the school yard. I finally managed to get up off the ground and was about to use a jūdō throw in self-defense, when I suddenly remembered my teacher's words of caution. Although I was pretty beaten up by this time and had a bloody nose, I immediately ceased resisting the other boy's assault, meekly allowing him do what he would. Once he no longer got any response from me, he decided it was pointless to inflict any more injury and left the school yard bloated with pride. After he was gone, I got up smiling to myself, proud in the knowledge that I had obeyed the words of my jūdō instructor. I went home, cleaned my wounds, and never told another soul what happened that day.

Reflecting on this fight when I was older, I realized that it was not the jūdō teacher's warning alone that held me back that day. Even though I was still in elementary school, I already possessed a sharp awareness of the racial implications this sort of incident could have. I knew that if I used a jūdō throw on the boy, he might have ended up in the hospital, possibly with a broken back, and the responsibility for his hospital bills would fall on my mother. A white family would almost certainly do all they could to give a Japanese American family trouble in a case like that. Despite the powerful urge to avenge my own personal humiliation, my reluctance to add to my mother's already heavy burdens was even stronger. I would never have let a Japanese American boy attack me like that without a fierce fight, but it was clear to me that I had better not be too successful in any altercations with white boys.

To apply for visas for our journey to Japan, Mother and I had to visit the Consulate General of Imperial Japan. The office was on a corner of Sansome Street in San Francisco's trade and commercial district, an hour by trolley from Japan Town. Although this was my first visit to the consulate, I felt a kinship with the officials there as we approached the building.

They're Japanese like me, I told myself naively.

My naiveté, however, vanished the moment we arrived at the front door of the consulate. This imposing entrance, with its huge Imperial chrysanthemum crest, seemed designed to intimidate any ordinary mortal. And the bureaucrats who presided inside the building took that Imperial crest as their shield, arrogantly flaunting their power and authority over others. Common Japanese citizens could only bow and mutter "Yes, sir," "I see, sir" to the officials' every haughty utterance.

The time came at last for me to bid farewell to my Caucasian teacher and my San Francisco classmates. My father, however—always the faithful servant—did not see fit to take off time from work to tell his son good-bye.

It was April 1934, and the United States was still in the grips of the Depression. On the docks, pickets from the longshoremen's union confronted armed police officers in an atmosphere thick with animosity and mistrust. Mother and I walked past the picketers and up the gangway onto the *Taiyō Maru*, one of the Japan Mail Line ships that I had dreamed would one day take me to Japan. This ship was a huge 10,000-ton passenger liner that had been captured from the Germans during World War I. It was to make a port call in Honolulu and then sail straight on to Yokohama.

As third-class passengers Mother and I were crammed into a three-family compartment in the hold of the ship. With almost no ventilation, the air was stifling. For the first twenty-four hours the ship pitched about in rough waters, and Mother took to her berth with seasickness. I felt just a bit dizzy but not sick and quickly adjusted to the odor of the hold. Then, after that initial twenty-four-hour period, the large, gentle undulations of the sea began to sway in a quieter, fixed rhythm. Two or three days later, I spotted flying fish leaping lightly over the waves and occasionally spied a pod of dolphin swimming nearby.

The spray thrown up by the bow of our ship as it cut through the waves would now and then spill over the deck. At the stern, the propeller created a great whirling vortex with a trail extending far into the distance. Over the roiling waters fluttered a Rising Sun flag, just like the one I had spied from my hilltop vantage point in Sacramento Park when I was a small boy. Now as I gazed at that flag I was filled with a mixture of nostalgia for the city I had left behind and a sense of adventure for what lay ahead.

Like any young boy, I was fascinated with the ship itself. I spent my days exploring its every corner, stymied only by securely locked doors barring the way to the first- and second-class sections. Soon the sailors began to notice me doing my rounds of the ship and included me in their good-natured banter. They even let me join them in the crew's large Japanese-style communal bath, the first I had ever seen, and allowed me to take my meals with them.

All in all, that two-week Pacific journey was the happiest time I could remember in my young life. It was a fitting prelude to my stay in Japan.

Mother grew up in the town of Hiratsuka in Kanagawa Prefecture southwest of Tokyo. Although Hiratsuka had a population of fifty thousand or more, it was still a country town dotted with rice paddies and vegetable fields. In feudal days it had been a post town on the Tōkaidō Road, the famous east-west highway immortalized in the prints of the woodblock artist Hiroshige. An active pleasure quarter just a few hundred yards to the west of Mother's childhood home was a living memento of that earlier era.

East of Hiratsuka flowed the Banyū River. On the west was another stream named the Hanamizu, and beyond it could be seen Mount Kōrai in Ōiso. To the north towered Mount Ōyama, site of Shugendō mountain religious practices, with the villages of Hadano, Isehara, and Atsugi clustered about its base. Quiet pine forests stretched along the lovely shoreline to the south. The waves there were high, however, and a swift undertow near the shore made it a dangerous place to swim, so most people in the area went to Ōiso to swim in the ocean.

During the Meiji period the British Armstrong Company had built a naval powder depot in Hiratsuka, and a railway spur extended out to it from the main Tōkaidō line. An old-fashioned steam engine periodically chugged to and fro on those tracks, tranquilly pulling a freight car. My grandparents lived not far from this siding.

When Mother and I arrived at her family home after our long sea voyage, her parents welcomed me—their only grandchild—with beaming faces and open arms. As instructed by my mother, I left my shoes in the large entryway, and then stepped up onto the polished wooden floor of the front hall, gazing about in wonderment at the tatami-matted rooms before me. Steam whirled upward from the spout of a large iron kettle set over a charcoal brazier in the spacious parlor. I was standing there, enthralled by this scene, when Grandmother came and drew me by the hand into another room, almost as large, on the south side of the house. There she served us dinner.

According to Mother, Grandfather once operated a geisha restaurant in this sprawling residence. That was the reason for the decorative garden in the central courtyard, with its pond full of leisurely swimming carp, and for the spacious rooms that opened onto the garden from every side. In the courtyard, unripe grapes hung heavily in inviting arbors, but I was more intrigued by the pathway leading from this garden to another in the rear of the house. The path led under a huge oak tree and past a small fox-deity shrine originally placed there to draw prosperity to Grandfather's restaurant.

Four leafy paulownia trees stood sentry along the western border of the large garden in the back, their shadows shielding the house from the rays of the late afternoon sun. Grandmother's vegetable garden was in one corner of this large plot. In the field next door I could see an old man slowly making his way along with buckets of night soil balanced on a pole over his shoulders. Far in the distance towered Mount Fuji, looking exactly like its pictures in the books Mother had shown me in America. When I saw the grandeur of that mountain peak, city boy though I was, I began for the first time to feel an affinity with the natural world.

My grandfather was a large man, nearly six feet tall and over 175 pounds. He told me that he was the oldest son in his family. They were landowners in a village about twelve miles from Hiratsuka. For some reason that I never learned—whether the family had fallen on hard times or had disinherited him—Grandfather moved from the village to Hiratsuka while still a comparatively young man.

I never could quite figure out Grandfather's business. Every once in a while he would set off on his bicycle with a small package—heading toward the village of Isehara or sometimes toward Atsugi. He may have been a dealer in curios and antiques, for there were old swords, Buddhist images, scroll paintings, and other collectibles all over the house. Mother simply commented that Grandfather was always trying something new. She didn't seem much concerned about exactly what he was doing. My grandparents did own two houses in Hiratsuka: the large two-story mansion where they lived in the old Asama section and a smaller, two-room house on the other side of a broad avenue. The smaller house was let out to renters, but—looking back—I doubt that the rent brought in by one small house could have supported a household of the size my grandparents maintained, including a maid.

Certainly Grandfather was a man of many talents. He did all the cooking himself when he operated the restaurant, and he built the rental house entirely with his own hands. And he was no amateur in the art of garden design—he had personally laid out the garden in the central courtyard of the main house. In addition, Grandfather was said to be exceptionally astute at appraising antiques.

If Grandfather had a flaw, it was that he was quick to become enthused about something and just as quick to cool off. Perhaps that was due to his firm confidence in his own ability to do well at just about anything he tried. He didn't seem to worry about money, in any case. On the contrary, he always appeared to have plenty to spare. He was away from home at least one or two days a week, ostensibly on business—but it did make me wonder. No doubt about it, he was a fascinating man.

Grandmother was the daughter of a wealthy farmer. She could not read, but she was honest, spirited, and hardworking. One time she stumbled in the garden and broke her wrist, but she never mentioned her pain to anyone. Instead, perspiring profusely, she located a piece of wood, bound it tightly to her wrist with a cord, and went on with her work. Only when urged by the maid did she go to a doctor to have the bone set and then immediately went back to her housework the minute she got home.

Grandmother always worked right along with the maid. Japanese families in those days left open the sliding doors of rooms facing onto the garden except in the coldest winter months, for they considered the garden to be an extension of the house. As a result, those rooms needed to be swept and dusted twice a day. The women did the laundry by hand with a washboard, made their own starch from leftover rice, and ironed the clothes with a heavy iron heated over hot coals. The daily bath was prepared by filling the deep bathtub with cold water pumped from the well; this was then heated by building a fire under the tub. All these tasks along with meal preparation kept Grandmother and the maid busy from dawn until dark.

About ten days after I arrived in Japan, Grandfather came home with a puppy for me. It was a midget Shiba, just like one I'd seen in Miss Tuft's pictures when I was in grade school in America. I was speechless with delight. Grandmother—with characteristic lack of imagination—christened the dog with the English name, Pooch. But the name didn't matter—this dog was the first pet I had ever owned. Every morning when I got up, there would be Pooch jumping all over me, licking my face, hands, and feet. I hugged my puppy, glowing with the pleasure of having another creature to care for and love.

Twice a week a tradesman called "Yassan" would come by my grandparents' house pulling a heavy cart full of fruits and vegetables behind his bicycle. Unlike most Japanese tradesmen, he did not call out loudly to advertise his wares as he went down the street, so if the neighborhood housewives weren't on the alert, they sometimes missed him. Occasionally Yassan took the liberty of entering our garden gate and helping himself to a drink of water at the kitchen pump. Pooch would jump all over him, tail wagging furiously. Neither my grandparents nor the maid seemed to mind these unannounced visits from the vegetable dealer.

Yassan always carried a wooden sword in his cart. Knowing this, the neighborhood boys and girls would gather with anticipation whenever he came, in hopes that he would pull out his weapon for a lighthearted mock sword fight with them. Indeed, he may well have had some experience with kendō, the Japanese art of fighting with wooden swords, for he possessed both a decisive downcut and enough control to avoid touching the children with his weapon.

In the midst of these playful sword fights, Yassan appeared to forget all about his produce business, but meanwhile the merchandise disappeared from his cart. When he had finished entertaining the children, the neighborhood women came up one by one, told him what they had taken, and paid him what they owed.

Occasionally a woman would give him a few extra coins. "For last week," she'd explain.

When Yassan wasn't engaged in mock sword fights, he frequently sat down with the children in a circle around him for a lively chat. It wasn't long before I became fast friends with this man. One day Yassan brought along a book for me, a storybook about a medieval Japanese swordsman named Tsukahara Bokuden. Right then and there he sat down and began to read the book to me. Four or five other children soon appeared out of nowhere and pressed in close to listen. In those days you could find popular storybooks very cheaply in the used bookstores. With their gripping tales of courage and human drama, they were the perfect textbooks to teach the Japanese language to a young boy like me.

But alas, Yassan also had his weaknesses—he was afraid of anything having to do with death. The road in front of my grandparents' house led to the outskirts of Hiratsuka and several villages beyond, but it was also the route to the local crematorium. One day, a long, snakelike funeral procession came down the road with eerie gongs clanging and high-pitched bells ringing. The pallbearers surrounding the casket were strange looking—all robed in white, their white headbands adorned with white paper triangles. Behind them, dressed in black, followed the family and friends of the deceased, handkerchiefs dabbing at swollen eyelids.

As soon as Yassan caught sight of this frightening procession he paled, rushed into our courtyard, and crouched under the big oak tree, terrified at the approach of the corpse. As he cowered under the tree in our garden that day, the maid poured him a cup of cool water from the well and patted his back reassuringly. But soon even she was unable to contain herself any longer and burst out laughing at Yassan's timidity. From that day on, Yassan could never again lift his head in the presence of our maid. For some reason that I could not fathom, though, the two of them seemed nevertheless to be on extremely intimate terms with one another.

Then there was the toothless old priest from the Zen Buddhist temple where my grandparents had been parishioners for decades. Well over eighty years old, the elderly cleric still walked the twelve miles to our house from the temple, steadying his tottery gait by grasping the handle of the old baby carriage he pushed before him. The only things in the carriage were the priest's Buddhist scriptures and his smoking paraphernalia. When he arrived at our front door he called out a perfunctory greeting and then went into the parlor without waiting for Grandmother to invite him. There he sat down by the charcoal brazier and lit his pipe. Even when Grandmother entered the room with tea and formal words of welcome, he barely acknowledged her presence. Perhaps he was hard of hearing.

The priest eventually seated himself on his knees before the household altar, assumed a dignified pose, and began to chant the scriptures. After he completed this memorial ritual in honor of deceased members of the household, Grandmother brought in two small decanters of unheated sake for him. The old priest quickly downed the contents of both decanters, laid his head on a floor pillow, and promptly fell fast asleep, snoring loudly. An hour or so later, he got up and left the house without a word of farewell, pushing the baby carriage before him back to the temple. This priest never offered a homily. Indeed, he appeared entirely incapable of doing any such thing. Still, he possessed a certain charm. I had to admire a man who discharged his official tasks with such dignity and then completely relaxed and revealed his true self—an old man who forged ahead at his own deliberate pace, traveling the twelve miles to his destination and back again, entirely on his own.

"Oh no! He forgot his money!"

Grandmother rushed out to give him the offering envelope he had left behind, but she soon returned. That old priest did move quickly. Assuredly, he was an unconventional clergyman, but he was far more approachable in all his humanness than any awe-inspiring holy man.

It was early spring when Mother and I arrived in Japan, so school was in session. Mother wanted me to adjust to Japanese school life as quickly as possible, so she took me without delay to enroll in the nearby grammar school, Hiratsuka No. 1 Elementary School. That morning, she paid her respects to the teacher, left me in his care, and returned home.

In honor of this important occasion in my life—and as an expression of regard for my new teacher and classmates—I had dressed up proudly like a young gentleman. I neatly combed and parted my hair, put on a new shirt and tie, and polished my shoes. Thus attired, I was led into the classroom by my new teacher. The other pupils stared at the strange newcomer with enormous curiosity.

Then someone yelled out, "It's an *Amerika-jin!*"

In that instant I was given a premonition of things to come. Of course I was an *Amerika-jin*—an American—but the tone the boy used when he said that word bespoke a sense of exclusiveness, of discrimination against the outsider. It turned out that my desire to show respect to my new classmates—which had inspired me to dress up in the only way I knew how—had unexpectedly become the source of my downfall.

There ensued a miserable time. American children, it seemed to me, would have included a newcomer from a foreign country without any question, using gestures to communicate if language failed. But these Japanese children seemed incapable of such easy acceptance of an outsider. They had no empathy at all for the feelings of a newcomer in their midst. I could not understand it then, but when I later learned more of Japanese culture and history, I realized that they had been raised with an island mentality, nurtured on its parochial, exclusive relationships. This was the heritage of the old feudal days, when Japan had isolated itself from virtually all contact with the outside world for over two hundred years.

On this my first day in school, the morning exercises now began. The sharp commands, the rituals, the sequence of calisthenics performed in unison by the class to the directions of a radio announcer—all of it was foreign to me. Everything about this highly regimented exercise routine took me by surprise. It was frightening, and it aroused in me a powerful feeling of defiance. Finally, I abandoned any attempt to imitate the others and decided just to stand still and watch their copycat antics. All of a sudden, someone reached out and yanked my hair and then someone else grabbed my necktie. I gritted my teeth and endured it, thinking disdainfully to myself how "uncivilized" these Japanese were. That was about all I could do in the situation. Back home, I said nothing to Mother about my humiliating experience at school.

One Sunday not long after that, I went with Mother and Grandmother to visit the cemetery at the temple outside Hiratsuka. On our twelve-mile trek we passed through several small villages. In each place the children pointed their fingers at me, with my American-style combed and parted hair, and whispered, or shouted, "*Amerika-jin!*" When we reached the village of Nakahara and the children there began to throw stones at me, my hot-blooded grandmother had had enough. She took after the offenders with a stick until Mother managed finally to grab hold of her and stop the assault.

The next day, at Mother's urging, I stayed home from school to go to the barber. As I sat in the barber chair watching my hair grow shorter and shorter, I became so sad that I began to weep. Surmising that I was upset at having all my hair cut off, the barber felt called upon to give me some advice.

"You know, when you come to Japan, you have to have your hair clipped like the other boys," he told me.

This man could not possibly understand my complex feelings at that moment. It was nothing so simple as being upset about the length of my hair. I was recalling as I sat there how happy I had been when I started school in San Francisco. That was my first encounter with white children, but despite my fears they had included me in their play without a moment's hesitation. I was crying for those happier times and because having my hair cut felt as though my ties with those friends in America were being severed. Beyond that, it meant giving in to the "barbarian" Japanese.

The barber went on, "You know, the Japanese people are kind to children."

Privately, I thought, Yeah, the Japanese spoil their children rotten.

Oblivious to my thoughts, the barber continued his vain attempt to console me.

"Japanese schools aim to train well-disciplined children, you know, and good discipline starts with having your hair clipped."

How I longed to escape from that barber chair!

I wanted to scream at the man, "A haircut has nothing to do with discipline! How can you call it discipline when Japanese teachers just cram it down their pupils' throats? Besides, when Japanese children meet someone from another country, they pull his hair and grab his necktie and throw stones at him. You call *that* discipline?"

I realized, of course, that it was useless to say any of these things to the barber, so I held my peace.

Little by little things did begin to improve—in part because I loved to play baseball. Slight of build, I was quick and agile. The Japanese schoolchildren played a variety of baseball that was not so very different from the version played in cramped city school yards in the

United States. In Japan, the children used a rubber ball with a wooden sandal for their bat, while in American school yards the pitcher bounced a tennis ball once on the asphalt surface of the playground for the batter to hit with his fist. It was playing this kind of school yard baseball—and the ensuing arguments—that finally broke the ice for me with my Japanese classmates.

The one thing I hated more than anything else, though, was being called *Amerika-jin*. Not that I disliked being an American, but I loathed the prejudice that was so tangible in the Japanese boys' use of the term. Fully aware of my sensitivity on this point, my classmates invariably taunted me with shouts of "*Amerika-jin! Amerika-jin!*" whenever we had an argument. Infuriated, I would attack my tormentors regardless of their size. I had no fear of a fight. I appreciated now, though, the reason my mother had sent me to learn jūdō in San Francisco.

Sometimes I lost these fights, sometimes I won. But it was through these confrontations that the other boys gradually came to accept me. They respected the fact that, win or lose, I fought for all I was worth. I was tenacious and did not give up even when I was hurt. And in the world of young boys that was the road to acceptance.

Just about the time I finally made some friends in this manner, summer vacation began.

One Sunday during vacation, Mother and I walked down to the ocean. As we strolled through the quiet pine forest along the shore, she gazed silently out toward the distant horizon. For lack of anything better to do, I squatted down and began stirring the sand idly with a stick.

Suddenly, Mother spoke.

"Minoru, I'm going to go back to America."

I was stunned. I knew my parents were estranged from one another, so I didn't see why she had to go back. But it seemed that Mother's plan was to leave me in Japan with my grandparents while she returned to the States by herself to earn the money to support us. I could readily understand her reasoning—it was just that these past few months had been the first time Mother and I were ever able to enjoy life together, and now that was going to end. I had been hoping that we could go on indefinitely living just the way we were. Here there were no scary white ladies yelling at Mother. And Grandmother and Grandfather were so good to me. I had Pooch; I was getting used to school; and by now I could even speak enough Japanese to get along reasonably well in day-to-day conversation. But my pleasure in all this depended upon my mother's presence nearby.

For a long time she gazed at the ocean in silence. No doubt she too was struggling with powerful emotions. Looking back, I realize that she had to be a very strong woman to return to the United States then, especially in her circumstances. The Japanese community in America would be extremely cool toward a young married woman living alone. She was doubtless well aware that they would look askance at her for that.

Mother took my hand and pulled me up from the sand. Silently we headed for home. That was a hot evening in the month of July.

The night before Mother's departure a few weeks later, we slept in the large room at the rear of the house. Grandmother and Grandfather were in the smaller room next door, the sliding doors open between us.

"I won't take you to the pier tomorrow, Minoru, if you're going to cry," Grandfather warned me repeatedly.

I promised absolutely that I would not cry. Mother caressed my head.

"Minoru won't cry. He's a big boy," she assured Grandfather.

After we were all in bed that night, Mother talked softly for a long time, telling my grandparents anecdotes about me as a small child. Eventually everyone fell silent. In the dark night, the wooden clappers of the fire patrol echoed forlornly, faintly, in the distance, warning householders to take care with their fires during the night. The clock on the wall struck midnight.

Pooch invariably pounced all over me first thing every morning, his tail pounding, but the morning of Mother's departure I brushed my puppy aside without responding to his greeting. In the front hallway Mother bowed deeply as she said her farewells to Grandmother. Then Grandfather, two or three other relatives, and I set out to see Mother off from the pier at Yokohama.

I sat beside Mother on the train, the moment of separation looming before me. Clickety-clack, clickety-clack, the train began to glide slowly over the tracks. The peach orchards beside the road leading to the shore grew smaller and smaller. The pine forests on Mount Kōrai in Ōiso slipped from sight. Only Mount Ōyama towering in the distance beyond Isehara Plain stayed in view, keeping silent watch over my grief.

In the seat ahead of us, two cheerful old country women chattered nonstop in the local dialect. I could not make out a word of what they said. In the aisle behind me, three robust, brown-skinned boys about my age teased one another idly, reveling in their day's outing on the train. No doubt they were going to Fujisawa on their way to Enoshima Island for the day. How I envied them their untroubled lives.

The train went on, crossing Banyū River, swiftly passing Chigasaki and Tsujidō and leaving Fujisawa behind. The simple rhythm of the unceasing clickety-clack, clickety-clack induced drowsiness. Then the huge hilltop stone statue of the Bodhisattva Kannon suddenly came into view as we approached the city of Ōfuna. When the train stopped in the station there, Mother bought me a sandwich of Ōfuna's famous ham from a vendor on the platform. I was so choked with emotion, though, that I could not possibly force it down. The boys on their way to Enoshima had long since gotten off the train. From Ōfuna to Yokohama there were no more stops. After the train pulled into Yokohama Station, we hailed a taxi to drive us to the Japan Mail Line pier near Sakuragi-chō.

I had not said a word to Mother from the time we left Hiratsuka. Nor had she spoken to me.

The harbor was cool, even though it was the height of summer. The luxury liner *Chichibu Maru* waited there, alongside the pier. Mother and I went aboard the ship. As before, the third-class cabins were rank and stifling. Mother stowed the few things she carried with her under the assigned bunk and then hurried off the ship, holding me by the hand. We went to Sakuragi-chō with Grandfather and the relatives for lunch at a corner sushi restaurant. The neighborhood around the restaurant was full of cheap lodgings designed for emigrants journeying home to the provinces for a visit or returning to the States.

The relatives enjoyed their lunch immensely, oblivious to the grief that threatened to overwhelm us. Mother managed to eat only one small piece of sushi. I didn't even touch the food. Next we all went to a department store in downtown Yokohama for Mother to do some last-minute shopping before hurrying back to the harbor. By now the pier was thronged with people. Family groups clustered on every side, bidding reluctant farewells to emigrants returning to the States after all-too-brief visits to Japan. With homes in two different countries, the expatriates were always filled with complex emotions at these moments.

With the inevitable separation pressing upon us, Mother and I went aboard ship once more to spend our final few minutes alone together in her third-class cabin.

"Gong-gong-gong-gong-gong-gong-gong!"

The insistent hammering of the warning gong penetrated to every corner of the ship's hold, its unwelcome sound boring into the very core of my being. Families and friends of the passengers began to make their way down the gangplank and back to the pier. As we said our good-byes, Mother gave me one final admonition.

"You study hard now, Minoru, and don't you let the Japanese children get ahead of you. *You're* going to *be* something when you grow up. So even if they give you a hard time, you just put up with it. I'll be back for you, I promise."

When the loudspeakers on the pier began the obligatory rendition of "Auld Lang Syne," a rainbow of paper streamers was all that linked the ship's passengers to loved ones on the shore. Here and there in the crowd handkerchiefs dabbed at tearful faces. Then from somewhere came a shrill cry.

"Banzai! Banzai! Banzai!"

To me, in my private despair, these irritating cheers rang hollow indeed. Silently and with all my might I clung to my end of the paper streamer that Mother had tossed to me from the ship, but I could not bring myself to look her directly in the eye. Soon I was engulfed in the crowd of adults, but through a tiny space between them I caught a glimpse of Mother's face, shining with tears. I took a deep breath and bit my lip hard, so that I wouldn't cry. In my mind I could still hear Mother's soft voice as she talked last night after we went to bed.

A tugboat nudged firmly at the stern of the ship, slowly moving its huge bulk away from the pier. A blast from the ship's horn silenced the clamor of the waiting crowd. Then the tugboat shifted positions to push the ship's side at its midpoint. The gulf widened between ship and shore, and one at a time the colorful paper streamers snapped in two. A voice on the pier shouted something unintelligible. I continued to gaze bleakly after Mother as her ship moved beyond the breakwater. At the end, the passengers on the ship looked no larger than tiny ants. By that time, only a scattering of people remained on the pier.

The summer's day was nearly over when we got back to Hiratsuka, and Grandmother had dinner almost ready. Pooch jumped all over me in welcome, but I ignored him and ran into the lavatory, closed the door, and stood there alone in the dark. I had forced back my tears all day, but now I could not stop them. I thought about the first time I went with Mother to her job in that cold Caucasian apartment house—how that scary white lady screamed at her and Mother just had to clench her teeth and endure it. I wanted to cry out "Mama! Mama!" but I told myself I must not do that. Instead, I just tightened my hand as hard as I could around the ham sandwich Mother had bought for me that morning, squeezing it into a tiny lump as I sobbed and sobbed.

"Minoru! Minoru!"

Grandmother was calling me to dinner.

Gradually I began to feel more comfortable in my Japanese school. I even got bold enough to raise my hand eagerly in class now and then, sometimes volunteering an answer to a question I hadn't fully understood. My teacher was a serious young man named Mr. Fukawa. He was extremely solicitous toward me, and I responded to his kindness with trust. My classmates, too, came to accept me. Even when I offered irrelevant answers to questions I didn't quite comprehend, the others would show their goodwill by simply smiling at me.

Then there was the physical education class. One day the teacher divided our class into two teams, red and white, and marked a circle on the ground with the heel of his shoe for a sumō wrestling tournament. This was the first time I had ever seen the sport. Thanks to my jūdō lessons in San Francisco I was no weakling, but jūdō and sumō are not at all the same thing. A sumō match is decided quickly, within a small defined space, so it requires a great deal of concentrated strength for a short span of time. There is no chance to plot a strategy as you wrestle.

The matches began with the largest pupils and proceeded downward in order of size. I observed attentively the various techniques used by the larger boys. When my turn came I plunged into the ring just as the others had done, established a hold on my opponent, and deployed an aggressive left-right leg movement. But my opponent had a grip on me too, and it was a standoff.

"You can do it! You can do it!" I heard someone cheer.

I pressed my head against my opponent's chest and started to force him down, but by this time he had shoved me to the side of the ring. He gave one final push. At the very edge of the circle I twisted aside, but it was too late—my foot went over the line. My opponent then fell, but he was declared the winner.

The match was over. It was a fair fight.

After all the matches were finished, the teacher told us to line up in two rows: winners in one row, losers in the other. I lined up with the other boys who had lost their matches. The teacher walked along that row, boxing the head of each loser with his fist. My turn was coming. I braced, closed my eyes, and lowered my head, waiting for the blow. It came. But the teacher just patted my head with his open hand. Stunned and resentful, I watched him pass on down the row, boxing the heads of the other losers. I didn't like being treated differently from the other boys.

Japanese boys do enjoy a scrap. One day a boy called Gon lashed out at me for no apparent reason.

"You stupid *Amerika-jin!*" he snarled.

I hadn't heard *that* for some time now, but all the old familiar anger boiled up inside me. Gon was much bigger than I; he was the class bully and not a very bright student. He proposed that we settle the matter after school in the playground out back. That was a challenge, and I was determined to meet it with every bit of strength I possessed. I spoke to no one of the imminent confrontation and after school went to the appointed spot.

I had given my strategy a great deal of thought. It would not be a sumō match this time, so I would be able to make full use of the space available. But my opponent was a good deal larger than I and clearly stronger. It was plain that if he caught me off guard, I wouldn't have a chance. Thus I planned to surprise Gon first with a quick attack. Then, once he was off balance, I would grab his leg and topple him. When I had him down, I would stomp on his wrist and break it. If, on the other hand, my opponent managed to get the initiative and attack me first, I would grab hold of his shirt and flip him, jūdō-style, then get him in a necklock from behind and choke him until he lost consciousness. If neither of these strategies worked, I would let him hit me, then I would sink my teeth into his neck and never let go, even unto death.

I was pale but calm in anticipation of the fight. My mind held no other thought than the defeat of this formidable enemy. The fury aroused in me at being called *Amerika-jin* had that powerful an effect.

When we met after school, Gon appeared to sense my suicidal determination and looked a bit nervous. But then I noticed something that threw me into a state of confusion: a girl with a baby on her back was standing quietly over by the swings not far from the battleground, watching. It was the neighbor girl, Toyoko, who was three or four years older than I, a girl who was always especially kind to me. Sensing that something was afoot, she set the baby down softly on the ground and, ignoring its howls, ran over to me with her back to Gon.

"Don't fight, Botchan. Come on now, let's go home," she urged me gently.

She drew me away by the hand and returned to the sobbing baby she had left on the ground, lifting him up onto her back again. Then she started for home, pulling me along with her.

Apparently Gon hadn't really wanted to fight at all, for as soon as Toyoko interrupted our confrontation he grabbed his schoolbag and ran. It seemed he had only meant to taunt me a bit. In one moment, all the emotion that had coiled so tightly in my breast went slack and left me feeling utterly dejected. I was embarrassed, too, at the cowardice of letting a girl rescue me from the showdown. Still, I couldn't help but be grateful to her. And I thought her a brave, warmhearted person, wise beyond any adult. She never told anyone of my near humiliation that day.

People in the neighborhood called Toyoko's father Tora-san, meaning "tiger," probably because he was known as a heavy drinker. He crafted bambooware to support his wife and three children, but the family was extremely poor. A few weeks after the unconsummated showdown, Toyoko suddenly vanished from the neighborhood. After a time I heard that she had been sold as a geisha, but I had absolutely no idea what those words meant. All I knew was that she was a beautiful girl with lovely translucent skin and bright eyes and that she was a brave and gentle young woman.

It was also around this time that someone pointed at Toyoko's house and said in my hearing, "They're *eta*."* I didn't know the meaning of that, either. What a strange word, I thought.

All this happened during my first year in Japan, when I was in the sixth grade.

I missed Toyoko after she left the house across the street. She had been like an older sister to me. Soon I took to milling about in front of her house for no particular reason. Her father Tora-san was busy in his workshop from early morning on, so I began to watch what he was doing. With his sharp-edged hatchet Tora-san would split yard-long

---

* A term now considered taboo, referring to a group of Japanese long discriminated against for their historical association with the killing of animals and the processing of animal products. Also called *buraku-min*.

lengths of green bamboo pieces into regular widths and then feed them into his manually operated weaving machine, sitting there hour after hour fashioning bamboo screens. The clear, sharp report of his weaving machine echoed throughout the neighborhood all day, imparting a certain energy to the rhythm of life there. Toward evening, Tora-san would gather up the bamboo scraps and cut them into tiny pieces with a knife to make toothpicks.

"Young man, why don't you take these pieces of bamboo home with you and see what you can make with them?" he suggested to me one day.

I accepted the bamboo pieces he gave me without comment, but I had no inkling of how to make anything with them. Unlike ordinary wood, it was necessary to have a pattern to make something out of bamboo and that limited what could be made with it.

Several weeks later, however, I was given an assignment at school to do a craft project. Not knowing what to make, I shyly crossed the street to consult with Tora-san, who suggested a bamboo smoking tray. He cut off at the joint a piece of bamboo about two and a half inches in diameter, which he said would be the tray itself. Then he split a seven-inch piece in two for the stand. He handed me a knife and some glue and carefully instructed me in the procedure for putting the tray together. I went back home in high spirits and set to work on my project, following Tora-san's directions. Two or three days later I showed him the finished smoking tray. The craftsman made a few little improvements here and there, and I then had a wonderful tray. Moreover, I had learned the joy of creating something with my own two hands.

That night I proudly set my handiwork by my pillow before going to sleep. When I opened my eyes in the morning, I gazed with great satisfaction on my creation. After breakfast I set out for school, bearing my smoking tray with great care. It was only a five-minute walk from home to the back gate of the grammar school, but on my way, just thirty yards or so from the house, I noticed a large, unfamiliar black car parked by the fork in the road. It had a Tokyo license plate. The driver was at the wheel, and in the back two black-suited men sat hunched forward with their heads down. It looked a bit strange, but I didn't think too much about it and started to go around the car. At that moment the two men in the back jumped out, grabbed hold of me, and started to shove me into the car with them. I struggled wildly to escape their grasp, bucking and kicking them in the shins. Desperately, I yelled for help. Tora-san, already in his workshop, heard my cries and came running out barefoot, waving his hatchet.

"You let that boy go!" he shouted.

Startled, the two men loosened their grasp for just a moment and Tora-san took that chance to pull me away from them. He pushed me behind his back and glared at them with his hatchet held high. The driver spoke urgently to the two men. They jumped back into the car and it roared off down the street.

At that moment Grandmother and Grandfather finally arrived on the scene and Tora-san told them what had happened. They had not seemed very pleased earlier at my friendship with this *eta* neighbor. They knew he was helping me with my school project, though, so had not said anything about it. Today, however, both my grandparents dipped their heads in gratitude to him. Tora-san bowed even lower.

"It was nothing, sir. I'm just glad everything turned out all right," he said.

This "*eta*" was not uncultured. He knew the proper etiquette just like anyone else, I thought.

My smoking tray, meanwhile, lay on the ground in pieces, a pitiful sight after being trampled underfoot by the two men. I walked back home under my grandparents' watchful eyes.

"We'll have to report this to the police," Grandfather said.

"Grandfather, that was Papa," I told him.

He looked up sharply.

"What? He was trying to kidnap his own son? Well, I guess we can't very well report *that* to the police."

"That's the sort of thing Papa would do," I stated flatly, without emotion.

"Well, what should we do now?" Grandfather wondered aloud.

"Nothing. He could see I didn't want to go with him. He won't come back."

I was calm. Even if my father did succeed in kidnapping me, I had no intention of living with him. I planned to stay right here until Mother came back to Japan to get me.

A deep hatred for my father stirred within me—not so much because he tried to kidnap me, but because he trampled all over the smoking tray I had worked so hard to make. As a father, he had trampled on his family in just about the same way, I reflected bleakly to myself. Young as I was, I intuitively understood what was in his mind and despised him for it. My father hadn't cared enough about me to take time off from work and tell me good-bye when I left San Francisco, but now it had occurred to him that he was going to need me for his future security. That had always been his all-consuming preoccupation. He probably figured he should bring me back to the United States and make sure I got a high school education so I could support him in his old age.

The maid came into the room bearing the remains of my smoking tray. I glanced at it, banished it from my thoughts, and hurried off to school alone.

Several weeks after the unfought battle, Gon came up behind me and tapped me on the shoulder.

"I'm sorry I called you that," he mumbled, dipping his head in apology.

I ignored him. The feelings generated in me by a confrontation I had faced with such intense determination could not be let go so easily. But at least I was no longer afraid of Gon.

But I got into innumerable small scraps even after that. I often scuffled with Fuku-chan, whose father was a policeman, and Dekun, a rather timid, good-natured boy who was the son of a railway worker. These fights were never serious, though. Even when one of us ended up with a bloody nose we would be playing together again, the best of friends, the next day. Then there was Toshi-chan, the dyer's son. He was strong but never got into fights. Gantetsu and Gakera, too, were gentle people who didn't fight. All of these boys became my close friends.

One day I went with Toshi-chan and Dekun to the new swimming pool at Ōiso. After they taught me how to swim in the pool, the three of us ran to the beach, leapt into the ocean, and swam to a rock about a hundred yards out. The waves were pretty rough, but before long I worked up the courage to try riding the big ones. I loved the ocean.

> We are sons of the ocean,
> children of the white caps
> and the pine groves by the sea.

We sang loud and long as we played in the surf all day together. Other times we went fishing in the Hanamizu and Banyū Rivers. My friends taught me how to catch fish there.

Good friends, however, can sometimes be bad friends. When I was invited by one of the boys to go with him to steal watermelons from a patch near the shore, I was perfectly happy to participate in that, too. Rare is the young boy who can resist the thrill of doing something just a bit dangerous.

Near my house was an area of vacant lots and sand dunes. I loved to play war with my neighborhood friends in those open spaces. Occasionally when I came home from these battles I went directly into the living room without bothering to clean the sand off my feet. Grandmother was furious when she caught me in her clean house with those dirty feet and chased me out with her broom. Then I would escape into the garden and scramble up the huge oak tree by the path to the rear garden, hoisting myself up by a rope I had tied to one of its upper branches.

This tree was one of my favorite spots. In it I had a tree house where I could recline and read for hours. The orange-crate bookshelf beside my perch held *The Heroic Tales of Plutarch for Young Readers*, the lives of Napoleon and Bismarck, and a collection of Byron's poetry. Many such books were written in relatively simple Japanese and published for young readers in those days. The neighborhood children laughed at me when they saw me reading books in the treetop, and they nicknamed me "Tarzan." Fictional heroes like Tarzan did not interest me, though. It was the heroes of history and the poets who intrigued me.

I had written to Mother about the friends I had made in Hiratsuka. One day she sent a box of one hundred chocolate kisses from America with a note saying that they were to share with my friends at school. Delighted to have something to give my classmates, I took the box to school and presented it to the teacher, telling him what my mother had said. I asked him to distribute the candy to the other children in the class.

To my great surprise, the teacher called the pupils to his dais one at a time and presented each with a single piece of chocolate. Each boy in turn bowed politely, accepted his piece of candy with great respect, then bowed again before returning to his seat. I was astounded that they would respond with so much formality to such a little thing. One boy, who was from a fishing family in Suka, made a point of coming over to my desk, bowing deeply, and thanking me.

"It would be a great shame to partake of this by myself, so I will take it home to share with my father and mother and little sister," he told me.

Then another child, one who rarely said a word in school, came over and bowed.

"I will place this on the family altar as an offering for my late grandfather," he said.

After that, each boy came to my desk to express appreciation. Finally, at a complete loss for the proper response to all their polite words of gratitude, I put my face down on my desk and my arms over my head.

I had known that most of my classmates were from poor families. Some came to school wearing wooden sandals that did not match. At lunchtime, these children would take their lunch boxes out of their schoolbags and go through the motions of eating, although many times I could see that those boxes were empty to begin with. Still, they would hide their hunger and not complain, pretending out of pride to be eating their lunch.

Thus I was deeply moved and somewhat embarrassed when I saw how these boys, who had so little in the way of material things, openly expressed their love for their parents, the older brother his affection for his little sister, the grandchild his love for the grandfather who had died. Moreover, they spoke of these feelings with such sincerity. It was not just the matter of a little piece of chocolate candy. They were demonstrating a feeling that is cultivated among the humble and the innocent, an unaffected simplicity that seems to be lost in more affluent societies. I was very grateful that I had been befriended by these boys. I envied them in a way, too, for, although poor, they had been raised in warm and caring families.

I was happy. My classmates had accepted me as a friend, my teacher was fond of me, and no one called me *Amerika-jin* anymore. My sixth grade year was coming to an end. It had been a year and a half since I arrived in Japan.

In the prewar Japanese educational system, after grammar school students completed the sixth grade, they were separated into two groups—those who advanced to middle school (the equivalent of an American secondary school) and those who went to an upper elementary school to complete their education. The former course was five years, the latter only two. My grandfather was a man of many talents, but he knew nothing about education. In particular, he had no understanding of my mother's plans for my education. Thus when I finished grammar school, Grandfather placed me in the two-year upper elementary course so I could complete the minimal education and learn a trade as soon as possible.

Hiratsuka Higher Elementary School was a ten-minute walk from home, over the high, embanked railroad tracks that led to the naval powder depot. Perhaps this plan was the best for me. I was not the type of student to cram for the entrance exams required for acceptance into the more academic course of the middle school. Not that I did poorly in school. I had even reached the point where Japanese language classes were rather easy, perhaps because I read so many books. I also knew a great deal about history and liked math.

But my favorite class in that school was kendō. I was agile and hated to lose. Moreover, I found that I was not at a disadvantage in this sport since body size was irrelevant—more than anything else kendō requires the power of concentration. I never did feel

entirely at ease with the kendō teacher, however. He was a balding
priest of the Buddhist Nichiren sect who was on the school staff.
One day when he was teaching us sword cuts, I made the mistake of
holding my bamboo sword blade side up.

"Is that the way you hold a sword in America?" he shouted
derisively.

I was embarrassed, but I didn't think a teacher should speak
to a student that way. Kendō instruction, like any other part of the
educational process, ought to help a student grow and develop.
Biased comments and vulgar sarcasm have no place in that process.
My classmates shared my chagrin at the teacher's insult—several
standing near me flushed and looked down as though they themselves had been reprimanded.

But I was determined not to let such an incident force me to
give up kendō. At home I pretended that the loquat tree in the garden was the Nichiren priest, and using it as my opponent I vigor-
ously practiced thrusts and slices with my wooden sword. In the end
I inflicted so much damage on that poor tree that it perished. To
punish me for killing her tree, Grandmother set me to work splitting
the family's firewood. After four or five days I gained full control of
the ax, my wrists firm and my stance secure. In high spirits, I volunteered to split all the firewood for the household from then on.

My time at Hiratsuka Higher Elementary School was great
fun, for it left me the leisure to do as I liked. I never bothered to
study for tests, since I had a strong aversion to that kind of regimented education and no interest at all in the insipid, government-
approved textbooks. At home, however, I continued to devour all
kinds of books up in my treetop aerie.

My mother's family was not poor. Mother worked as an elementary schoolteacher for a few years when she was young, but the family was affluent enough that she was able to resign from her job to
help at home before marrying my father and going to America. The
comfortable circumstances of Mother's youth, along with the age
difference between herself and my father and the assertive nature

she inherited from Grandmother, may all have contributed to the ultimate failure of my parents' marriage.

In any case, after arriving in America, Mother very quickly became acquainted with the harsh realities of the immigrant's life. She took it as a challenge, though, and responded assertively to the situation. Her first concern was to find a means of earning a living, and later an equally important issue for her was to devise a strategy for her son's education. She made detailed plans: first, to have me absorb Japanese culture and develop pride in my ethnic heritage; and second, to have me complete my higher education in the United States and make my home there. Entrusting me to Grandfather in Hiratsuka for a period of time had been the first step in this plan. But there she ran into an unexpected obstacle: Grandfather himself. His idea was for me to get the minimum education, learn a trade, and settle permanently in Japan. When Mother learned that he had placed me in the upper elementary course instead of a middle school, she was outraged. She prepared immediately to return to Japan and bring me back with her to the United States.

Meanwhile, I continued to enjoy my leisurely life in Hiratsuka. Then one day, after a rather long period of silence, a letter came from Mother saying that she would be arriving in Japan in just a few months. Almost four years had elapsed since we parted with such sadness at the pier in Yokohama. Meanwhile, I had been growing up as a Japanese schoolboy. But never for a moment had I forgotten my love for my mother in America.

By this time the atmosphere in Japan was changing. On July 7, 1937, the Marco Polo Bridge incident* had exploded on the tense Chinese mainland, triggering the Sino-Japanese War, and the conflict had spread rapidly across north China.

---

* Confrontation between Chinese and Japanese troops near the Marco Polo Bridge outside Beijing. Both sides were under political pressure to make no concessions, so this small incident eventually expanded into the warfare between Japan and China that was the prelude to the Pacific side of World War II.

"With courageous hearts we vow, we shall return victorious!" the Japanese soldiers sang as they departed for the front.

Day after day our teachers marched us to the train station, Rising Sun flag held high, to send the troops off to war. But it was not visions of soldiers that filled my head, it was the vision of my mother's face. And on the first and fifteenth of every month when the principal took us to Hachiman Shrine to pray for the welfare and success of the Japanese Imperial Army, I prayed instead for the safety and welfare of my mother.

The militaristic system was fast turning Japan into a closed society, not only in the international political arena but also in the educational world. Emigrant children whose parents sent them to Japan for schooling during that prewar period were subjected to all manner of humiliation. Ferris Girls' Academy in Yokohama, a distinguished school for young ladies, for example, refused to admit Japanese Americans. Apparently the academy did not regard the daughters of Japanese expatriates as "young ladies." After many a bitter experience of this nature, issei mothers elected to cut short their children's education in Japan and take them back to the United States. The strains felt throughout Japanese society were causing the Japanese educational system to close in upon itself.

The state of the economy was one source of tension in Japanese society during this period. On a snowy morning the year before Japan's war with China began, a group of rebellious young army officers staged the bloody February 26 incident, an attempted coup d'état that was not simply a political act—it was also a response to the dire economic situation in the provinces. Most of the rebellious young officers were from rural areas and knew all too well the desperate plight of the farmers. Poverty was not, however, restricted to the countryside. The cities were also full of people without jobs or economic support. The Sino-Japanese War that began in 1937 did bring a certain amount of prosperity to the country, but it was by no means a cure-all for Japan's troubled economy.

During this period, therefore, most fifteen-year-old males completing their schooling were extremely anxious about getting a job and making a living. I, on the other hand, never gave a serious thought to finding employment. It was Grandfather who was worried.

"How about getting a job as an interpreter at a resort hotel in the mountains at Hakone?" Grandfather suggested one day. "I know someone who can give you an introduction."

I rejected this idea with a laugh.

"Well, we'll talk it over with your mother when she gets here," he conceded.

In my own mind, I was thinking, I am *not* going to be any hotel interpreter! Your world is too small. My world is going to be much larger than that!

Grandfather was not inclined to press his views, however, and I was relieved when he said we would wait and talk it over with Mother. Grandfather knew very well that I was as interested in reading books as I was in amusing myself with my friends. In fact, he was always very generous in giving me the money to buy books that I wanted.

"I have no idea what that boy will end up doing," I once heard him confess to Grandmother.

At last the day I had longed for arrived. Grandfather and I went to Yokohama to meet Mother's ship. She came in on the *Asama Maru*, laden with gifts from the United States. But I paid no attention to the presents Mother brought with her; I wanted only to gaze at her face. She looked extremely worn and tired, but I was happy and relieved to have her safely back with me again.

When we got home to Hiratsuka, Mother lost no time in informing her parents in no uncertain terms that she would be taking me home with her to the United States. To my surprise, Grandfather voiced no opposition to her plan. By this time, he seemed to be at a loss as to what to do with his grandson.

During those years back in the States, Mother had officially divorced my father. As a result, she had to contend not only with the hardship of working as a lowly servant in Caucasian households but also with the stress of being cold-shouldered as a divorcée by the Japanese American community. Only her love for her son and her

Buddhist faith sustained her through the hardships of those years. She had a kind of severity in her tired face now, which tended to keep people at a distance. I wanted my mother to be a warm person, not this woman who lived by some rigid religious discipline. But young as I was, I could have no comprehension of her inner anguish.

Before we returned to the United States, Mother took me to Tokyo to stay for a few months at the main temple of the Buddhist sect to which she belonged. We arrived in the capital in December 1937, just as the foreign press was beginning to report the "Rape of Nanjing."* In Japan, however, they spoke of the "Fall" of Nanjing and celebrated on December 13 with a magnificent lantern parade through Tokyo.

Early the following spring, Mother and I were walking up a hill in Araki-chō in the Yotsuya section of Tokyo when all of a sudden a police officer began yelling at us, his voice harsh and loud.

"Hey! You stupid fools!" he shouted.

He ordered us abruptly to halt and stand at attention. Trembling, my mother followed his instructions and bowed her head low. Only afterward did we learn that the emperor and empress had been processing along Shinjuku Avenue only a hundred yards away from us, en route to visit the Shinjuku Imperial Gardens.

The police officer's angry shout that day seemed somehow emblematic of the tension that pervaded Japanese society in those days.

When Mother and I returned to Hiratsuka from our stay in Tokyo, the maid broke the news to me.

"While you were away, Botchan, we found Pooch one morning lying dead under that paulownia tree where he always played. It was so sad—he was holding the strap of your wooden sandal in his mouth."

---

* Atrocities committed by the Japanese army against the civilian population of Nanjing and vicinity when discipline broke down among the troops after taking the city. The rape and murder of civilians and POWs continued for six weeks.

Dismayed and unbelieving, I ran to the rear garden, where she told me they had buried my dog. Pooch had been the one who comforted me during those first days in Japan when the boys taunted me at school. And he had given me so much joy ever since. All these happy memories flashed through my mind as I ran to the garden.

There was my sandal, hanging from a branch of the paulownia tree. No doubt the thoughtful maid had hung it there. The tears burned my eyes as I dug deep into the earth to bury the sandal beside my dog. Then I gave in to my grief. I sobbed and sobbed.

"Oh, Pooch, you and I understood each other so well, even though we couldn't talk to each other in words. I know you died because you could tell I was going to leave you," I lamented.

Reluctantly, I bade a last farewell to my beloved dog.

It was a good time to be returning to the United States. Events in the Far East foreboded difficult times and were already causing severe strains in every sphere of Japanese life—political, social, and educational. For me, the death of my dog signified the end of four pleasant years in Japan. And Mother was in a hurry to return to the States.

Japan as a nation had betrayed its expatriates' nostalgic dreams of the homeland. It was a poor country, as even a youngster like myself could see. But that poor country had given me an enriching experience. It was the country of Yassan the vegetable man, the old Zen priest with his baby carriage, gentle, brave Toyoko, the kind "*eta*" Tora-san, my school friends Toshi-chan, Dekun, Gakera, Gantetsu, and Fuku-chan, my loving grandparents, and my dearly beloved companion Pooch. I would not forget them.

I boarded the ship in Yokohama with a lingering sense of regret—that morning when I left the house in Hiratsuka I had been so intent on not betraying my emotions that I failed to thank the energetic young maid for all the things she had done for me during my years there.

With mixed emotions I waved good-bye to Grandfather and the other well-wishers on the pier as the *Kamakura Maru* moved out to sea, carrying Mother and me back to the United States.

It was late spring in the year 1938.

3 *Kibei Youth*

Two enormous new bridges dominated the San Francisco skyline when I returned. The Golden Gate now spanned the entrance to San Francisco Bay and held the distinction of being the longest suspension bridge in the world. It had taken four years to build, from 1933 to 1937, and was finished the year before I came home to America. The channel under this six-lane bridge was narrow and deep, its current so cold and swift that it was already becoming known as a perfect spot for suicides.

When the *Kamakura Maru* slipped beneath that brightly colored span into San Francisco Bay, I feasted my eyes on nostalgic sights in every direction. To the north was Mount Tamalpais, named for an Indian goddess, its twin peaks swelling seductively. To the south, the hilly city revealed its lovely countenance between patches of drifting fog. Ahead lay one of the finest natural harbors in the world.

The ship now proceeded to its berth near the other newly completed bridge, the Bay Bridge, a double-decker span linking San Francisco with the city of Oakland to its east. The huge Japanese passenger liner eased up to the pier, its enormous weight heaving against it with tremendous force, and came to a halt.

After four years away from this port city I heard once again the nostalgic sound of deep-throated ships' horns and felt refreshed in every cell of my being by the chill of the harbor's early morning air. Ah, I'm back in *my* city, my beautiful city of hills, I said to myself.

That night I was home again with my mother in our humble but familiar apartment on the edge of San Francisco's Japan Town.

The following morning I walked to the corner grocery store to buy some bread and milk for my mother. The old storekeeper had not forgotten me.

"Where have *you* been?" he greeted me.

"In Japan," I replied with a smile, glad to see the old man again.

"Well, well. Welcome home!" he said warmly, selecting a piece of candy for me.

I was fond of this old grocer. A red-bearded immigrant from Eastern Europe, he spoke in heavily accented English. He was by now well over seventy but still managed his own business and lived by himself.

I recalled one day when I came to his store as a small boy to buy milk. On my way across the street to go home, I stumbled on the trolley tracks and dropped the heavy glass bottle. It broke and splashed milk all over my pants and shoes. The old man, glancing out the store window, saw what had happened. He hurried out and picked me up, gave me a new bottle of milk, and sent me safely on my way.

Another time when I arrived at his store early one morning I found him standing outside, pointing to a spot in the sky.

"Do you know what that star is?" he asked me.

"No."

"People nowadays call it the Morning Star, but the ancient Romans named it after the goddess Venus. They worshiped it," he told me.

After that, whenever I saw Venus on a summer's morning, I would think of that kind, red-bearded old man who always seemed such a romantic character.

Soon after we returned to the States, my mother went back to work as a domestic servant in the homes of white families. By this time, she had learned not to tremble in fear over such a trifling thing as a broken plate. She had even developed the courage to refuse unreasonable demands from her employers and to respond to their sarcastic remarks. And if an employer should ever displease her, she would walk off the job without a backward glance. Invariably the person would call and apologize, begging her to come back to work, but she always refused. She had no need to go back, for she was never at home more than a day before locating an even better job. My mother had acquired quite a reputation by this time for her culinary skills, so she was in ever-increasing demand among affluent Caucasian families. Her improved work situation made life somewhat easier for us than in the past.

Now that I was back in the States, I had to think more realistically about my future. School in America was different. In Japan, in due time, I was accepted as a Japanese and was surrounded by Japanese. There I was a member of the majority. But in America I became increasingly aware that, however my classmates might feel about me, I would always be a member of an ethnic minority. And I was not blind to the fact that prejudice abounded against Japanese and other minorities in America. I would have to be especially diligent in getting a good education if I were to overcome society's biases.

I was glad I had returned to America when I did, though, after spending only two years in the upper elementary school in Japan. Very likely I would have forgotten most of my English had I gone on to spend the full five years in a Japanese middle school. Other Japanese American youths who did complete the middle school course before returning to the States had spent so many years in Japan that their English was far below the American high school level. They had to struggle if they wanted to attend college in America. In fact, because they had spent so much of their childhood in Japan, they would always be handicapped with inadequate spoken English.

After my return to the States, I was admitted as a freshman at Lowell High School, a secondary school that was well known for its college preparatory course. There I had two hours of study hall every day, so if I used my time wisely, I could complete at least part of my homework at school. After I came home in the afternoon, I immediately set out again for a small Japanese school in Japan Town that was operated by Mr. and Mrs. Sano. Now that I was back in

America, I wanted to read as much Japanese literature as I could. I had a feeling that I might learn something about myself through the characters in that literature. Mr. and Mrs. Sano were Japanese intellectuals of a kind rarely encountered in San Francisco in those days. At their school I was able to devote myself to reading the novels of great twentieth-century masters like Natsume Sōseki, Mori Ōgai, and Shimazaki Tōson.

I resumed training in jūdō as well, spending two evenings a week at the gym on Sutter Street. After the class I came home for a simple meal with my mother before studying late into the night. Eventually I concluded that as a lightweight I was not physically adapted to jūdō and gave it up. Then I heard that Takano Hiromasa, son of the famous Japanese kendō master Takano Sasaburō, had come to San Francisco to teach kendō, a martial art that was still relatively unknown in America. Thereafter I went twice a week to the large gymnasium in the basement of the Buddhist church to continue the kendō training I had started in Japan. This teacher was unusual in that he was both a classical kendō practitioner and a modern gentleman. In his classes there were no angry pronouncements or silly preachments like those I had heard from the Nichiren priest in Hiratsuka.

After my kendō lesson ended and I was dripping with perspiration, I was physically and mentally exhilarated. As I headed for home along the eucalyptus-lined street beside the Buddhist church, the breeze moved the tops of the tall trees in great undulating waves. Gazing up at the distant sky between the swaying treetops, my ambitions soared. I vowed that I would become as strong and upright as those trees. Kendō infused in me the strength to face the hardships of life and taught me the Japanese virtues of courage and perseverance, qualities that helped me to work hard in school.

One of my high school classmates was a nisei boy named Hiro. He was a bright young man, talented at basketball, swimming, and dancing. He was thoroughly American in his every action and spoke not a word of Japanese. Hiro and I had very little in common. If I spoke to him, he would not respond. He deliberately avoided all contact with Japanese American students who had spent any time in Japan, and he held in particular disdain anyone who was interested in the Japanese martial arts.

Hiro and I lived in the same neighborhood. We could even see the lights in each other's windows at night. Early in my high school career, I regarded Hiro as my academic rival and made a point of never turning out my light before his went off at night. Even when his window went dark, I continued to study diligently into the early morning hours. Pretty soon, though, it dawned on me that while Hiro and I were studying late every night, our white classmates were compiling very respectable academic records without any particular effort at all. They didn't even seem to be consciously competing with their classmates. In fact, so far as I could tell, they behaved as perfect gentlemen toward one another and had a very casual attitude about their studies. I suppose that, born of affluent families and raised in privileged surroundings as they were, these white students had already absorbed so much culture from their environment that they felt relaxed about their education.

I began to realize that my future rivals were not the likes of Hiro—a product of the same insular Japanese American community as I—but the cream of Caucasian youth, people who inhabited a much broader world than either Hiro or myself. Now I became even more frenzied in my studies in order to compete with my true rivals. This was not grammar school, where Japanese boys and girls easily garnered the most stars on the teacher's chart. In high school it was the white students who began to excel, for at that level creative thinking was valued more highly than rote memorization. And creative thought was not a quality that was encouraged or cultivated within the narrow confines of the Japanese American community.

Possessed as I was with the conviction that education was the crucial factor for success in this Caucasian-dominated society, I became fiercely competitive in school. I saw academic excellence as my only chance. My Japanese teacher Mrs. Sano, meanwhile, shrewdly perceived my distraught state of mind and attempted to exert a calming influence on me through our readings in Japanese literature. I was very much aware of her efforts, and every day after my lesson with her, before I started for home, I secretly turned and bowed my head in wordless gratitude outside her door.

One day I was playing touch football with the other students at school. In the heat of the contest, a heavy shoe crashed into my left eye and knocked me flat on my back as blood ran down my face. I was momentarily stunned and almost lost consciousness, but then my embarrassment at the thought of passing out in front of a group of white students overcame the pain of my injury. I brushed away the hands of classmates offering to help me up, stood without any assistance, and took two or three steps forward. Then I fell again, this time face down. At least that way the others would not see the pain in my face. My kendō training had given me a strong aversion to bringing shame on myself in such a situation.

I was taken to the hospital in an ambulance. When I regained consciousness I could see nothing, for although only my left eye was injured, the doctor bandaged both eyes to avoid placing a strain on the good one. Mother rushed to the hospital as soon as she was called. I felt so badly to give her yet another cause for worry that I almost forgot my own physical pain. The tears that began to stream down my face when I heard her voice were tears of apology more than anything else.

After Mother went home, I lay in my dark world and examined my situation. I told myself that I had to get out of this hospital as soon as possible and return to school. I was impatient to get to the point where I could take care of my mother instead of just being a burden upon her. She had already devoted so much of her life to caring for me and providing me with an education.

Because of the pain in my eye, I did not sleep well that first night in the hospital. As I lay there awake, I suddenly recalled that a kendō match was scheduled with the Oakland team for the following week and that I had been chosen to compete in this match on the San Francisco team. When I remembered that, I felt compelled to be there to lead my team to victory. Early the following morning the nurse came in to wash my face.

"I have to get out of the hospital—now," I told her.

She was so astounded that it took her a few moments to reply.

Finally she said, very sternly, "You are in no condition to leave this hospital! Anyway, Min, you're scheduled to have an operation on your eye, you know."

"I'll come back for the operation after my kendō tournament," I promised.

Not surprisingly, however, the doctor would not permit me to leave the hospital for the kendō match. Now, of course, I realize that the idea was suicidal foolishness on my part. But kendō had that much influence over me—that I was willing to ignore my own physical pain in order to take responsibility for my part in the competition.

About ten days after the operation on my eye, when the pain had finally begun to subside, I heard the familiar voice of young Mrs. Sano, my lovely, intelligent Japanese teacher. I could not conceal my delight that she had come to see me.

"Is it still painful, Minoru-san?" she asked.

I smiled and shook my head a bit. No matter how much agony I was in, I would not admit it to this beautiful young teacher.

"I've brought a wonderful book with me today. Let me read it to you," she said.

She began in her soft, clear voice to read from the Bible. This was the first I knew that the Sanos were Christians. But the Bible could neither ease the pain in my eye nor calm the anxiety in my mind. Besides, what did Samaritans and Pharisees in ancient Israel have to do with my life, here and now? I could identify much better with the characters in the novels of Japanese authors like Sōseki, Ōgai, and Tōson. But the next day and the day after, Mrs. Sano came to the hospital to read the Bible to me. Then, after several days, she brought a different book.

"Have you ever heard of Helen Keller?" she queried.

Without waiting for my reply, she began to read aloud the autobiography of Helen Keller, finishing the entire book in ten days.

"Well, what do you think of Helen Keller?" Mrs. Sano asked.

"She's amazing. How could she possibly understand higher math so well when she was blind and deaf and mute?" I marveled aloud.

That was my honest reaction, but I was aware that Mrs. Sano was hoping for a different kind of response. I think she expected that I would see how Helen Keller's Christian faith had helped her to overcome her tremendous handicaps. Although I sensed my teacher's disappointment, I knew she was still gently smiling at me, for she was a cultured lady and a wise one as well.

The following week, Mrs. Sano read from *A Grain of Wheat*, written by Kagawa Toyohiko, a noted Christian social reformer who worked in the slums of Osaka. I was greatly moved as I listened—but not so much by the writer's Christian convictions as by the literary work itself.

For more than a month, Mrs. Sano came to the hospital virtually every day to read to me. I was profoundly, if mutely, grateful. Then one day, she asked me an unexpected question.

"Minoru-san, what do you plan to do with your life?"

I was not prepared to answer that. Right now I had no idea what I was going to do tomorrow, much less what I would do with the rest of my life. I did cherish some vague thoughts of finishing high school after I got out of the hospital and then going on to college to broaden my horizons, but I wasn't prepared to tell anyone that in so many words.

"Minoru-san, you must not think only of yourself. While your injured eye is healing, let your heart heal also. We must all do what we can for the world, for other people. I'd like to say a prayer for you today, Minoru-san," she said.

Before she went home that day Mrs. Sano murmured some sort of prayer in her gentle voice, grasped my hand firmly in her own soft warm one, and then left. That night I thought a great deal as I lay there sightless in my hospital bed.

Mrs. Sano was right. I *had* been thinking only of myself, I concluded. For the first time I began to consider what l might do in my life to contribute to the welfare of others. I began to perceive Mrs. Sano's intentions in her careful selection of the books she had been reading to me.

In the darkness, I listened to the unrelieved patter of lonely raindrops against the hospital window pane. It was late autumn.

After a lengthy stay, I was finally released from the hospital but still needed to convalesce for several more weeks at home. During that time, I continued to reflect. Several people of different religious persuasions had visited me in the hospital. Some told me menacingly that my injury was the result of my own sins, others that it was the curse of an ancestor's spirit, all sorts of strange things. But the one person who had been able to discern my innermost feelings was Mrs. Sano. She alone understood the complex emotions roiling inside me, and she had helped me to examine life from a higher perspective. I respected her for that.

Another person I had come to respect in those few weeks was the physician in charge of my case, Dr. Green. With my mother's meager earnings as our only resource, it was impossible for her to pay all the medical bills from my injury. Nevertheless, whenever I complained of pain in my eye, Dr. Green would come immediately to see me. It apparently made no difference to him, either, that we were Japanese Americans. One day as the physician was leaving our apartment after his visit, my mother bowed very low in the Japanese style, attempting somehow to convey to him her profound gratitude. Dr. Green hastened to reassure her, responding in his usual straightforward and modest manner.

"It's my job to heal my patient's eyes," he told her simply.

Dr. Green neither billed us for my operation nor did any insurance company reimburse him. Not many families had health insurance then, certainly not ours.

I had lost half a year of school by the time I was able to return. I still had two more years of high school before I could go on to college. I felt extremely restless and unsure of the direction I should take. I wished I had someone in whom to confide, someone I might ask for advice. Should I be a scientist? Should I become a great physician like Dr. Green? I agonized over these questions constantly, always recalling Mrs. Sano's words: "We must all do what we can for the world, for other people." But what *should* I spend my whole life doing? All through the night I thrashed about in bed, thinking of nothing else. When I woke in the morning my sheets were soaked with perspiration.

In September 1939 a cease-fire ended the Battle of Nomonhan (or Khalkhin-Gol as the Russians call it), which had raged for several months between Japanese and Russian forces on the border between Mongolia and Manchuria. Japanese Imperial headquarters reported the result as a victory for the Imperial Army, but in reality it had ended in a rout for the Japanese military—a bad omen for the struggle to come.

For the first time in a long while I visited the hilltop Sacramento Park, which I had known so well as a small child. I had not been there since returning to the States. From the park I looked down on San Francisco Bay, where a thin line of fog floated swiftly under the Golden Gate Bridge. I had heard that underwater nets were now stretched across the bay, to snare any enemy submarines. I could see artillery at either end of the bridge, and at times even in the city I could hear lengthy barrages of gunfire. Numerous artillery emplacements punctuated San Francisco's ocean shoreline right up to the harbor entrance, and the whole shore area was off-limits to civilians and patrolled by military dogs.

As I gazed at the bay below, I spotted a Japan Mail Line passenger ship floating leisurely through the harbor, its two smokestacks ringed with the distinctive red and white stripes. The *Asama Maru* was leaving port, apparently oblivious to the American military preparations surrounding it.

What were my Hiratsuka friends doing now, I wondered, my gaze drawn to the Pacific horizon.

The sun was beginning to set, and people who had been enjoying a leisurely day in the park were preparing to leave. I, too, turned to start home but stopped suddenly when my eyes fell on a particular park bench—the very place where I used to sit more than a decade ago, a small boy waiting for his mother to finish her day's work. Without thinking, I sat down. A few moments later I stood and walked on a little farther and there was the old water fountain. A large stone was set in front of it so that even a little child might reach the spigot. How often had I clambered onto that stone to get a drink of water? I certainly didn't need to do *that* anymore!

Although not particularly thirsty, I leaned over to drink from the fountain. As I swallowed the cool water, I was reminded that my debt to my mother was—as the Japanese proverb says—higher than the mountains and deeper than the sea. I was also deeply indebted to Mrs. Sano and to the kind ophthalmologist, Dr. Green. Strangely enough, the injury to my eye had given me a new and broader perspective on the world, much broader than what I had learned from kendō.

A year later, in the autumn of 1940, Japanese Imperial Navy tankers were still making periodic port calls in San Francisco. The sight of the Rising Sun flag flying over these ships invariably reawakened in the older Japanese immigrants feelings of nostalgia for their motherland across the ocean.

One Sunday afternoon that fall I spotted a group of four or five sailors on the street in Japan Town. I caught my breath when I heard them chatting in Japanese as they strolled along. How I would love to speak to them! It was so rare that I had a chance to converse in Japanese.

Approaching them boldly, I said, "Excuse me, would you like to come to my house for dinner?"

Usually I was the awkward, bashful adolescent, so issuing such an invitation to complete strangers was uncharacteristically forward of me. The sailors in their turn were absorbed in enjoying their shore leave and somewhat taken aback by my unexpected approach. Nevertheless, they did not hesitate for long. They smiled and accepted my invitation. Overjoyed, I led the way to our apartment. The sound of the men's heavy black shoes on the pavement recalled to me the clip-clop of wooden sandals on the streets in Japan.

It must have been these sailors' first visit to a Western-style home, for they sat stiffly in the upholstered chairs on the thick living room carpet while Mother busied herself in the kitchen, preparing a special dinner of roast beef for our guests. Then, while the roast was in the oven, we took them to the nearby market to buy gifts for their families in Japan.

The Caucasian manager of the market, an outgoing, jovial sort of fellow, tried to strike up a conversation with the Japanese sailors.

"Say, I'm a navy man myself—reserve officer in the U.S. Navy, as a matter of fact. It's a hell of a life in the navy, isn't it?" he remarked.

They, of course, did not understand a word of what he said, and I wasn't quite sure how I should interpret his comments for them. Japanese sailors in those prewar days were so earnest that they could not possibly have comprehended the humor lurking behind the man's perfectly straightforward remark about life in the navy.

"Things between Japan and the States aren't too good these days, are they? Guess I might be seeing you boys out in the Pacific pretty soon, eh?" the manager commented with a laugh.

I was astounded by his jocular manner. Then, as the sailors were leaving, the man handed each one a pack of cigarettes.

"Here, take home a little souvenir from Uncle Sam!" he said.

The men saluted smartly to express their thanks. The manager just laughed heartily and shook their hands, patting their shoulders as he saw them out the door.

This interchange highlighted the differences between Japanese and American educational systems. Too much discipline tends to make people rigid, I reflected, while freedom seems to exaggerate individual idiosyncrasies.

During the visit of the Japanese ship, Japan Town fairly bustled as officers and sailors were welcomed almost frenetically by the Japanese American community. Golden Gate Institute, the Japanese language school, invited the officers for ceremonies that were full of military overtones.

Then, before leaving port, the sailors reciprocated by inviting members of the Japanese American community aboard their ship for a party. They served all manner of Japanese delicacies to their guests.

"Oh, how delicious!" the issei marveled as they savored the Satsuma soup.

"A real taste of home," they sighed to one another.

The captain gave a little welcoming speech, personally expressing his appreciation for the generous hospitality he and his men had enjoyed during the ship's call in the Port of San Francisco.

"Ladies and gentlemen, this Japanese naval vessel is an extension of the mother country. Please, make yourselves at home here today and consider that you have returned to Japan," he said.

Those words "mother country" reverberated with countless overtones of nostalgia for the issei, arousing in the oldest immigrants particularly a deep longing for the land they had left behind decades before. Many of the expatriates shed tears as they listened to the brave words of the gallant young Japanese officer.

"My fellow countrymen, do not be anxious about the well-being of Japan. We shall defend the soil of our nation against all foreign enemies for as long as we live!" he declared.

All too soon it was time for the ship to set sail. The party drew to a close and the Japanese Americans went ashore. A rousing instrumental rendition of "The Battleship March" was followed by cheers of "Long Live the Emperor!" and a final military salute from the ship's officers and sailors. Then the vessel disappeared into the fog of San Francisco Bay.

I did feel a sense of kinship with those Japanese sailors, but I could not share the enthusiasm of the other people on the pier as we watched the ship sail away. I remembered all too well the tense atmosphere I'd experienced in Japan before I left that country—the social unrest aggravated by the February 26 and the Marco Polo Bridge incidents, the strains on Japanese society that lay concealed beneath the festive celebration of the "Fall" of Nanjing. To me, this ship was symbolic of the troubled Japan I had seen just two years before—a country fast on its way to becoming a militaristic state.

After the sailors left, I settled into my old routine—going to high school, reading Japanese literature with Mrs. Sano, and taking kendō lessons in the evening. But the departure of the Japanese ship left me increasingly puzzled by questions of my own identity. Am I Japanese or am I American? If I am going to live my life in the United States as I intend to, what am I supposed to do as a member of an ethnic minority here? How can I overcome the inferior status that seems inherent in being a minority in this country?

Questions like these motivated me to take a new interest in the history of Japanese Americans. There were not many books on the subject then, but from listening to my elders I learned about the difficulties Japanese immigrants had always faced in America: that for a period between 1906 and 1907 Japanese children were barred from San Francisco public schools; that in the 1920s the government cut off all further immigration from Japan; that Japanese immigrants were not allowed to own real estate in this country (although some managed to get around the restriction by purchasing a home or land in the name of an American-born child); and that issei were not permitted to become naturalized American citizens. I knew, too, from accounts that I read in the local Japanese American press, that white farmers in California were now accusing Japanese farmers of being a threat to the Caucasian population's economic well-being. How? By working too hard!

As I thought about who I was in the light of all this, I also became more aware of the differences between kibei like me and the other nisei in California—especially that our two groups of second-generation Japanese Americans had very different attitudes toward assimilation. The nisei tended to believe that successful assimilation was vital to their survival in American society, so most of them struggled to mold themselves after the patterns set by the dominant Anglo culture. They hoped that would somehow assure their future security and success in this country. But we kibei, who had received much of our childhood training in Japan, still had a spiritual foothold in Japanese culture. On the one hand that foothold gave us a firmer sense of identity, but on the other it rendered some kibei less capable of fully assimilating into American culture—and also perhaps less motivated to do so. Thus, as a result of very different experiences in childhood, both cultural and language barriers separated these two second-generation groups, creating a tension between us.

When I considered the generally biased attitude toward Japanese Americans in this country, added to the peculiar difficulties facing a kibei, I was increasingly convinced that earning a college degree was going to be crucial to my own survival in America.

But the issue of my education was overshadowed by the ominous international situation. In November 1941, Japanese Ambassador Nomura Kichisaburō and special envoy Kurusu Saburō met several times with American Secretary of State Cordell Hull and President Franklin D. Roosevelt. The Japanese Imperial Army had already occupied French Indochina, and Tōjō Hideki had replaced the more moderate Prince Konoe Fumimaro as prime minister of Japan. Clearly, a crisis was threatening to break over the Pacific.

I heard rumors at church that the Christian evangelist E. Stanley Jones was desperately trying to mediate between Japan and the United States. But the local Japanese American newspaper reported that the government of Japan regarded as an unacceptable ultimatum the "note of November 26" handed by Cordell Hull to the Japanese emissaries. This note set forth detailed terms stipulated by the U.S. government as conditions for an amicable settlement of outstanding differences between the two countries. But that amicable settlement was not to be.

Less than two weeks later Japan bombed Pearl Harbor. Japan and the United States were at war.

Not quite four months after the Pearl Harbor attack, on April 1, 1942, an unprecedented military order was announced in San Francisco. Despite its timing, this was no April Fool's joke—West Coast Army Commander Lieutenant General John L. DeWitt was dead serious when he ordered all persons of Japanese ancestry excluded from a large portion of the city of San Francisco effective April 7. Identical orders were issued up and down the West Coast, until the states of Washington, Oregon, and California were effectively off-limits to all Japanese Americans, U. S. citizen and resident alien alike. At the same time, executive orders were issued by the federal government to establish the machinery for evacuating Japanese American residents from the entire coastal area and forcibly interning them in designated facilities inland. Notices of these orders in both Japanese and English were posted on every street corner in San Francisco's Japan Town.

The Japanese American Citizens League (JACL), a nisei organization, offered an immediate response to these orders, but I was shocked when I heard it: all members of the Japanese American community were strongly urged to comply fully with the government's directives. This despite the fact that members of the JACL's own constituency were angered and dismayed at being stripped of their constitutional rights as citizens of the United States and forcibly evacuated from the West Coast to be interned in unfamiliar places far from their homes.

In flagrant violation of the Constitution, on the pretext of a national emergency, the United States government effectively deprived West Coast Japanese Americans of the freedoms guaranteed to all citizens by the United States Constitution. How could our nation so arbitrarily revoke constitutional guarantees for one particular group of citizens, I wondered. Doesn't that undermine the Constitution itself and weaken the protection it is supposed to give all Americans?

I found it hard to believe that so far as I knew not a single influential politician, public figure, or organization was speaking out to defend and protect the rights of American citizens who were about to be forced into what amounted to concentration camps. Indeed, the vocal supporters of the exclusion and internment of all West Coast Japanese Americans included such political and social leaders as President Franklin D. Roosevelt, champion of democracy and architect of a New Deal designed to ensure the well-being of all American citizens; Earl Warren, attorney general and later governor of California and eventual chief justice of the Supreme Court; and internationally known journalist Walter Lippman.

I did understand very well that America, the country of my birth, had been attacked by a foreign enemy and now needed its cit-

izens to join in its defense. But I was outraged at a compulsory evacuation order directed exclusively against Japanese Americans. It
wasn't just that my rights as an American citizen were being violated—I was frustrated and infuriated by the dark shadow that the
exclusion order seemed to cast across my entire future. I had yet to
graduate from high school, and now this turn of events was going to
stand in the way of the college education that was so crucial for me.

Japanese Americans living in our section of San Francisco
were put on notice that we would be required to vacate the city by
twelve noon on April 7, 1942, after which time we would be subject
to compulsory internment by the U. S. government. All West Coast
Japanese Americans would first be transported to "assembly centers"
without delay. The orders stipulated that we were to take with us
only what we could carry ourselves.

With just a few days before the deadline, we had no choice
but to sell off virtually all our furniture and other belongings for
whatever price we could get. Our white fellow citizens did not hesitate to take full advantage of this situation. They forced us to cut
prices so low that in many cases they were able to walk away with
people's family treasures and personal possessions for practically
nothing. My feisty mother, however, rebelled, refusing to sell her
most treasured belongings. Instead, she expressed her rage openly by
smashing to bits every valuable piece of pottery she had brought
with her to this country—to the evident astonishment and dismay
of a cluster of white onlookers who had been panting to acquire her
beautiful Oriental pieces at bargain basement prices.

The night before we were to be sent away, I lay on the floor of our
apartment—our beds were already gone. I could not sleep. Restless,
I got up and walked over to the window. The light was out in Hiro's
room. His family must have had a fair amount of savings from their
business, for as soon as the exclusion orders were announced, his
entire family moved away—I suppose to someplace farther east
where the orders did not apply. People with money were fortunate;
they could protect themselves and their families by buying their way
to freedom. Hiro always showed great disdain for the martial arts,

but his family were certainly adept at the art of self-defense. Now he would be able to finish high school in another city, to complete his education and assure his own future security. *He* would never think of becoming caught up in things like Japanese culture and literature, in tradition and ethnic pride. Hiro had no dreams, so life was easy for him. He was clever. And I despised him for it.

I gazed out my window, past the darkened houses and beyond to the boundless reaches of the night sky. The moon shone brilliantly, and, even farther away, the delicately shining stars whispered among themselves. I gazed at them for a long time, recalling the refrain from the old Christmas carol:

> O star of wonder, star of night,
> Star with royal beauty bright.

Mrs. Sano had sung that carol to me. I wondered what she was doing now—what she would be thinking. She had done so much for me. She was so kind and beautiful. I hoped that all would be well with her.

I awoke early the next morning. The time had come.

Mother was truly the Japanese housewife who, like the proverbial flying bird, leaves behind no trace. She had cleaned every nook and cranny of that apartment until it sparkled, even though it did belong to that nasty landlord who badgered and insulted us.

Mother and I ate a simple, unhurried breakfast and gathered our baggage. I took one long, last look at the spot where my desk had stood for so many years. Then we set out to walk to the nearby YMCA, where we and our Japanese American neighbors had been ordered to report.

As we passed the corner store, the red-bearded old storekeeper left his customers inside and came rushing out to bid us a tearful farewell. For the first time I learned that the man was a Russian Jew. Although he must have already been middle-aged at the time of the Russian Revolution in 1917, he had been forced to flee persecution by the Communists and came to the United States seeking freedom.

"And now I am furious at this country for taking away *your* freedom!" he shouted in a loud voice, shaking his fist heavenward.

I smiled inside to know that at least here was someone who was still on the side of justice. I said good-bye to the kind, passionate man who had been so good to me over the years and wondered whether I would ever see him again.

Several buses were lined up and waiting in front of the YMCA, and a crowd of people had gathered. Japanese are invariably polite, no matter what the occasion, and even this horrendous day was no exception. People smiled and greeted each other, asking after one another's health. But then everyone fell silent when the armed soldiers supervising the operation began to treat us like so many pieces of baggage, handing out large tags with numbers to be hung about our necks.

Our initial destination turned out to be the Tanforan Assembly Center, a hastily remodeled racetrack in the suburbs of San Francisco, about an hour's bus ride away—where the large, chic Tanforan Shopping Center was later built near San Francisco International Airport.

To the north of this assembly center were the San Bruno hills, with "South San Francisco Industrial City" spelled out in large letters on their slopes. To the east, the P–38 high-speed pursuit planes that were active in the South Pacific took off or landed every few minutes at the airport. To the south was Burlingame, an upper-class, restricted white residential area where Asians were not allowed to live. A highway leading into San Francisco formed the western boundary of the compound. Sturdy barbed wire fencing surrounded the assembly center, and sentries with bayonets were posted along the perimeter every thirty yards or so.

The upper part of the grandstand on the east side of the Tanforan racetrack had been converted into one large dormitory room for single men, and most of the unmarried kibei were placed there. Young couples were assigned rooms in a small, remodeled horse barn that still reeked of horse manure. In the center of the track stood row upon row of barracks, the housing designated for families.

In this hastily constructed shantytown, a single plywood panel divided the quarters of each family from its neighbors. We could hear the slightest whisper next door. There was no privacy anywhere.

Here began the first phase of our life in confinement.

Meanwhile, on the outside, the Hearst newspapers led increasingly vicious attacks on Japanese Americans, inciting the people against us, warning their readers that they must never relax their vigilance against people of Japanese ancestry. And the populace accepted their every word uncritically. This was understandable. Even though we Japanese Americans had nothing to do with it, the husbands, sons, and friends of many readers of the Hearst papers had died or been wounded in the Japanese attack on Pearl Harbor. Also, a large number of servicemen who were from nearby Salinas, California, were among those taken prisoner by the Japanese Imperial Army and subjected to the infamous Bataan Death March in the Philippines. The families of these victims of Japanese military actions now turned the brunt of their anger against the Japanese Americans, and newspaper pages were laced with scare stories about us, with headlines such as "California Overrun with Japanese American Spies" and "Japanese-Americans Organizing Secret Societies in Assembly Centers."

The nerves of the American people, already frayed by wartime panic and fear, became more and more agitated. Indeed, the propaganda was so effective that Chinese Americans frequently suffered from being mistaken for Japanese. Finally, so that they might walk down the street unmolested, many Chinese Americans began to wear signs declaring "I am not a Jap!"

Sometimes people contrast the internment of Japanese Americans to Nazi Germany's treatment of the Jews, pointing out the obvious truth that Japanese Americans in the United States fared far better than the Jews in Germany. The two situations can hardly be compared. The United States is purportedly a democratic nation. Nazi Germany was a totalitarian state that never pretended to guarantee rights to all citizens. It is absurd to speak in the same breath of the internment policies of two nations with such diametrically opposed political ideals and forms of government.

Moreover, the fact that Japanese Americans were singled out for mass imprisonment was blatantly a matter of racial prejudice against Americans of Asian ancestry. No such attempt was made to intern entire populations of German Americans or Italian Americans, even though the ancestors of these people had likewise immigrated from Axis nations. Hypothetically, they could have engaged in fifth column activities aiding and supporting the enemy from within the country much more easily than racially identifiable Japanese Americans.

One common explanation for the unconstitutional internment of Japanese Americans attributes this aberration in American ideals of justice and human rights to a temporary mass hysteria that erupted only in the context of a war. Clearly it was nothing so spontaneous as that. The roots of the internment of Japanese Americans in 1942 are to be found in the long history of oppression faced by the Japanese American-community on the West Coast. This oppression was not directed solely against immigrants from Japan and their children. All groups of Asian ancestry in America look back to an appalling history of maltreatment in this country.

This history of racist oppression and maltreatment is the backdrop to my own story as an American teenager of Japanese ancestry who was incarcerated in internment camps for four long years by his own government.

There was not a single case of sabotage by a Japanese American during World War II.

4 Introduction to Life in a Concentration Camp: The Tanforan Assembly Center

The U.S. government provided three main types of concentration camps for the evacuated West Coast Japanese American population during World War II: assembly centers, relocation centers, and one segregation center. (There also were a number of smaller internment facilities where Japanese nationals and others were detained by the Justice and State Departments.) Assembly centers were the temporary camps into which we were initially herded on an emergency basis. The so-called war relocation centers, of which there were a total of ten, were the more "permanent" facilities where interned Japanese Americans were placed to remain for whatever length of time the U. S. government deemed necessary. These camps were administered by a newly created government agency called the War Relocation Authority (WRA) and thus were often referred to as WRA centers. One of the ten WRA centers, Tule Lake, was later redesignated a segregation center. So-called disloyal and dangerous elements were placed there, isolated from the other, more cooperative internees.

No matter what these centers were called, those of us who were sent to them were without exception civilians, noncombatants. We were forcibly incarcerated in these camps and deprived of our civil rights with no regard for the fact that the majority of us were American citizens—and for the sole reason that our ethnic heritage was Japanese. The residents of these internment camps were in no sense criminals but were nonetheless kept behind barbed wire under the constant surveillance of armed guards. To that extent, these "war relocation centers" were undisguised prisons or concentration camps.

For the first time in my life, I was forced to relieve myself on the toilet in the presence of total strangers. Or rather, to make the attempt. I don't believe anyone, no matter how thick-skinned, would find it easy to use a toilet that is just one long plank of ply-wood with holes in it—with no semblance of privacy and with mag-gots swimming in the tank below. Adjusting to this novel way of going to the bathroom was our initiation rite into communal living, a rite that took most of us a good long time to pass. Many of the women in the camp would go to the bathroom only in the middle of the night. Mothers accompanied daughters and screened them with sheets so they might have a little privacy.

Although we had no freedom in these assembly centers, we *were* guaranteed three meals a day without any particular effort on our part. But it is not enough for human beings just to be fed like so many animals in captivity with nothing to do. With no work to do, there is nothing to aspire to. And a society where there is nothing to aspire to loses all sense of purpose and order. In my own need to escape the aimlessness and chaos of this existence in the camp, I began to look for some kind of work.

The Tanforan Assembly Center was divided into several "blocks," each with over two hundred residents. Mother and I had been assigned to the block on the east side of the center, near a highway. After a time I heard that our block had a position open for a cook's helper in the kitchen, so I applied for the job and was hired at the grand salary of sixteen dollars per month. (There were two main wage levels for camp residents: $19 a month for skilled work and $16 a month for general labor. There was also said to be a $12 category, but it was rare to see a person earning $12.)

Two shifts worked in the kitchen. One prepared breakfast and lunch and the other dinner, with the two groups trading duties weekly. My shift was headed by a young nisei called Kō, a corpulent fellow in his early thirties. Normally a quiet person, he could be rather terrifying when angered, for he was a big man. But he was so self-conscious and apologetic after losing his temper that I couldn't help but like and respect him. I also enjoyed working with a vivacious young woman named Mrs. Hashimoto, who taught me how to handle a kitchen knife to dice up vegetables, bone a young hen, or slice beef. Feeding over two hundred people three times a day kept the kitchen crew very busy, but we did our best to serve the other residents cheerfully, and the food provided to us during this initial period of internment was not too bad.

I gained much from my work in the kitchen, but perhaps most valuable was the opportunity to become acquainted with nisei like Kō and Mrs. Hashimoto, both of whom were older than I. They were college graduates who had already experienced the hardships of life in American society. They were well acquainted with white America's anti-Japanese bias, which had existed for a long time before the tragedy of World War II. Still, these two nisei were good American citizens. They were unconditionally but quietly loyal to the United States and even forgave the American people who persecuted them. Neither did they hate the Japanese—born and bred in the United States, they didn't know enough about the Japanese to hate them. I liked these two individuals because they did not whine and complain about their plight like some of the kibei, nor did they prate about "loyalty" and "patriotism" as did some of the other nisei.

Kō, although discouraged in the present situation, seemed firm in his private belief that someday he would be called upon to demonstrate his loyalty to his country—even to the extent of putting his own life on the line. He never identified with Japan's military successes even when the Japanese Imperial Army was advancing rapidly through Southeast Asia during the early stages of the war. On the contrary, Kō was determined to volunteer for the American military just as soon as the government would allow him to do so. After the war ended, I learned that Kō had indeed been given the opportunity to demonstrate his loyalty as a citizen of the United States. He gave his life for his country on the battlefields of Italy.

One day after I began to get somewhat used to life in the assembly center, word came around that an armed platoon was about to search every block in the camp. The guards must have had plenty of time to spare, for they were preparing to comb all the barracks in the camp, to locate and confiscate any contraband items in the possession of residents. Contraband items included weapons (such as pistols and knives) and shortwave radios—things that could not possibly have been smuggled past the soldiers into the assembly center in the first place—plus anything printed in the Japanese language.

I had brought several Japanese novels and biographies with me, as well as some volumes of Chinese-style poetry, so I decided I'd better hide these suspect publications before the search began. Accordingly, I headed for a remote corner of the grassy area beyond the racetrack fence and located a spot there to conceal my precious books. This done, I threw myself down on the grass, looked up at the sky, and drew a deep breath.

A cluster of white clouds drifted quietly eastward. Suddenly—as if purposefully to destroy the peacefulness of the scene— a P-38 pursuit plane plunged into the mass of clouds with a deafening roar, returning me to the real world with a start.

"Oh yeah, there's a war on," I said aloud to myself.

"Hey, Min, what are you thinking about over there?" asked a soft, rather effeminate male voice close by.

I turned my head slowly to see a boy named Mickey, who had been a high school classmate in San Francisco. He had been lying quietly in the deep grass not too far from the spot where I had concealed my books. Mickey had asthma and was always so sickly that he had received a special exemption from gym classes at school. It didn't look as though he had a very happy family life either—his widowed mother had remarried a man much older than herself. I hadn't known Mickey very well in high school, but from what I knew about him, I felt a bit sorry for him. Mainly, though, I thought of him as kind of a weakling.

"What are you reading?" I asked.

Without answering my question, Mickey strolled over amiably and sat beside me. He was carrying a Bible.

"Min, what are you planning to do?" he asked.

I turned on him indignantly.

"What the hell does it matter what I plan to do? They've thrown us into this place and we aren't going anywhere or doing anything until this war is over!" I fumed.

"Min, do you know what war is?" Mickey asked.

What a dumb question, I thought, not bothering to answer.

"War is evil. It's a sin. There is no such thing as a 'just war.' It's murder. No matter what the reasons for it, war is evil. It's a sin."

I listened without comment. Where on earth did a weakling like Mickey get such strong convictions? Statements like "war is evil" and "war is a sin" were taboo in America then. Such talk would definitely be frowned upon by the House Committee on Un-American Activities!

"What are *you* going to do, Mickey?" I asked.

"I'm going to go to college. And God willing, I'll study to be a doctor and a missionary. When this war is over, I want to help the people who have suffered because of it," he replied.

After a moment, Mickey continued, "Min, you speak Japanese, don't you? Do you suppose you could teach me some Japanese? Maybe just an hour a day?"

I'd been a little startled and unnerved when I realized Mickey must have seen me hiding my Japanese books, but now I was surprised again—to hear that he actually wanted to learn the language. He hadn't been someone I particularly noticed in high school, but I did remember that his name was always on the honor roll, despite his frequent illnesses. No doubt he was intelligent. Some of our other nisei classmates were smart, too, but I had consciously kept my distance from them. They were so blatant in their efforts to be as American as possible. Besides, they seemed concerned only about their own welfare and had nothing but scorn for anything Japanese—as though they were ashamed of their own ethnic tradition. Hiro was one of those.

But Mickey was different from that bunch. True, he hardly knew anything about Japan, but he was making an effort to learn. Not only that, he also seemed more concerned about helping other people than about ensuring his own future best interest. I realized that behind Mickey's weak appearance was a very strong will. He had love and hope and faith. What a strange, skinny fellow he was!

Not long after our encounter, Mickey received permission to leave the assembly center to take a scholarship at a college affiliated with his denomination. His church would act as his guarantor. After Mickey left the camp, thick letters arrived from him faithfully every month. Each time he wrote to me, he talked about the love of God. I wasn't much affected by this talk of God's love, but I did write to Mickey several times and sincerely wished him well in his endeavors.

I wanted to get out of the assembly center, too, and continue *my* education. I glared resentfully at the barbed wire enclosure that cut me off from the outside world. Beyond that fence an endless stream of cars moved along the highway, those in the northbound lane heading toward my hometown of San Francisco. In the city, I knew, could be heard the nostalgic plaints of ships' horns in the harbor. Here, we only heard the roar of bloodthirsty fighter planes.

"Min," called a feminine voice behind me as I paced along a road in the assembly center one day, deep in thought.

When I turned, I saw Nancy, an attractive young woman about my age whom I had met working in the mess hall. I did not respond, however. I just kept on walking. I had to do some serious thinking about my future, and I really didn't feel like talking to anyone.

Apparently surprised and hurt at this rebuff, Nancy was silent for a few moments.

"Well! Good-bye!" she flung out angrily, and ran off in a huff in the opposite direction.

Suddenly returning to my senses, I turned around to apologize. But by that time she was gone, and it was too late.

In the early days of our incarceration, notices called "Japanese Imperial Headquarters Communiqués" managed to filter into the assembly center rather frequently. These news summaries informed us proudly of Japan's victories in Southeast Asia, which the Imperial Army had by then almost completely overwhelmed. But by the late summer of 1942, these bulletins from Japan were becoming more and more outdated. The Japanese Navy, moreover, had already tasted decisive defeat at Midway, yielding naval and air supremacy to the Americans in the Central Pacific.

It was clear by this time that there was no longer any threat whatsoever of a Japanese attack on the West Coast of the United States. Consequently, the removal of Japanese Americans from coastal areas to prevent fifth-column activity in the event of a Japanese invasion—the ostensible reason for the exclusion orders in the first place—was patently unnecessary.

Nevertheless, U.S. government officials chose to ignore both the lack of military necessity and the unconstitutionality of rounding up and interning the entire West Coast Japanese American population. The War Relocation Authority had received its orders, and its directives were to be implemented as planned. Accordingly, we were now informed that we would be moved further inland— from the assembly center in California to a relocation center in the interior of the country.

We bade a terse farewell to the racetrack that had been our host for the past four months—and to its benchlike toilets. Southern Pacific Railway cars stood on a siding beside the assembly center. Mother and I climbed aboard the train under the watchful eyes of bayonet-carrying soldiers. We were told that our group was headed for the Topaz Relocation Center in the state of Utah.

As the train began to travel up the coast and I realized that I was leaving the Pacific shore for months or maybe even years, I longed to take one last look at the familiar scene. But every window on the train was covered with a thick black curtain, and we were under strict military orders not to open them. The reason? Because air force and navy bases and fortifications were located along our route. I smiled bitterly at the thought of this precaution. Not a soul among us would have had the desire or the gall to commit any kind of sabotage.

We learned that our trip was to last two days and two nights. The train was crowded, but the food was surprisingly good. We were even served by black waiters in the dining car, but as none of us had any money for tips, the service wasn't particularly good.

The train slowed significantly once it began the climb into the foothills of the Sierra Nevada. When at last we were allowed to open the curtains, we could see giant sequoia trees and beautiful rivers flowing through deep, verdant valleys. Then the luxurious evergreen forests around Lake Tahoe spread before our eyes. The train switched engines in Reno, Nevada, and immediately started on again, hurtling headlong into the vast expanse of the Nevada desert. The desolate landscape stretched on and on, not a tree or blade of grass, not a single house in sight, only an occasional tumbleweed blown along by the wind. The train moved slowly over the desert like a tiny boat navigating a vast ocean. Here and there large outcroppings of rock salt tricked the eye into seeing snowdrifts.

We went on and on through the desert for a full day and night until at last the train halted on a siding in the tiny, remote station of Delta in central Utah. We got off the train and soldiers loaded us onto buses to be jostled about for another half hour under the sizzling heat of the September noonday sun.

Finally, we saw in the distance—like a mirage in the desert—row upon row of barracks, plunked down in the midst of crazily blowing clouds of sand and dust and surrounded by high barbed wire fences and watchtowers.

5 Sand Capital Topaz

I stepped off the bus and fell as the thirsty desert sand swallowed up my feet. The wind whipped about, lashing my face with sharp grains of sand. In the midst of this confused arrival, I noticed a young woman holding an infant and standing there hopelessly, immobilized. But how could I help her? How could any of us help her? We were all in a daze, searching about in the blinding sandstorm for the right barracks. It took Mother and me a full hour to locate our assigned quarters in the blowing dust and sand. We hurriedly took refuge inside, but the sand was blowing in through the poorly fitted frames of the closed windows. All our possessions were soon covered with a layer of sand and the room was full of it.

Our throats were painfully dry, so I went in search of the lavatory to get some water. When finally I located the latrine in our block I heaved a sigh of relief—this camp actually had flush toilets separated by partitions! But the water was so lukewarm and salty that I gagged on it. And I spotted three large scorpions nesting by one of the toilets.

Once we had adjusted to life in the Tanforan Assembly Center, it was relatively peaceful there. We were still in the suburbs of San Francisco, close to familiar San Francisco Bay. We were in known surroundings and a climate to which we were accustomed. But Topaz was utterly foreign to us. It was frightening to California Japanese Americans to be taken so far from the West Coast, and we despaired at the thought that as long as the war continued we would be held prisoner in this desolate camp in the middle of the Utah desert.

But the Japanese do have a tendency to accept what comes, and the older generation had inculcated this quality in their offspring as well. Although caught in this bizarre twist of fate, the majority of Japanese Americans submitted docilely, without resistance. They resolved to persevere even in the midst of this desert. They would make a home here and get the trees to bloom. The trees, however, balked at putting down roots in the alkaline desert soil. And when it rained, the ground turned to clay and the mud stuck to our shoes so that we could hardly lift our feet. Still, the residents of Topaz persevered, studied the situation, and tried again. They planted strong-rooted flowering plants in front of their barrack homes and trampled down and graveled the clay paths until they were hard enough to walk on even in the rain. Some people created a miniature pond in front of their quarters and planted a decorative sagebrush or two beside it in lieu of a bonsai. Others decided to create more living space for their families than was provided in the cramped barracks. They pulled up the floorboards and dug down nine or ten feet to fashion a fine basement room with floor and walls and ceiling. These underground chambers proved cool in the summer and warm in the winter. Thus was this desolate desert hamlet rapidly transformed into a desert metropolis full of vitality, dubbed "Sand Capital Topaz" by its ten thousand residents.

About the time the struggling plants put forth a few little green buds, a public high school opened its doors in Topaz. Many of the adult nisei had college degrees, so it was no problem to recruit a teaching staff from within the camp itself. Nevertheless, the officials brought in a Caucasian teacher specifically to teach classes in civics and American history. It seemed that the government authorities felt these two subjects could not safely be entrusted to Japanese American teachers.

Recalling the precedent of Mickey's release from Tanforan to attend college, I registered in the camp high school to complete the final term of my senior year. In my college prep school in San

Francisco, math, science, and foreign languages had been emphasized more than civics classes. But, perhaps because of the peculiar nature of the Japanese American concentration camps, the high school in Topaz stressed civics and American history. According to the requirements of this school, I still needed these two courses in order to graduate, despite the fact that I already had plenty of credits in math, science, and foreign language.

The instructor for the social studies courses was a tall, haughty white woman with a forbidding manner. She appeared ill at ease at first, trying to pronounce our unfamiliar Japanese surnames, but eventually she learned to say them almost correctly. It was about this time that she began to give lectures in our class on the Bill of Rights. I was astounded. What was this anyway? The fundamental human rights of every student in that room had been flagrantly violated by the United States government when it imprisoned us in this concentration camp. And now that government was going to force us to study the Bill of Rights? I could not believe the gall of these hypocrites! I longed to stand up and shout, "There's a limit to how much you can humiliate people!" But I held my peace for the time being and refrained from confronting the teacher.

One day, however, in the class on modern American history, the same teacher began to discuss the history of diplomatic relations between the United States and Japan. Needless to say, the study of the history of diplomatic relations between any two nations requires a sophisticated understanding of the culture and history of both countries. Our teacher, however, summarily dismissed Japan as a country with a long tradition of militarism, which had repeatedly acted as the aggressor against other nations, while the United States by contrast had a tradition of freedom and democracy. That statement was an easy one to refute, but not a single student in the room appeared inclined to do so. I could not restrain myself any longer. I raised my hand and stated that I wished to take exception to the teacher's presentation, beginning with her definition of an "aggressor nation."

Taken aback by my unexpected challenge, the instructor immediately counterattacked by citing the historical facts of Japan's invasion of Manchuria, China, and French Indochina.

"And was it not Japan that attacked Pearl Harbor?" she concluded in a loud voice.

I refused to lose my composure.

"That is not a definition. Those are simply historical examples. If we are going to give historical examples, then didn't the United States invade the territory of the American Indians and subjugate them as it moved westward? Didn't Russia invade Siberia and subjugate its native peoples as it developed eastward? Didn't America's allies, England, France, and Holland, invade South and Southeast Asia and subjugate the people of those countries?" I asked.

"Min, are you a fascist?" the teacher accused, betraying her increasing agitation.

"I am not a fascist. But if you are going to talk about history, before you judge that a certain country is an 'aggressor nation,' I think you first have to look at the historical circumstances to understand *why* that country acted as it did," I persisted.

The teacher glared at me, but I would not be intimidated. All the indignation I had felt since being imprisoned in the camps suddenly exploded. Throwing caution to the winds, I was determined to speak my piece.

"You said America has a tradition of freedom and democracy. If that's true, why were we Japanese Americans forced out of our homes and thrown into concentration camps?"

"That is enough, Min! What you are talking about has nothing to do with what we are studying," she said.

"The imprisonment of Japanese Americans is a part of American history," I insisted.

"That is *not* what we are discussing in this class," she retorted, dismissing out of hand the questions I was trying to raise.

After class ended—perhaps out of deference to the teacher—not one of the other students spoke to me. I realized that I probably should not have said the things I did. I knew it wasn't the teacher's fault that Japanese Americans had been interned. I had gotten carried away by the force of my own rhetoric and attacked her too harshly. But, still, I thought it was very inappropriate for someone who fancied herself a teacher to become so enraged by a student's disagreement as to denounce him as a "fascist." Besides, even though the teacher did know her American history fairly well, she clearly knew very little about Asian history. I was deeply disappointed in an instructor who had to resort to brainwashing her students, who refused to listen to a student's opinion, and who believed without question that the United States was always and absolutely in the right. Concluding that I had nothing to learn from a teacher who was so self-righteous and narrow-minded, I decided to quit going to school. I did not go back to class the following day.

About a week later I ran into Nancy in the mess hall. She lived in the same block in the camp. Nancy and I were in the same year in high school, but she was younger than I. Because of my years of schooling in Japan and the time I lost with my eye injury, I had fallen a little behind in the American school system. Even though I was older, however, Nancy was a forthright young woman who would not hesitate to speak her mind when she wished. Now she approached me with every appearance of having forgotten that awkward incident when I ignored her at Tanforan.

"Min, why haven't you been in school this week?" she asked abruptly.

One reason was that I had decided none of my classmates had any guts, but I couldn't very well say that to her. So I didn't say anything at all.

"Min, it's not your fault. And it's not the teacher's fault, either. Everybody's nerves are on edge with this war going on. Why don't you come on back to school? You want to go to college, don't you? You know you can't get into college without a high school diploma. Besides, it's only a few more months until we graduate anyway."

Having thus delivered her opinion, Nancy turned and breezed out of the mess hall without a backward glance.

She is right, I suppose—actually, she's pretty perceptive, I admitted to myself, but I did hate facing that teacher again. The next morning, however, I braced myself and went to school. The teacher welcomed me back to her classroom with a perfunctory smile. Inwardly, I was screaming, "You bitch!"

I soon realized that the teacher now carefully avoided any mention of delicate issues in her class. It was cowardly of her, but with her limited knowledge of Asian history it was probably the wisest course for her to take. Her boring, insipid lectures droned on and on, day after day.

About a week later, the teacher approached me after class to ask if I would serve as interpreter for an upcoming PTA meeting. Apparently Nancy had told her that I was fluent in Japanese. No doubt she had been full of good intentions to attempt a reconciliation between the teacher and myself, but it annoyed me and I did not want to do it. Still, I couldn't very well refuse, so I agreed to be there. After the meeting ended, the teacher handed me a thick, recently published book on American history as a thank-you gift for my services. I guessed this gesture was her way of trying to make amends, but I was sorely tempted to tell her that I was far more interested in eighteenth-century French history. Nevertheless, I accepted the book without comment and hurried out.

I wanted so badly to get out of Topaz. And good news was surprisingly soon in coming. It came in the form of an announcement from the WRA that students would be able to apply for permission to leave the camp to continue their studies. I went to the administration office immediately to submit my leave application. About a month later I received a summons for an interview. This invitation was not, however, from WRA officials as I had anticipated. It was from the FBI. When I saw that, I had a certain premonition about it.

Trembling, I reported to the administration office.

"Take a seat, please," I was told.

The investigator was a rather paunchy middle-aged man. He smiled as he spoke in a deep, powerful voice. I always feared the smile of a Caucasian. You never knew what lurked behind that pleasant face. Apprehensive, I took the proffered seat without saying anything.

"You were educated in Japan, right?" he began.

"I spent four years there."

"So—you're a kibei," he stated.

I knew well the negative connotations of the term *kibei*, and that the FBI were keeping an especially close watch on the kibei. I hesitated a moment before answering, thinking over the implications of his question. In that I had been educated in the States, was completely fluent in English, and was comfortable in the American milieu, I was a nisei. By the same logic, inasmuch as I had been educated in Japan, was fluent in Japanese, and was comfortable in the Japanese milieu, I was also a kibei. I wondered exactly what my interrogator understood by the term *kibei*, but—intimidated as I was under the circumstances—I dared not ask him to clarify.

Evidently my failure to respond promptly made a bad impression on the FBI agent, for his smile suddenly vanished and he became agitated.

"You dirty Jap!" he shouted, pounding the table in front of me with his pudgy fist.

I paled. He continued to shout. Not quite sure what was happening, I was terrified.

"I suppose you'd be *glad* if Japan won this war, wouldn't you?" he said accusingly.

I just sat there with my mouth open at that absurd suggestion, for I knew very well from my boyhood experience in Japan how poor the Japanese were. How could Japan win a war against a rich and powerful country like the United States?

"Well, why don't you say something?" he shouted.

Again he banged the table sharply, then sat on it, glaring down at me from his perch.

Finally, I found my voice.

"I am an American citizen," I said.

It had taken all my effort to say that much, and my voice trembled as I spoke. It was no longer fear, however, that made me tremble. It was the wretched feeling of having to endure such humiliating insults from this man. Utterly oblivious to any human feelings I might have, he continued to throw out questions, his voice harsh and thick with ridicule.

"What were you doing while you were in Japan?" he asked.

My voice became harsh as well.

"I was a child. I went to school there from the time I was eleven until I was fifteen. That's on my leave application, if you'd read it!"

"And what were you doing in San Francisco?"

"I was in high school," I replied.

"Not school. What kind of organizations did you belong to?"

"I didn't belong to any organizations."

"It will do you no good to lie," he warned.

"I did not belong to any organizations," I repeated.

"Liar! You were a member of the Butoku-kai,* were you not?"

"I just took some kendō lessons. I guess the San Francisco Kendō Club was affiliated with the Butoku-kai, but I never knowingly became a member of that."

"I am not asking you what you *knowingly* did. I am telling you that the Butoku-kai is a reactionary organization. What kind of training did they give you? What sort of orders did you have when you came into this camp?" he asked.

"I took kendō lessons as a sport!" I retorted.

"Why do you lie? The head of the Butoku-kai is General Araki Sadao. What orders did Araki give you? Orders to commit sabotage, right? You speak Japanese—you're a perfect candidate for sabotage. You're a kibei, and a member of the Butoku-kai. You are a dangerous individual! And you are *not* getting out of this camp!" he concluded, shouting.

By this time, I was shaking with a hatred that boiled up from deep within me, and I no longer cared whether or not I got out of the camp. It was all right with me if I never went to college at all. My future didn't matter anyway. If I had possessed a knife at that moment, I have no doubt that I would have plunged it into the FBI man's heart. From my kendō training, I knew how to kill another and to kill myself in the tradition of the ancient samurai. And kendō had trained in me the determination to accomplish what I willed. I knew that I could kill him, and myself. Such was the intense hatred and rage that the FBI agent provoked in me.

---

* Martial Arts Association.

I have no memory of leaving that office. Once outside, I began to wonder how the American government could be so suspicious and afraid of a youth like myself, a minor who had not yet even graduated from high school. Why on earth was the government persecuting me? Why wouldn't they let me out of the camp to go to college? I tried to puzzle it out rationally. The only reasons the man had given, though, were that I was a kibei, that I had taken lessons in kendō, and that I was a member of the Butoku-kai!

In those few hours, all my hopes for this world, my trust in other human beings, and my confidence in myself were utterly decimated.

"The FBI is cruel! They're tyrants! They're abusing their power!" I was screaming inside.

That afternoon I paced up and down the dusty roads of Topaz, feeling completely and utterly alone. Enviously, I watched a hawk soaring high in the sky, free to fly wherever it wished to go. Finally I found a deserted corner of the camp where, away from the curious eyes of others, I could release my feelings in tears of vexation and rage. I could not help recalling my boyhood days in Japan. Innocently chasing dragonflies and cicadas in the garden in Hiratsuka, playing with Pooch, swimming with my classmates, stealing watermelons with the bad boys—those had been the best years of my life. I had never had such freedom in San Francisco. Life there had been a much more serious business for me. Once I entered high school, I became all too keenly aware of the realities of the struggle involved in living as a member of a minority in this society—and those realities had pressured me to work as hard as I could at my studies.

High school in San Francisco had also been a period of social isolation for me. Alone in a corner of the school yard during the lunch hour, I would sit quietly, eating the simple sandwich I had made for myself and observing with a cool eye as my Caucasian classmates enjoyed lunch together, chatting and joshing with one another. And my nisei classmates had always eaten their lunches in a certain spot, in the same group, repeating the same simpleminded conversations. I had not been accepted by that group either, for I was a kibei. I don't *care* what they do, I had told myself. I reacted against them with contempt, becoming more and more attracted to the Japanese tradition that had been the source of so much solace to my soul. In fact, I had begun to take great pride in that tradition.

They don't know anything about Japanese tradition at all, I had thought. They don't understand it, but *I* do.

Still, I could not altogether deny the fact that I had been lonely. I had had no friend with whom to share confidences or discuss the future. More and more, I had turned inward. Kendō lessons had given me a physical outlet for my resentful feelings, and Mrs. Sano had helped to soothe my troubled spirit through the Japanese literature she had read with me. But, all in all, high school in San Francisco had been a lonely time for me.

Darkness fell in Topaz.

The howls of coyotes from outside the camp's enclosure were almost tangible in the night. Every few moments the eerie beam of the searchlight from the watchtower swept across my feet and moved on.

That evening, idly flipping through the pages of the book of Chinese verse that I kept beside my bed, I found these lines:

> Behind his words he tends the dark flame that annihilates
> bones;
> In his smile he stealthily sharpens a rapier to pierce the
> other through.

That's what it is, I thought, reflecting on the day's events. America misleads people with its clever words about freedom, only to persecute them in the end. America preaches equality as its loftiest ideal, smiling as it leads people to their destruction, I concluded.

I would never forget my hatred of that FBI agent. I cursed the government of the United States, which had thrown me into this camp—I would curse it forever. In my powerlessness, this was the only means I had to express my defiance toward those in power.

Morning came. I decided I would quit going to school for good, no matter how close I was to graduating. This time it was not just because I found it unbearable to listen to the teacher's hypo-critical preachments about civics and American history. It was because I knew how excruciating it would be to watch my class-mates complete their studies with prospects of going on to college and to witness their elation when they received permission to leave the camp. Now I knew that I would not be leaving the camp. I would not be going to college. I was distraught. I despaired of ever finding a way out of here.

It was at this point that I began to think seriously of escape.

I recalled our arrival in the camp. The little freight station called Delta had been about thirty minutes away by bus. I should stay away from there for sure. Local people would know as soon as they saw my Asian face that I was an escapee from Topaz, and they would lose no time in informing the authorities. I would avoid Delta, then, and head north into the desert. I would skirt around population centers altogether, moving along the southern edge of Salt Lake at night and then into Ogden. That was about 150 miles from the camp. It should take me about ten days to get that far.

The desert is bitter cold at night in the winter and is beastly hot in the summer, so I figured it would be best to make my break sometime in the spring or early summer. I would need a magnet for my compass. I had spotted a surveyor's instrument at a construction site in the camp and one night went to the worker's shed, broke open the instrument, and stole the magnet. I would need at least five leather water bags—or botas, as they were called—to carry enough water. These, too, I began to take one at a time, at intervals, from the construction site. At each meal in the mess hall I saved a portion of my rice, dried and salted it, and stored it in a bag. I knew that I would perspire in the desert so I would need to replace the salt in my body if I were not to collapse.

I whittled a hardwood stick to make a weapon for protecting myself against wild animals in the desert. Coyotes are shy, so I knew that I didn't need to worry about them. Wolves can be vicious, but I figured that if they attacked me in a small pack of two or three I could handle them. With that in mind, I practiced kendō every night—targeting a low object and hitting it vertically, whirling around instantly and making a horizontal slash, then stepping back to make another vertical hit. There was no way, though, to protect myself from rattlesnakes that might slither up while I slept—I just had to hope I wouldn't encounter any. But I equipped myself with a first-aid kit just in case.

Finally, I began to think about what would happen once I got through the desert. If I could slip into Ogden under cover of dark, then I could get on an eastbound freight train. Once I got farther east, I should be able to buy sandwiches or something in the stations. All races of people lived in the eastern industrial cities, and, in any case, the exclusion order didn't apply in that part of the country. I envisioned that I would live in one of those cities, get a job there, and attend school at night.

The problem was how to get out of the camp. I certainly could not escape in broad daylight, for the soldiers in the watchtowers were constantly on the lookout. It would have to be done at night. But even at night, they continually swept the perimeter with searchlights from the towers. I tried to estimate the range of the searchlights. They illumined a stretch of about two hundred yards at five-minute intervals. I thought I could make it if I could get past the range of the inner searchlight, cut through the wire fence with pliers, then move quickly beyond the range of the outer searchlight.

Again I visited the shed at the construction site, this time to steal a strong pair of pliers. I practiced cutting steel wire of the same thickness as the fence, but discovered it would take me well over ten minutes to cut a hole in the fence that was large enough to crawl through. I practiced and practiced, but still I could not get the time under nine minutes. Just thirty seconds of cutting with those pliers and my hand was so numb I could barely move it. I realized that if it took me that long to cut the fence, then I couldn't possibly avoid being caught in the sweep of the inner searchlight. I was sure in any case that the soldiers in the guard tower would immediately notice a hole that big in the fence. Besides, I was afraid that if they caught me in the act of escaping, they might well shoot me on the spot. (Later I learned that I was not far wrong on that count. On April 11, 1943,

James Hatsuaki Wakasa, age sixty-three, was taking a perfectly inno-cent morning stroll near the fence inside the camp when he was fatally shot by a guard from a watchtower about three hundred yards away.)

I gave up the plan of cutting my way out through the fence.

I now recalled the enormous sewer pipes in the city of Paris that I had once seen in a movie in San Francisco. It wasn't likely there were any sewer pipes that large in the camp, but perhaps there would be some kind of pipe big enough for me to crawl through. During the daylight hours I searched diligently for the openings of any pipes inside the camp, but none that I found were large enough for a person. Apparently camp sewage was discharged through rather narrow pipes to a spot about half a mile away. So escape through a pipe would not be possible either.

I had seen those basement rooms that some residents dug out under their living quarters. They worked on them very openly, and no one thought anything about it when they saw a pile of dirt out-side the barracks. But if I were to dig a tunnel, say from our living quarters all the way to the outside of the fence, the pile of dirt would be so gigantic it would be sure to invite suspicion. And if I did suc-ceed in escaping through a tunnel leading to the outside from our quarters, it would bring certain trouble for Mother. So a tunnel escape was out of the question, too.

I thought and thought about it.

Then one day, as I was walking near the camp entrance, I spotted a truck full of men in work clothes leaving the camp. I asked a middle-aged man where they were going. He said that the camp had a farm about five miles away, and that the men on the truck were going to work there. I headed straightaway for the camp employment office and signed up as a farm worker. What a beautifully simple way to get out of the camp! I smiled to myself and forgot all about the pre-vious obstacles I had encountered.

I drew a deep breath as the truck carried me and the other farm workers out the front gate. It was the first time I had left the con-fines of the camp since they put me here. The very air seemed full of hope. As the truck moved along the road, the barracks of the camp receded into the distance until they looked like so many tiny matchboxes.

The truck bounced along for about twenty minutes over the narrow, dusty road to the farm. There were no soldiers anywhere in sight. We were surrounded by desert, of course, so they probably figured there was no place to run and hide. But that was where they were wrong. Still, an escape would require meticulous planning. And, before anything else, I needed to develop a feel for the surrounding terrain. I decided to take my time and perfect my plan without rushing things.

Someone was waiting for us with a fire burning when we got to the farm. The workers all walked over to the fire to warm themselves, and there I saw a tanned, robust young kibei from Hawaii. Near the fire he had an old wooden plank that he proceeded to prop up at one end with a small stick. To the bottom of the stick he attached a string, which he led off some distance to the side. He pulled a piece of bread from his pocket and broke it into small pieces, scattering them about under the board. Within five minutes a dozen sparrows had gathered to feast on the bread. The boy then jerked the string, dropping the board, and the men all shouted and dived after the sparrows. The boy from Hawaii casually shoved the birds he snared into his pocket. Then, one by one he took them out and plucked their feathers. He rinsed the naked birds in water, placed a wire mesh over the fire, and began to roast them. When they were done he picked one up and ate it with great relish. The other men followed suit, preparing and roasting their sparrows to eat. I just stood there watching. Then the boy handed me one of his roasted birds.

"Try it. It's tasty," he urged.

I took a bite of the thigh. I couldn't truthfully say it was tasty, but everyone was having such a good time roasting and eating the sparrows that I found the whole thing immensely enjoyable. I smiled again.

The young man was about my age, but hard work had given him a physique and maturity that I still lacked. Everyone called him Yoshida. He had a friend two or three years older named Yoshino, who was also from Hawaii. Neither of them could speak a word of English but they had a kind of unsophisticated charm. Because they were kibei who had returned to Hawaii from several years of schooling in Okinawa just before the war broke out, they were regarded by the U.S. government as particular security risks. Thus, they had been sent to this concentration camp on the mainland even though most Japanese Americans in Hawaii were not interned. I liked the two of them, and they seemed to like me as well.

Yoshida and Yoshino were friendly with a third young man originally from Okinawa named Nakasone. One day Nakasone suggested to Yoshida, Yoshino, and me that we steal a pig. This suggestion rekindled my own youthful fondness for such pranks. The four of us remained at the farm after the usual quitting time that day, telling the others we would be working late that night. We laid our plans. I had little to contribute as a novice at this particular endeavor, but each of the others readied a rope.

After dark, we stole into the hog house on a neighboring farm. Yoshida grabbed the back legs of a hog while Yoshino got the front legs and tied them up. Meanwhile, Nakasone firmly bound its nose and mouth. Their movements were so swift and simultaneous that the pig was easily bound before it had a chance to make a noise. It must have weighed over two hundred pounds. The four of us struggled to carry the heavy bound animal to a tree about a hundred yards away. Nakasone hung the pig's rope-bound hind legs over a branch of the tree. As it swung there upside down, he swiftly slit its throat and the warm blood began to gush out. The three young men sat on the ground and lit their cigarettes. As much blood as possible had to be drained from the animal before it could be butchered, they explained.

After they all finished their cigarettes, Nakasone cut the pig down and they proceeded swiftly to cut off its head and legs, split open the belly, and rip out the entrails. It was truly a skillful job. I just stood there observing the whole process in silent admiration until they pressed me into service as well, instructing me to dig a deep hole at the spot where the blood had drained onto the ground. Then the bloodstained soil, along with the pig's head, legs, entrails, and any other parts that would take too long to cook, were all dumped into the hole and buried to eliminate all evidence of the slaughter.

Back at our farm, my companions lit their cigarettes once more for a well-deserved rest. Then they went to work again, carefully cutting up the parts of the hog that could be easily cooked and wrapping them in waxed paper. We dug a deep hole near the shed, buried the waxed-paper packages there, and placed a large stone on top so that our treasure would not be stolen by coyotes or wolves. Neither the manner of butchering nor the method of storage was particularly sanitary, but this was not the time or place to be concerned with such niceties.

It was the wee hours of the morning before we got back to the camp. It had been a thrilling evening.

The next day all of us working at the farm ate our fill of stone-roasted pork. Nakasone bewailed the fact that we couldn't roast the pig whole, but all in all it was a very pleasant day.

The manager of the farm project was an issei man in his sixties, a soft-spoken fellow with a powerful build. He taught me very carefully how to do all kinds of things—to plant potatoes, to transplant tomato and celery seedlings, to drive a tractor. I learned firsthand just what backbreaking labor it is to transplant seedlings or plow a huge farm. But hard work did have its compensations. The three rice balls I wolfed down every day at lunchtime were more delectable by far than the sandwiches I used to eat all alone in the corner of that school yard in San Francisco.

Summer was on its way. The manager began to give me, the city boy, work that was less strenuous but that carried greater responsibility. In one leap, I was put in charge of the irrigation ditches. I drove a small truck all around the farm, and when I discovered a break in one of the ditches I would plunge into the water with a shovel to fix it.

With the truck at my disposal, I took the opportunity to investigate thoroughly the territory surrounding the farm. Once I even accompanied the manager and the Caucasian supervisor to the

train station in Delta to pick up some fertilizer and farm imple-
ments. While there, I discovered that eastbound trains did make
stops in Delta, and I concluded that this would be my best route of
escape after all. I checked the layout of the station and glanced over
the train schedule, committing it to memory to note down at a later
opportunity. Eastbound departure times varied depending on the
day of the week but were generally between four and six in the
morning. All were freight trains headed for eastern industrial areas
by way of Ogden. The boxcars looked securely locked, so the only
"open seating," so to speak, would be on the coal cars.

I readied my compass, botas filled with water, food, clothing,
and even blankets, and hid them in a shed at the farm, awaiting my
chance. Then one night I stayed at the farm after the others left, on
the pretext of doing some necessary night work. To make certain it
was safe, I went first to check the outer perimeters of the farm. Having
made sure that no one was about, I went back to get my provisions. By
this time it was already beginning to get light—I had to hurry.

But just as I started down the road in the truck I glanced out
over the fields and was startled to see in the distance that one of the
large scallion fields was entirely flooded with water from an over-
flowing irrigation ditch. Had I altogether forgotten to close the
sluices at the end of the day yesterday, or was there a sudden influx
of water from upstream? I hurried to close all the gates, rushing up
and down every road on the farm, then proceeded to shovel the
water out of the field. It took me hours. By the time I finished, it was
morning and I gave up all hope of escaping that day.

Presently, the truck carrying the other workers arrived for
the day. I hurried over to tell the manager.

"Sir, I did a terrible thing," I confessed.

My words tumbled over one another as I explained how the
ditch had broken, flooding the field, and how I had shoveled it out.
I hung my head with shame and apologized. The manager laughed
loudly at my excessively downcast expression.

"Why, that sort of thing happens all the time!" he reassured me.

Then he got into the truck with me and we went to take a
look at the situation. The gates were all closed by this time, and the

drainage outlets neatly repaired. Assuming that I had stayed up all night just to fix the outlets, the manager praised me so generously that I was really embarrassed. I knew very well that the whole thing had happened only because I was so absorbed in my escape plans that I failed to check the water level upstream.

At lunchtime, I sat down beside the manager and apologized to him again.

"I'm really sorry about that mess," I said.

"You don't need to apologize. Everybody makes mistakes. You just keep up the good work. You do amazingly well at this work for a city boy!" he said encouragingly.

Indeed, as he sat there next to me, the manager seemed to be genuinely enjoying his lunch, altogether unconcerned about my lapse. I was tremendously relieved. I resolved that I would not make another mistake like that one.

I had great respect for the farm manager. The oversight of this huge farm required careful attention to all its many aspects, but he had such a firm grasp of the entire operation that in an emergency he could quickly make the appropriate decision. Moreover, he encouraged people, gave them responsibility, and had excellent judgment when it came to putting the right person in the right place. When a job was well done, he saw to it that the workers got all the credit for the results. When something went wrong, however, he took the responsibility himself and never blamed the others.

The men working on the farm were all either issei or kibei who spoke little or no English. Their conversation tended to be dominated by prewar reminiscences. Whenever I broached the subject of what might happen after the war, they would smile and say, "Who knows?" It wasn't that they didn't know, though. They were afraid. When they were evacuated from the West Coast they lost the farms they had labored to build up over many years, so they knew that after the war they would have to begin again from scratch. But they did not want to think about that right now.

"What do you think you'll do, though, Minoru-kun?" they asked.

"I want to go to college," I told them.

Despite the situation in which I now found myself, I still had not given up my determination to finish school. I remained convinced that the only way to make a decent life for myself in America was to get an education.

"You're right. If we were educated, we wouldn't have spent our whole lives working like peasants," the manager muttered.

"But farmers do honorable work, don't they?" I asked.

The manager just grinned and patted me lightly on the shoulder. He got up slowly, dropped his cigarette, ground it out with his boot, and headed back to work. Perhaps my youthful earnestness recalled to him the aspirations of his own youth. He had been born and raised in Meiji period Japan and came to America right after the Russo-Japanese War in the early 1900s. People said he had no family and no property of his own. Apparently he had experienced something of the seamier sides of life—he was no stranger to alcohol, gambling, or women. He was a man well acquainted with the pain of living, with the ironies of life, and a heavy, lonely shadow always seemed to trail in his wake. But he would never dream of demeaning another human being.

The three young kibei from Hawaii continued to sit there with me.

"What are you going to do in college?" one of them asked curiously. College was an alien world to these young men.

"Well, first I want to study Western philosophy. Then after I graduate from college in the States, I want to go to Japan and study Asian philosophy. I want to do something to create better understanding between Japan and the United States."

Suddenly embarrassed at revealing so much of my own inner thoughts and ambitions, I fell silent. But the others were unperturbed. They looked at me with new eyes.

"You study hard and do that, okay?" one of them said.

"You won't forget about us when you're famous, though, will you?" another kidded with a grin.

The three stood up to go back to work. Like the farm manager, these were not the kind of people who would ever criticize or hurt anyone. They were a little unsophisticated, but they were humble, hard working young men.

I remained sitting there for a while after the others returned to work. I *do* want to hurry up and go to college, I thought. When can I get out of here? When will I ever be able to go to college? Will all *my* plans end up as empty dreams, too? I wondered.

I slipped my hand into the pocket of my work pants and took comfort from the touch of a small, well-worn paperback book I carried there. It was the biography of Benjamin Disraeli—born a despised Jew, he was an adventurer who overcame poverty and illness and rose to become prime minister of the great British Empire.

Ten days had passed since the break in the irrigation ditch. Once more I remained at the farm overnight. This time I was very careful to check the sluice gates and ditches. All was as it should be. Once more I gathered my gear and started off through the darkness in the truck. I drove with the headlights off, for I knew the roads well enough. I headed for a mosquito-infested alfalfa field about a mile from the Delta station and there I parked the truck. Shouldering my gear, I walked silently through the dark toward the station. There was the freight train standing just where it was supposed to be. I climbed into one of its coal cars, made an indentation for myself in the midst of its black contents, and spread out the blankets I had brought to conceal myself and my belongings. As I settled in to wait for the train to begin its journey, I looked up at the stars twinkling in the early summer sky.

At last I was out of the camp! My heart was already in the East. When I get there, I'll be able to study! I thought, elated.

And the FBI can go to hell! I added bitterly.

Thirty minutes went by. I began to feel a little calmer. But then something started to bother me: How would the manager at the farm explain my escape to the white supervisor? They might interrogate him pretty harshly. It could affect the other workers, too—those men who'd been such good friends to me. Maybe they wouldn't be allowed to leave the camp to work on the farm anymore. Or perhaps they would be sent to a special detention center, locked up as criminal accomplices of the escapee. The men would surely hate me for what I had done. They would question my integrity.

Slowly I folded my blankets, gathered my belongings, and forced myself to begin the long walk back to the truck.

Frustration seething within me, I gunned the motor and raced the truck through the darkness. Tears fell on my hands as I gripped the steering wheel. My body shook with uncontrollable sobs.

"*Damn* the FBI! *Damn* the FBI!" I screamed over and over inside the truck as I drove back to the farm.

I heard a whistle in the distance. It was daybreak. Time for the train to depart.

In February 1943, a few months before my brief escape from the camp, an explosive manifesto had arrived in Topaz. All residents would be required to complete a government questionnaire, a copy of which was posted on the notice board in the mess hall. Entitled "Application for Leave Clearance," the implication was that those who completed the questionnaire satisfactorily would be allowed to apply for release from the internment camps and be free. The most crucial question included in this document was number 28:

> Will you swear unqualified allegiance to the United States
> of America and faithfully defend the United States from
> any or all attack by foreign or domestic forces, and
> forswear any form of allegiance or obedience to the
> Japanese emperor, or any other foreign government, power
> or organization?*

I paled when I read these words. I had to think what to do. I did not want to answer such a question. The point was not whether I was loyal to the emperor of Japan or loyal to the United States.

---

* Commission on Wartime Relocation and Internment of Civilians, *Personal Justice Denied* (Washington, D.C.: The Commission, U.S. Government Printing Office, 1982), 192.

The point was the excessive coercion being exercised against me—an American citizen—by the U.S. government. That government had incarcerated me against my will, taken away my freedom, prevented me from getting an education, subjected me to the intolerable humiliation of an interrogation by the FBI, caused me to despair of ever leaving the camp, and now—on top of all this—it was trying to coerce me into pledging my unconditional loyalty to it. I did not want to yield to that kind of oppressive force. Then, to underscore the government's demand, the WRA administration warned camp residents that those who did not respond to the loyalty question would be subject to a $10,000 fine or twenty years in prison. Much later it was revealed that this threat was nonsense fabricated by the WRA without any legal basis whatsoever. It is a cruel hoax when a government chooses to practice that kind of deception on its own citizens.

The loyalty question was initially intended for all camp residents, with complete disregard for the fact that those in the older generation were still Japanese citizens and that citizens of any country who are living abroad when a war breaks out might legitimately retain feelings of affection and loyalty toward their own homeland. Even the thickheaded U.S. government bureaucrats finally realized how absurd it was to demand that the issei declare their undivided loyalty to America—particularly given the fact that the laws of this country had denied these same Japanese immigrants the right of naturalization. Thus the government eventually dropped its demand that noncitizens answer question number 28.

It was a fundamentally different issue for us nisei, however. We were Americans. We did not have Japanese citizenship, so it was not at all surprising that the majority of our generation responded "yes" to the loyalty question. Still, even in our case, it was hardly a simple yes-or-no matter. We were members of the same ethnic minority as the issei, and together we had a long history of being persecuted as Asians in the United States. Moreover, our two generations were naturally related as members of the same households, as parents and children. It is not surprising that some nisei felt compelled to refuse to declare their loyalty.

The dilemma of loyalty versus disloyalty that faced internment camp residents was not just an idle topic for dinner table conversation, a simple choice between two alternatives. To choose the
one (pledging one's loyalty to America) meant hoping for the total
destruction of the other (Japan), and here lay the cruel ramifications of the issue. To pledge our loyalty to America meant collabo-
rating in the killing and wounding of people who lived in Japan, a
denial of a personal connection based on a shared culture. This
denial was the source of particular anguish for kibei like myself who
were American by birth and citizenship but who had also lived and
studied in Japan.

Issei, nisei, kibei—all had to live through this war between
the United States and Japan, each in his or her own particular situation experiencing an individual anguish. It is impossible to say who
made the "right" decision at the time and who the "wrong." We all
had to endure a period that was rife with ironies, and each of us had
to act with integrity in accord with the dictates of conscience.

Of course—as in any group of people—there were some who
seemed to lack this quality of integrity, who based their decisions
more on opportunism than anything else. One such person was the
principal of a San Francisco Japanese language school. When a
prince of the Japanese Imperial family had come to the United
States in the prewar years, this principal invited him to visit his
school and did his best to encourage a spirit of emperor worship
among the other Japanese Americans. Again, when the Japanese
Imperial Navy's tanker put into port, the same man invited the
Japanese naval officers to his school and loudly advocated the community's support for the Japanese military. Strangely enough, however, soon after the war broke out, this same principal accepted a job
as a Japanese language instructor working for the American military, training U.S. intelligence forces for the war in the Pacific. At
that point he boasted to all who would listen that *he* was supporting
the struggle against "fascist Japan, imperialist Japan, aggressor
Japan." It seems that there will always be those in every age and
nation who feel that integrity, when inconvenient, is a dispensable
commodity.

Even young nisei children got entangled in the discussions about loyalty and disloyalty.

"Mama, I'm an American. I want to hurry up and get out of this camp and be free," says the little girl.

"Me, too!" chimes in her little brother.

"What do you mean?!" the mother replies. "I'm Japanese. If the Japanese Army lands in San Francisco, I'll go out and greet them with the Rising Sun flag!"

"If you carry a Japanese flag, Mama, I'll carry the Stars and Stripes and fight those Japanese soldiers!"

Such were the absurd interchanges that the loyalty issue provoked between issei parents and their American-born children. But if the Japanese Army had indeed landed in San Francisco, what would have become of this family?

There was another scenario that was at the same time less hypothetical and a great deal grimmer. In a number of Japanese American families, one son living in Japan was drafted into the Japanese Army while another son in the States enlisted in the United States Army. Thus it came about that brother was pitted against brother—as enemies fighting one another on the ephemeral stage of a global war. This was not some fictional scene from Dante's *Inferno* or an imaginary description of the Buddhist hells related by the monk Genshin in his *Essentials of Deliverance*. It was a real situation created by a war between Japan and the United States in the very twentieth century that advocates love for humanity and prides itself on rational, scientific thinking. Brothers screaming at one another about loyalty and fidelity while devouring one another in the name of "justice"—what is this if not a scene from hell?

The war in the Pacific created some very strange scenes in the camp at Topaz—scenes curiously similar to some I had witnessed on the streets of Japan during the Sino-Japanese War. A soldier's mother would go from door to door begging other women to contribute one stitch apiece to a "thousand-stitch belt" for her son who was going to war. Each fervently hoped that this traditional good-luck charm would ensure her son's safety on the battlefield. Even though some in the camp scoffed at these women, they would persist until they acquired all of the one thousand stitches for their sons' belts. Whether or not their American-born sons ever actually wore those belts as they went into battle is another question. But many a nightly tear was undoubtedly shed by these young men on their army-issue pillows when they thought of the love that their issei mothers had sent with them as they went to war armed with this traditional protective charm. This was the tragic dilemma of the nisei soldiers: Even as they took up arms against the homeland of Japanese tradition, they realized they themselves were heirs to that same tradition.

The nisei in Topaz held meeting after meeting to explore and discuss among themselves the ramifications of the loyalty question. Extremist elements among the kibei in the camp had been rather quiet, but with this new provocation from the government they became vocal once again. The pro-Japan group tried everything they could do to discourage other nisei from cooperating with the U.S. government. They would barge into nisei meetings, heckling, ridiculing, and threatening the participants. It was an extraordinarily tense atmosphere in which the nisei had to decide what they should do.

At one of the meetings, a group of very rational young nisei men were working to draft a declaration of their intent to comply in every respect with the laws and regulations of the U.S. government, to fight against imperialism, and to meet their obligations as good American citizens. As I sat listening to the debate, I became so disturbed by the tenor of the discussion that I could no longer contain myself. Their arguments only magnified the sense of indignation I had been feeling, particularly since that humiliating interrogation by the FBI agent. I raised my hand and was recognized by the polite young nisei presiding over the proceedings.

"I have two objections to all of this," I stated. "First of all, the term 'imperialist' is very ambiguous. It would be easy enough to demonstrate that America, too, is imperialistic. Second—as to meeting the obligations of a good citizen—what on earth does 'good' mean here? And exactly what *are* those obligations? When you make a blanket promise to 'meet your obligations as a good American citizen,' aren't you just committing yourselves blindly to doing whatever the U.S. government orders you to do?" I asked.

The young chairman's gentlemanly attitude suddenly vanished and he responded with anger to my outburst. "There is a war going on, you know!! We don't have the luxury to deal with all these abstract, philosophical questions you're talking about. The point is, we have to prove to the U.S. government that we're loyal Americans. We *have* to make the government see that we're sincere!"

Obviously there was no point in my pursuing this argument any further, so I held my peace and left the meeting. True, the things I'd said were rather abstract. I didn't make any practical suggestions about what we ought to do in the situation we were facing. But I really did feel that the questions I'd raised were the crux of the matter. I wasn't so much concerned about what we ought to do right here and now as I was about the war itself. It galled me that the other nisei just accepted the war without question and were simply calculating what they should do to ensure their own future best interests.

After I left the meeting, the group drafted a resolution of their intent to declare their loyalty to the United States government and to cooperate in every way possible with the war effort. This declaration passed by a majority vote of those present that evening and was duly forwarded to the camp administration.

A few days after that meeting, as I was leaving the mess hall one evening, I was accosted by the mother of the young nisei man who had argued so vehemently against me the night of the meeting.

"Minoru-san, you are still young. You are too idealistic. My son is enlisting in the U.S. Army because this is his country. He is a courageous young man—he's no coward. When this war is over, we'll see who was right," she declared.

Having no desire to discuss the matter with this woman, I turned on my heel and walked away.

"It's ridiculous, all this talk about who is courageous and who is a coward! History will be the judge of that!" I muttered to myself.

I felt more and more isolated. I found that I could sympathize neither with the ingratiating, opportunistic attitude of the nisei, nor with the violence of the radical pro-Japan kibei group. I knew no one who shared my feelings.

I began to see the loyalty question as my only opportunity to take a stand against oppressive government authority. I decided that I would no longer allow myself to be led around by the nose doing as I was told by the U.S. government. Accordingly, I responded with a decisive "No" to the loyalty question. At this time I was yet a minor, just nineteen years of age and totally oblivious to the far-reaching consequences of giving such an answer on the government's questionnaire.

One of the consequences of my refusal to declare my loyalty to the government became clear enough in short order, however. I was informed that because I had answered "No" to question number 28, I was now considered to be a member of the dangerous, anti-American element. As such, I would presently be transferred out of the Topaz Relocation Center to the Tule Lake Segregation Center located in northern California.

Thus it was that I bade farewell to the residents of Sand Capital Topaz, to my nisei friends, to the issei and kibei who had befriended me at the farm—and to my mother. My father, who was also interned at Topaz, was subsequently given leave clearance and later died.

It was autumn 1943.

6 "Disloyal and Dangerous": The Tule Lake Segregation Center

Tule Lake is a desolate spot in northern California near the Oregon border. Inland from the coast, this drained lake bed is out of reach of the moderating influence of the warm Kuroshio current, which runs along the Pacific Rim. Winters in Tule Lake are severe.

One of the regular war relocation centers had operated at Tule Lake since May 1942, but beginning on July 15, 1943, this camp was designated as a segregation center, where "disloyal" and "dangerous" individuals would be isolated from the main body of Japanese American internees. Segregation center inmates were to be brought from the nine other WRA camps, while "loyal" internees among Tule Lake's original residents were either given leave clearance or transferred to one of the other centers. Of all the Japanese American internees held in WRA centers during World War II, none were treated by officials of the United States government with so little understanding—indeed with such cruelty—as the residents of this Tule Lake Segregation Center.

The population of the segregation center was approximately eighteen thousand. The preponderance of these inmates were either issei or kibei, but among them were also some nisei who had never laid eyes on Japan. The mood of this population was one of uniform gloom. I arrived in this depressing place in late September 1943, along with the remainder of the "disloyal" and "dangerous" contingent from Topaz.

By the time we got there, the previous residents of Tule Lake had graveled the roads and dug simple drainage ditches beside them. Like Topaz the camp was divided into blocks, each with a mess hall and lavatories at the center. On either side of these shared facilities were ranked ten barracks containing three or four rooms each. Each room was equipped with a coal stove for heat in the winter, although with no insulation in the walls the room became cold the minute the fire died down. The only way to stay warm was to burn coal in the stove all day long.

But fuel was also in demand to heat the baths. Virtually the only pleasure for people in my block was to soak in a large, Japanese-style communal bath. Coal and kindling for the entire block were left in great piles in front of the bathhouse, and the grouchy old man who tended the fire to heat the bathwater kept a constant guard over this fuel supply, shouting at people to "Leave my fuel alone!" He made it extremely difficult for us to get any coal to heat our rooms.

I was assigned to share a room with a pair of kibei brothers who were several years older than myself. I'd known them a bit at Topaz—they'd gone to middle school (high school) in Japan before the war and were students at the University of California, Berkeley, when the war broke out. They were gentle fellows with a good bit of common sense, but I saw very little of them. Both young men were engaged to be married and were for all practical purposes already living with their fiancées, who were also at Tule Lake. So most of the time I had the room to myself.

The bugle sounding reveille reverberated to every corner of Tule Lake in the frosty dawn. I rubbed my eyes and peered out the window, dimly discerning a group of people floating toward me out of the morning mist.

"*Wa-shoi*! *Wa-shoi*!"

It was a group of forty or fifty young men feverishly yelling out in unison as they ran along the road behind my building. Each had a shaved head and wore a headband emblazoned with the rising sun insignia. Behind them came an equally fervent band of their female counterparts. I shuddered.

These were members of fanatic pro-Japan groups called the Young Men's and Young Women's National Defense Associations (Hokoku Dan) and the Service Association (Hōshi Dan),* led by Nishi Honganji Buddhist missionaries, teachers from the Japanese language schools, and other loyalists to the cause of Imperial Japan. Males in the two groups invariably shaved their heads, while the females wore braids. Both groups were known to be violent at times.

The first major incident of violence that erupted at Tule Lake was triggered by an accident involving internee farm workers who were not themselves members of these groups. On October 15, 1943, a truck carrying a group of inmates to work on the project farm over-turned, killing one man and injuring several others. The farm work-ers demanded compensation for the victims and safety measures to ensure that such accidents did not occur again. They refused to go back to work until those two demands were met. Tule Lake's incom-petent director, Raymond R. Best, not only rejected their demands but also completely barred segregation center residents from any agri-cultural work thereafter. On October 29 he called in strikebreakers from other relocation centers to run the Tule Lake farm.

Now forbidden to return to their jobs, the Tule Lake farm workers sought permission to hold a public funeral for the man killed in the accident. The administration's denial of this request resulted in mass demonstrations in the segregation center on November 1. Taking advantage of this discontent in the camp, the gangs of fanatics surrounded the administration office. The army intervened on November 4, but the demonstration only grew. Finally, on November 13, martial law was imposed on Tule Lake. Two weeks later the entire camp was subjected to a sweeping search for contraband, and residents thought to be agitators were rounded up and arrested.

---

* The full names in Japanese of these organizations were Hokoku Seinen Dan, Hokoku Joshi Seinen Dan, and Sokuji Kikoku Hōshi Dan.

The imposition of martial law at Tule Lake involved the mobilization of one entire battalion of armed soldiers, thirty-one officers and 899 troops, equipped with six tanks, several armored vehicles, and dozens of jeeps with mounted machine guns. As they charged into the camp, the army vehicles fired warning shots in every direction. In a futile gesture of defiance, one of the Hokoku Dan members leapt onto a tank with a baseball bat, but he was immediately thrown to the ground.

The military did not limit its activities to suppressing gang members, but generally harassed and intimidated the entire population of Tule Lake, including ordinary, peaceful residents. In addition to firing warning shots from tanks speeding through the camp, they even in some instances killed unarmed residents. James Okamoto, a nisei who had never been to Japan, was returning to the segregation center from a work assignment outside the camp on May 24, 1944, when he was shot by a guard at the front gate. Okamoto died the following day. The soldier was of course disciplined. The charge against him? Wasting a bullet. His punishment? A fine of one dollar.

The violence of ultranationalist groups was also turned against any camp resident who opposed their purposes. Even homicide was not unknown. Soon after the Hōshi Dan and Hokoku Dan were formed in the camp, the manager of Tule Lake's consumer coop, Yaozo Hitomi, was found with his throat cut. This crime was never solved, but the very fact that such a murder could take place and not be solved illustrates the psychological hold these violent gangs had on the general population of the segregation center. Their frequent attacks on individuals of whom they disapproved, while usually not fatal, made for raw nerves throughout the camp.

The violence perpetrated by the Hokoku Dan and Hōshi Dan on their fellow segregation center residents was inexcusable. It was, however, a symptom of the tremendous frustration caused by the extended unlawful detention of these young Japanese Americans. The incident involving the agricultural workers was just the fuse that ignited the violence that was waiting to happen. The subsequent indiscriminate arrest of group members and imposition of martial law, far from daunting these hot-blooded youths, only served to intensify their violent expressions of defiance—against both camp administration and fellow residents.

The extremists who were arrested (primarily members of the Hōshi Dan and Hokoku Dan) were thrown into the stockade, beaten, dragged about by the feet, and generally treated like animals. Although the administration arrested in all more than four hundred members of these gangs, others continued to rampage through the camp, turning Tule Lake into an abnormal, terror-ridden society.

The residents of Tule Lake Segregation Center had no protection whatsoever, either from the reign of terror imposed by violent gangs inside the camp or from the repression imposed by the army from without. The living conditions there were so severe that Dr. Richard Drinnon wrote years later that Tule Lake was "an 'extreme situation' whose psychological manifestations were comparable to schizophrenic phenomena observed by Bruno Bettelheim in the Nazi camps."*

The abuse suffered by Japanese American internees at Tule Lake was neither reported to the American public at the time nor did most Americans learn about it even after the war. Incidents of abuse at the segregation center were, however, observed and documented in a series of reports by Dr. Marvin K. Opler, an anthropologist working in the camp at the time. Clandestine photographs of some abusive incidents were also taken and should still be on file in the San Francisco offices of the late attorney Wayne M. Collins—the only legal advocate who worked on behalf of the unfortunate residents of Tule Lake.

Tule Lake residents were the victims of cruel and ridiculous administrative policies. The director of the center, its officers and guards, were demonstrably war criminals. It makes no sense that after a war has ended, only the war criminals of the defeated nation are punished. Meanwhile, individuals in the victorious nation who have cruelly and illegally violated the rights of others during that

---

* Richard Drinnon, *Keeper of Concentration Camps: Dillon S. Myer and American Racism* (Berkeley: University of California Press, 1987), 157.

same war go scot-free. The ancient political wisdom that "might makes right" clearly still holds in the modern world.

D uring that first autumn at Tule Lake, I was equally repelled by the tactics of the militantly pro-Japan gangs in the camp and by the oppressive measures taken against them by the U.S. government. But initially at least I had enough sense to refrain from challenging either the army or the gangs, and I certainly was not fool enough to join the Hokoku Dan or Hōshi Dan. The whole place simply terrified me. I was afraid to venture to the latrine alone at night. I was even scared to hold out my plate for food in the mess hall, because I never knew—maybe the server was a gang sympathizer. At night, alone in my room, I slept fitfully, wondering when the gangs might come bursting through my door in a surprise attack.

Finally, I developed such a severe nervous disorder that hives broke out all over my body. A Japanese American doctor in the camp examined me but did nothing to help. I lost my appetite. I knew I had to take some food, but the more I ate the worse the hives became. Malnourished as I was, I began to have repeated nightmares. Whenever I dropped off to sleep, I would dream that I was falling over the edge of a cliff into a black, bottomless pit. Then I would jerk awake, bathed in perspiration.

I had reached my physical and psychological limits. Not knowing what else to do, I finally decided to appeal to the camp administration for some relief from my suffering and for protection from this terrifying environment. One afternoon, I struggled to my feet and, confiding to no one what I was about to do, I walked toward the front gate where the office was located. Between the segregation center itself and its administrative office, however, stood two barbed wire fences some ten yards apart. Several sentries were posted at the gate. As I approached them, my throat was so parched that I could have breathed fire. The closer I came, the stronger the feeling that I was doing something terribly wrong. With effort, I asked a young sentry to let me through so I could go to the office. He told me to show my pass, but I had no pass—and no idea of how to get one.

"So you're one of those Hokoku Dan guys, huh?" he snarled.

"You can *tell* I'm not one of them, can't you? I don't have a shaved head," I replied.

The soldier snickered. "Well, wait here a minute. Lemme check with the office."

I looked around. Standing out there in the open made me exceedingly nervous. I knew that I was in full view of any gang members who cared to look. I could even be killed like Okamoto by one of the other sentries—it wasn't far from here that the guard had shot him.

After a while a heavyset, middle-aged guard emerged from the office.

"Hey you, Jap. Whadda you want?" she asked.

It was not an auspicious beginning, but I braced myself and said, "I want to talk to someone in the office."

"What about?"

"Please, let me come in," I pleaded.

"Whatsa matter? You don't like the segregation center?"

"Please let me come in," I repeated.

"I know—you're one of that anti-American gang. You go on back now," she said.

At that moment, two or three guards came running toward me, pistols drawn.

"Get out of here, you Jap!" they yelled.

Without bothering to ask why I was there, one of them—a big fellow—grabbed me and shoved me back inside the camp fence.

At that point I lost all control and began screaming: "Is this what you call America?! I was born in the U.S.! I grew up in this country!"

"Shut up, you Jap!"

Crazy with frustration and rage, I kept on shouting.

"So this country is really just for white people, isn't it? America's for the white people! There really isn't any such thing as freedom in this country, is there?!"

At that point a shot rang out. And another. And another.

Three times the guards shot their 45-caliber pistols at my feet as I scrambled back into the camp.

Before long, a rumor was spread among the gangs that I had gone and talked to the camp administration.

A few evenings later I was resting on my bed when the dinner bell rang. I had no appetite, but I forced myself to get up and go to the mess hall. I knew my health would never improve if I didn't eat. I went through the line and held out my chipped dish for a modest helping of that night's entrée. I salted the food and took a bite of the pasty, tasteless rice. I managed to swallow that much but gagged when I tried to eat the pan-fried liver. As usual, I left the mess hall that night with an empty stomach.

It was getting dark outside as I headed back to my room. I could see a newly delivered pile of coal in front of the bathhouse, but the old man was there glaring at everyone who went by. It was going to be another night without coal. The mess hall crew got all the coal they wanted, because they were in cahoots with the old guy. Tule Lake was like all abnormal, oppressive societies where individuals grasp any little vestige of power they can get hold of, just so they can throw their weight around and make other peoples' lives miserable. The old bathkeeper and the kibei bunch running the mess hall were like that—they had absolutely no conception of performing a service for others.

I recalled those first days of internment at Tanforan, where the nisei I worked with in the mess hall always did their best to serve the other residents. They created the tastiest meals they could with the limited materials they had available. They sympathized with their fellow camp residents, so they treated them as humanly as they possibly could. At that stage the fragrance of civilization still lingered in the camps. As I dragged my malnourished, exhausted body back to my quarters, I wondered how all those people I had known at Tanforan were getting along now.

Suddenly, three shaved heads lunged out of the shadows between the barracks. One of them hit me in the face, but I did not retreat. I threw myself at him with all my strength in a counter-body blow. My lip was cut and bleeding badly, but I wasn't going to worry about that. I stuck my right foot deep into the other guy's thigh and twisted my body, giving him a hip throw. The trouble was, I was so weak from not eating for several weeks that I fell with him. When I hit the ground his two friends started kicking me in the sides.

"Guys with long hair are *inu!*"* one of them taunted.

"Guys who speak English are traitors!" the other said.

Then the fellow I had thrown got to his feet and kicked me in the face.

"You asked for this!" he screamed.

Then the three of them scattered, disappearing into the darkness. I lay on the ground for a few moments, writhing with the pain in my sides. I could feel the blood running down my face. Two or three people started toward me to take a look, but I wasn't about to let them witness my agony. I willed myself to stand and limp back to my room. None of the onlookers made any move to help. They were all scared to death of retaliation from the gangs.

I had gotten a good look at the guys who jumped me, but to whom could I report them? Tule Lake was an unpoliced community. Besides, by this time, both the camp administration on the outside and the right-wing gangs on the inside regarded me with so much suspicion and hostility that neither would help.

Back in my room I didn't even bother to cleanse my wounds. It just didn't matter. Instead I followed my first impulse, which was to pull my record player from under my bunk. It was just a cheap one that I had bought from a friend at Topaz with the pittance I earned working on the farm. At this moment it wasn't so much the physical pain as my frantic emotions that needed soothing. I had only one record, Beethoven's Third Symphony, the *Eroica*. No matter how many times I played it, I found myself enthralled by its music.

Reputedly, Beethoven initially intended to dedicate this symphony to Napoleon the Great, who was one of his heroes. However, when Napoleon took the title of emperor for himself, Beethoven—a man of republican principles—felt outraged and betrayed. In the end, the composer refused to dedicate the piece to Napoleon.

---

* Stool pigeons. Literally, "dogs."

I went to sleep that night listening to the *Eroica* and thinking how I, too, had been betrayed—both by my government and by my fellow residents in the camp.

On July 1, 1944, the so-called Renunciation Bill, which had been passed by the Seventy-eighth Congress, was signed into law by President Roosevelt. This new law allowed Americans to renounce their citizenship in time of war. Implementation of renunciation procedures under this law began at Tule Lake in the fall of 1944.

By this time, I was physically and mentally at the end of my rope. I had been ridiculed and humiliated by the FBI agent at Topaz, denied permission to leave the internment camp to attend college, shot at by the guards in Tule Lake, and attacked by ultraright gangs in the segregation center. In my rage, I had only one thought: It was the government of the United States that threw me into this place. Why should I want to be a citizen of a country like that?

I decided to do the one last thing I could do to express my fury toward the government of the United States. I would renounce my U.S. citizenship.

I handed the application for renunciation of citizenship to the woman at the desk. She took it from me without even looking up, totally oblivious to everything I had been through in these last few years. She finished processing my papers in under ten minutes—as though this were the most routine, everyday matter in the world. I was very young, in fact just barely old enough to renounce my citizenship under the new law. But neither this woman nor anyone else ever said a word to me about the gravity, the far-reaching consequences, of what I was doing.

As I walked out of the camp administration office, I was conscious of a vague but growing sense of discomfort. Then it dawned on me: They got me! The American government threw me into a concentration camp, labeled me dangerous because I wouldn't declare my loyalty, intimidated me, and subjected me to extreme mental and physical stress. In fact, the government did such a good job of manipulating me that I just gave up my United States citizenship—voluntarily! Now they could deport me to Japan without any trouble at all, I realized.

Well, it was too late. I'd walked right into the trap set by the U.S. government—for this law that enabled native-born Japanese Americans to renounce their citizenship was by no means hastily constructed. In retrospect, it was the culmination of decades of calculated discrimination against Japanese Americans.

Some nisei still have not forgiven those of us who renounced our citizenship at Tule Lake, but they have no idea of the abnormal psychological state that prevailed in the segregation center. Renunciation was not a criminal act; it was simply the last act of defiance available to human beings who found themselves in an intolerable situation. Granted, it was a stupid thing to do. But that stupidity was fostered by years of persecution under the U.S. government. Long years of rage and accumulated resentment spawned that stupidity.

One of the renunciants was a nisei named Joe Kurihara, a man who had served in the U.S. Army artillery during World War I and garnered a distinguished war record with numerous honors. On several occasions in the relocation camps and again in the segregation center, he attempted to represent camp residents in negotiations with the authorities, pressing for better treatment. But invariably the officials ignored him, and all his efforts were fruitless. When he persisted in appealing to their conscience, they began to regard him as dangerous. He was thrown into the stockade and beaten.

Kurihara was not very tall, but he was a powerful, muscular man. Ordinarily an individual of few words, he could express his opinion with passion when the occasion demanded. He was straightforward and honest and despised anything the least bit dishonest or hypocritical. Kurihara would never kowtow to the authorities, no matter how much they beat him.

Betrayed by the country of his birth and despairing of the American conscience, Kurihara was one of those Japanese Americans who renounced his U.S. citizenship during the war. As a consequence, not long after the war ended he was "repatriated"—at age forty-nine—to a country he had never seen. He remained in Japan for the next twenty-seven years, firm in his resolve never again to set foot in the land of his birth. He died in Tokyo in 1971.

Joe Kurihara's renunciation of his U.S. citizenship was a protest against the persecution and maltreatment he suffered at Tule Lake. Even after the war ended, the U.S. government never offered a word of apology to Kurihara or to others like him. Was Joe Kurihara stupid? Or was the U.S. government stupid? History will judge.

The end of the war was close at hand and the winter solstice fast approaching. At Tule Lake black smoke rose from the bleak barrack rooftops into the evening sky, and the chill air turned my breath into white puffs that vanished into the surrounding darkness.

I recalled the leisurely strolls that I used to take through the streets of San Francisco. I could hear the lonely bellowing of ships' horns through the evening mist. In the fog, I would barely be able to see ten steps ahead. The tap-tap of footsteps would be the only clue that someone was approaching. Ah—those footsteps. Perhaps it would be some gorgeous young woman. A moment of anticipated pleasure. But that beautiful creature never did materialize. Life is like that, I told myself. Hope always meets with disillusionment somewhere just out of sight. Pleasure exists only in the moment of anticipation.

Deep in thought, I walked the nighttime roads of Tule Lake just as I had wandered the nighttime streets of San Francisco. I was no longer afraid of the gangs. By this time my despair was so deep that I just figured they could go ahead and kill me if they wanted. My steadily deteriorating physical condition contributed to an overwhelming sense of resignation.

"Guys who need three-to-one odds to attack somebody haven't got the guts to kill anyone!" I'd tell people.

"They say they belong to the National Defense Association?! Those guys couldn't defend a thing!"

"Service Association? What did they ever do to serve anyone? Those birdbrains!"

Those were the sorts of things I would say to anyone who would listen. Then I would walk through camp with a homemade billy club hidden under my jacket, ready for whatever might befall me. This was decidedly a self-destructive tactic.

As I wandered through camp that December night, I started to reminisce about Christmas in San Francisco long ago. I pictured the glittering yuletide displays in department store windows on Market Street, Christmas celebrations at church, and especially the holidays when I was a small boy. These memories made me smile for the first time in a very long while.

When I was little, there was a boy named Jōji living in my neighborhood in San Francisco. He firmly believed that it was Santa Claus who brought his Christmas presents. I thought that was pretty funny. But Jōji was a happy, trusting, overindulged little boy who had a warm family life, full of dreams and full of ease. His father was a kind doctor who was fond of children, and his mother a sweet, gentle lady. Every Christmas they would outdo themselves buying presents for their little son, telling him that Santa Claus had brought them. On Christmas afternoon Jōji would hurry to my place to tell me what Santa had given him. He'd always bring me a nice gift, too.

"Min, what did Santa give *you?*" he'd ask.

"Come on, Jōji, you know there's no such thing as Santa Claus!" I'd tell him.

Thus our yearly argument would begin.

Soon after the Manchurian incident in 1931,* Jōji's parents decided to leave San Francisco and return to Japan. Given the tenor of world events, they decided they had best abandon their plans for a future in America. Japanese doctors in those days were tacitly prohibited from treating white patients, particularly females, so Jōji's father's practice as a gynecologist had necessarily been restricted to the small Japanese American community.

---

* Seizure of the Manchurian city of Mukden by Japanese troops on September 18, 1931, followed by the Japanese invasion of all of Manchuria and creation of a military colony.

I remember begging my mother to let me buy Jōji a pair of woolen socks as a going-away present. I hated so to see my friend leave. As I recall, the family came from somewhere around Fukuoka, in southern Japan. They were good people, gentle people.

I wondered what Jōji was doing now. Were you drafted into the Japanese Army? Please don't die in this awful war. It's not your war. It's the politicians' war.

I was so engrossed in this reverie that I lost all track of time and walked to the far corner of the camp. Suddenly, I heard music coming from one of the barracks. When I listened closely, I realized that it was a hymn I had learned in church years ago:

> My faith looks up to Thee,
> Thou Lamb of Calvary,
> Savior Divine!

I stood there alone, rooted to the spot outside that barrack room, drinking in the music that flowed softly toward me. These were the sounds of a peaceful world, a world that seemed light-years away from the deranged place where I now lived. I found myself singing the rest of the stanza:

> Now hear me while I pray,
> Take all my guilt away,
> O let me from this day
> Be wholly Thine!

At that moment, the door of the barrack room opened softly. I stepped back involuntarily as a pretty young woman of seventeen or eighteen emerged from the room carrying a bucket. She hesitated for a moment, apparently startled at the sight of the strange, scar-faced young man standing outside. But then she smiled, came out, and went to fill her bucket with coal. Through the partially open door I caught a glimpse of the room inside. Fourteen or fifteen people were gathered there. The young woman returned.

"Won't you come in?" she asked.

"Oh. No, thanks," I said.

Flushing, I lowered my head to conceal the scar on my cheek and began to walk away. She came after me.

"Please come in. We've just finished singing hymns, and we're going to have tea now. We'd love for you join us. My name's Cindy."

She was so charming and innocent. At a loss for words, I turned to follow her toward the simple little barrack church. I felt a bit sheepish, for I hadn't really wanted to leave. Unobtrusively, I dropped my billy club on the ground before going in.

A young Caucasian minister was standing at the front of the room. His suit was old and shabby, but his face revealed a self-composed, intelligent individual. When he saw me, he hurried over and shook my hand. His handshake was warm, full of love.

"My friend. Welcome!" he said.

There was instant communication between us, even in that first encounter. Our eyes locked for a moment before I could drop my gaze. I did not want to meet his eyes. I didn't want him to see the ugly, desolate state of my soul. I didn't want him to notice the tears in my eyes. But how could I hide the tremendous sense of relief that rushed through me in that moment? At last, I had met a true human being again.

Tom Grubbs was a Presbyterian minister. Everyone called him by his first name. He had been born and raised in Los Angeles and graduated from the University of California, Los Angeles. He then spent three years at San Francisco Theological Seminary and came to Tule Lake immediately after his ordination. He was a committed pacifist, a conscientious objector.

> All they that take the sword shall perish with the sword
> (Matt. 26:52).
> For whosoever will save his life shall lose it; but
> whosoever shall lose his life for my sake and the gospel's,
> the same shall save it (Mark 8:35).

These words formed the core of Tom's faith, and he firmly believed that unconditional service to humanity was to be his life's work.

As he was not a government employee, Tom could not live in the housing provided for the center's Caucasian staff. Thus he commuted daily to the segregation center from his lodgings five miles away, riding his battered old bicycle through rain, wind, and snow. He was in every way an admirable man, quietly giving of himself in service to others while never pressing his religious views upon them. But a person's convictions can be communicated without words. Tom's very presence was a beacon of light radiating hope in Tule Lake's deranged and desolate sea of darkness.

The day after my first visit to the church, I heard a knock on my door. I was lying in bed, by now so weak from loss of appetite, hives, and general debilitation that I spent more than half my time there. Tom opened the door and entered my room, loaded with delicacies the likes of which I had never before seen in the segregation center—fresh oranges, cheese, ham, and bottles and bottles of vitamins. Welcome as these gifts were, I hesitated to accept them, for I knew that as a poorly paid young minister, Tom himself had little to spare. But he insisted.

"Your body is the temple of the Lord—you must not abuse it," he told me firmly.

I suppose my poor physical condition was blatantly obvious to anyone. But Tom had not come just to give me fresh food and medicine. He had come to talk. Our conversation started casually enough, but Tom became increasingly passionate as he spoke.

"People who genuinely want peace cannot sit idly by and do nothing! They have to have more courage than it takes to fight on the battlefield. It's not a primitive, physical kind of courage, though. It's the courage of the tactician—of someone who carefully works out ideas and plans. It's a courage that is awakened to love. We have to fight together like warriors, Min, to build a more peaceful world, a new era of justice," he concluded fervently.

It seemed that Tom was well aware that I had acquired the scar on my face by refusing to cooperate with the fanatic gangs in the camp. The two of us talked together for hours, and then Tom said a prayer and headed for home on his old bicycle.

I mulled over this conversation for a long while. I really could not see all this business about God and faith. But what I *could* see clearly were the hope and the courage that seemed to well up out of the heart of a person like Tom, a person who burned with such intense faith. In my own state of despair, I was deeply moved by the young minister's passion. It was the same kind of passion I had seen before in the lovely Mrs. Sano and in that "weakling" Mickey. People who had hope in their hearts seemed to possess this kind of passion; and these passionate people had so much courage!

In addition to vitamins and hope, Tom began giving me food for my intellectual hunger as well, recommending books for me to read. One was *The Fall of Christianity: A Study of Christianity, the State and War* by the Dutch theologian G. J. Herring. The thesis of this book was that in the early years of its existence the Christian Church had consistently challenged the power of the state, but since the time of Constantine it had retreated from its original critical stance and compromised with state power. In addition to his historical analysis of religion vis-à-vis political power, Herring set forth in this work his proposed tenets of belief for a true Christianity in the modern world. I found this book to be engrossing.

When I attended the Christmas Eve gathering at the little church, Tom introduced me to a radiant, youthful lady in her forties named Miss Thomasine Allan. She had been a missionary in Iwate Prefecture in Japan for a decade or more, but in the early years of the war she was sent home on the exchange ship *Gripsholm* by order of the Japanese government. Back in the States, she came to work at Tule Lake, where she put to use her fluency in the Japanese language, assisting with the relocation of residents who had received leave clearance to resettle outside the camp.

Miss Allan never failed to pray for the friends she had left behind in Japan. According to Tom, when the Japanese government ordered her out of the country, local police officers came to the train station when she left—not for surveillance purposes, but to express their gratitude for all she had done over the years to help their community. Boy, I thought, if that was true, you had to admire those police officers, too. It would have taken a lot of courage in wartime Japan to go to the train station and publicly give a friendly send-off to an "enemy alien."

Very likely Miss Allan had some pretty unpleasant experiences in Japan after the war began, but she never alluded to anything of the sort. Invariably she had only words of kindness for everyone she met—policeman, soldier, or otherwise. Miss Allan knew nothing of enmity or hatred. She truly loved all human beings and labored tirelessly for the sake of others.

Idealist though she was, Miss Allan had her practical side. She took me aside soon after we met and told me in no uncertain terms that I must go to the segregation center high school and complete my secondary education.

"Min, without an education you will never be able to teach anyone else or make any of your own dreams come true. The way the U.S. government has treated Japanese Americans is wrong. But there are people in this country even now who have not abandoned their ideals, people who reject militarism and hatred and are sincerely working for the freedom of all and the defense of human rights. To meet people like that, though, you will need to study and to inform yourself. You need to do a great deal of reading."

Not long after that conversation, Miss Allan introduced me to Mr. and Mrs. McCartney, a couple in their early thirties. They were solid, God-fearing Minnesotans who had come to Tule Lake to teach in the high school. He taught biology and she taught English. Music-lovers both, they were strict Lutherans. Mrs. McCartney was a quiet person who rarely spoke in the group, always listening to the others, nodding and smiling while they talked. It was a long time before we learned that before the war, between her high school and college years, she had worked in Japan as a secretary to an American missionary in a fishing village northeast of Tokyo. One day she told us about her wonderful experiences there and confided that she hoped to return after the war ended. None of us had any idea until then that Mrs. McCartney was fluent in Japanese.

Mr. McCartney directed the church choir and on occasion would sing a solo in his rich, tenor voice. He came to my room one day bearing two records.

"These are just a small token of our friendship, Min, but we thought you might enjoy them," he said, giving them to me.

One of the records was called *By the Banks of Lake Minnetonka*. It was a recording of his own solos. The other was the well-known St. Olaf College Choir singing Martin Luther's "A Mighty Fortress Is Our God."

Tom had shared with me his passion as a pacifist, Miss Allan had encouraged me to continue my education that I might realize my ideals, and now Mr. McCartney had given me music to soothe my soul. After the long months and years I had spent in the camps, it seemed simply amazing that these people should care so much about me.

That little church was home to a number of other unusual characters. One was Ruthevelyn Pim, or "Pimmy," a young woman from the Midwest. The daughter of a Chicago industrialist, she had recently earned her master's degree in educational psychology from the University of Chicago. Even though her job as a preschool teacher in the segregation center was anything but glamorous, she seemed to love it. The rather serious Tom and the McCartneys were just a trifle reserved with the exuberant Pimmy, but I always thought I detected a twinkle in Miss Allan's eye when she smiled at Pimmy's impishness. Pimmy faithfully attended Sunday worship services and evening meetings at the church, but back in her own room she would fling her feet up on her desk and light a cigarette. Perhaps even more shocking to the other Christians, her bookshelves were adorned with wine bottles.

One day Pimmy invited me to stop by her apartment. When I arrived, someone else was there before me—a Caucasian gentleman from the camp administration office. He was energetically urging Pimmy to purchase some high-yield U.S. government bonds.

She looked down at him coolly and asked, "Why should I?"

When he launched into his sales pitch again, she cut him off.

"I refuse to buy any government bond that will be used to finance a war!" she said, putting an end to the conversation.

Pimmy was strong-willed and had definite convictions, and she refused to compromise those convictions regardless of the personal cost. Why on earth had this young woman come to such a godforsaken place as Tule Lake? Certainly not out of idle curiosity. The belief that drew Pimmy and the other members of that church together was pacifism. A haven for war-resisters, the little church in that far corner of the camp was a breath of fresh air amidst the strife and tumult of the Tule Lake Segregation Center.

Nourished in body, soul, and mind by my association with this group of Christian pacifists, my physical condition began gradually but steadily to improve. Clearly, my health problems had been the direct result of the psychological stress of living in the segregation center, for now that my will to live had revived, my body began to heal itself.

With Miss Allan's encouragement, I did return to high school. It had been more than a year since I had quit the high school at Topaz in frustration and disgust. Social studies had been my nemesis there, but the social studies class at Tule Lake was wonderful. The teacher, Miss Murphy, was a vivacious Berkeley graduate. She was athletic and unaffected, preferring simple clothes and the lightest of makeup, which did not conceal her true beauty—the beauty of a person on fire with idealism. Nor did Miss Murphy content herself with dry, theoretical lectures. She would introduce real issues to illustrate theoretical problems, fearlessly expressing her own opinions on the issues raised. She even discussed the delicate matter of Japan-U.S. relations, startling the class on occasion by criticizing U.S. government policy. She invariably encouraged us to consider every angle of an issue before she revealed her own conclusions. Her nondogmatic approach was the antithesis of the attitude demonstrated by my social studies teacher at Topaz.

Miss Murphy was engaged to be married to a young man she had met in college. He enlisted in the marines right after the war broke out and was now serving in the South Pacific. One day Miss Murphy read our class a letter from her fiancé. He wrote movingly about the cruelty of war, vividly describing the agonizing death of a fellow marine and then depicting a pathetic last-ditch attack by some desperate Japanese soldiers. She even read to us the love poem with which he ended his letter:

> Though the wars of men be muddied with contradictions,
> My love for you is crystal clear.

About three weeks later we heard the tragic news that this brave, romantic man, the fiancé of our beloved teacher, had been killed in action. Miss Murphy did not miss a day of school. Keeping her pain and grief to herself, she applied just a touch of makeup to her swollen eyelids and carried on with her teaching.

The intelligence, human warmth, and sense of responsibility demonstrated by this young teacher made a lasting impression on me. I felt especially indebted to her for her guidance during those last months of my oft-interrupted high school education. As young as she was, she was a remarkable educator.

Like Pimmy, Miss Murphy's choice to work at Tule Lake was a matter of conscience, though not in her case tied to any particular religious belief. It was truly remarkable that these two young women had chosen to devote themselves selflessly to service in the tempestuous world of that segregation center during World War II. Perhaps it was their way of bucking the tides of the time. Both women were passionate idealists with great dreams of creating a new, more perfect society after the war. In my view, they deserve to be recognized as forerunners of the civil rights movement in America.

At long last I completed the requirements for graduation from high school. On the day of the commencement ceremony, I was startled to recognize Nancy in the audience.

"Hey, what are you doing here in the segregation center?" I asked her after the formalities had ended. For once, I was the one to initiate the conversation with her. Maybe I'm finally learning to be more relaxed after all, I reflected.

"Oh, I'm a dangerous character. Didn't you know that?" Nancy retorted.

Good old Nancy. She hadn't changed one bit.

"Congratulations, Min," she said. "I'm really glad you finished high school. What are your plans now?"

Of course I hadn't any plans, with no apparent prospects of getting out of Tule Lake. But as soon as Nancy learned that, she eagerly told me about the research center where she was working in the camp. She thought I might be able to get a job there, too.

"I'm working as a typist, but I know they're looking for someone who can read and write both Japanese and English—and you'd
be perfect for that," she asserted.

I asked her to put in a word for me. The next day I went to visit
the research center and was hired on the spot as a research assistant.

Research centers had been established by the WRA in each
internment camp to study the residents, their cultural background,
and their behavior, with a view to helping administrators cope with
problems that might arise in the camp. The director of the
Anthropological and Sociological Research Center at Tule Lake
was cultural anthropologist Dr. Marvin K. Opler. A tall, red-haired
Jewish American with thick glasses, he would stroll casually
through the camp wearing the same cheap regulation jacket as the
segregation center residents. People who did not know him probably thought he was a workman. Because of his size, he was rather a
forbidding presence at first, but in actuality he was a very kind-
hearted human being. Apparently, he tried to enlist in the army at
the beginning of the war but was rejected because his unusually long
legs made his movements sluggish. But Opler had the stamina to sit
day after day writing his perceptive reports with complete concentration. Nor was he lacking in courage. Every day he walked through
the camp to his office in his shabby jacket, entirely unconcerned
about the riots, demonstrations, and terrorist incidents raging all
about him in Tule Lake.

Opler's job was to analyze the social psychology of the populace of Tule Lake and to report his findings both to the director of
the center and to WRA headquarters in Washington, D.C. He had
opposed converting Tule Lake into a segregation center from the
beginning and later warned in his reports to the WRA and the
Tule Lake administration that the society within the segregation
center was abnormal, that the resulting tension could be expected
to erupt into violence. He urged the administration to ward off this
possibility by devising policies to foster a more normal society
within the center. He maintained that in order to determine the

most appropriate policies for the center, administrators would need to inform themselves fully about the cultural background and social psychology of the residents.

Dr. Opler is said to have been the most productive of the several community analysts in the WRA centers, offering the most perceptive analyses as well as the most accurate predictions of resident behavior. Nonetheless, the most frequent and most extreme incidents of violence and abuse occurred in the Tule Lake center. But that was not the fault of inadequate analysis or mistaken predictions on Opler's part. The problem lay in the incompetence of WRA Chief Dillon Myer and Tule Lake Director Raymond Best. These two officials either ignored Opler's reports or lacked the ability to apply his analysis of social psychology to their administrative policies. Best dismissed Opler's proposals out of hand, proclaiming that his "theoretical" advice was completely unrealistic in controlling the "fanatics" housed at Tule Lake.

The premises upon which anthropologist Opler and administrator Best based their respective ideas about camp policy were fundamentally at odds. As Dr. Opler explained to me, he regarded the residents of Tule Lake as essentially normal human beings, while Best considered them fanatics. The former sought to restore the normal social conditions necessary for human beings to function. The latter was entirely preoccupied with controlling the behavior of people he perceived to be fanatics.

In any case, the task of Japanese-speaking internee researchers like myself was to study the traditional Japanese culture of the residents. We would submit our findings to Opler and he would incorporate them into his analysis of the social psychology of the segregation center and the policy advice he submitted to the camp administration.

One researcher was a single issei man in his fifties named Mr. Ōbayashi. He was a man of great integrity, an intellectual with degrees from both Japanese and American educational institutions. He worked diligently in the research center from 8:00 A.M. to 5:00 P.M. every day, never allowing a facetious remark to pass his lips. But he was so straightlaced that the rest of us found him quite unapproachable.

Mr. Tominaga, a bachelor in his late sixties, was just the opposite of Mr. Ōbayashi. He had been a journalist in the Japanese American community for several decades, but no one knew much more about him. He had a luxuriant mustache and always wore a neatly tied necktie so that at first glance he appeared to be quite the gentleman. There were subtle differences from Mr. Ōbayashi, however. The latter always wore a spotlessly clean and pressed sport shirt, open at the collar, while Tominaga—even in white shirt and tie—invariably had stains on his clothing and unmistakable holes in the heels of his socks. He never showed up for work before ten or eleven in the morning and went home long before anyone else. No one criticized him, however—we just couldn't. With all his solemn air, he radiated a boyish innocence, a kind of naiveté, and a wonderful sense of humor. He possessed at once an epicurean streak and an Oriental fatalism.

"As a former journalist, I can see very well where this war is going to end—Japan is bound to lose," he informed us.

"If you're so convinced Japan is going to lose, then why did you end up here in Tule Lake?" I asked.

"Well, at my advanced age, I do not wish to remain in America after it wins the war. I am, after all, Japanese. All I really want to do is take one last look at Japan after it is defeated and spend the night with a geisha in Shimbashi. Then I shall be prepared to die."

He said this with such gravity that everyone had to laugh.

Whenever the old newspaperman got on the subject of geisha, he would rhapsodize like a man many years his junior. Mr. Ōbayashi, meanwhile, would be radiating palpable disapproval from his desk across the room.

One Sunday morning I skipped church and stopped by Mr. Tominaga's small room, where he lived alone. He greeted me at the door with a sleepy look on his face and a cup of saké in his hand. I never did learn how he had managed to get hold of that! I declined his offer of a drink as we both settled down beside his coal stove. Mr. Tominaga, saké in hand, was clearly pleased at the prospect of a good chat.

"Minoru-kun, have you ever been in love?" he asked abruptly.

Without waiting for my answer, he then embarked upon a monologue.

"You know, the person who has been in love is truly fortunate, and people who have never had this experience are really to be pitied. I have wanted all my life to fall in love because, well, as long as I've lived I never have really done anything worthwhile," he confessed.

I had no idea how to respond.

Mr. Tominaga was silent for several moments and then he continued: "You know, even if you live to be a hundred years old, you have to die sometime. What do you suppose a person thinks about just before he dies?"

I had no ready answer for that either.

"My guess is that, no matter how rich or famous they are, most people probably think about how useless their lives have been. But I imagine that when they look back, they probably feel they were happiest when they were in love," he said.

Tominaga looked utterly content as he sat there philosophizing and savoring his saké. He talked on, recalling with ingenuous pleasure the experiences of his student days and expounding further on his view of life.

"It's a mistake, you know, for students to get all involved in political movements. They really ought to be studying literature and philosophy and falling in love. These things will be far more useful to them later on in life. Do you know why? Because people who have been in love are openhearted and tolerant. The ones who have never loved another person are narrow-minded and all closed in on themselves. This world would be a much pleasanter place to live if everyone would just fall in love. But I'm afraid that so long as the Christians and all those other pious people think that sex is so sinful, we'll keep on having these wars."

Tominaga talked about his student days in Tokyo in the early nineteen hundreds. As the second son of a Japanese baron he had enjoyed a life of unusual privilege, but apparently he came to the United States in search of greater opportunities than he would have had at home. I'm not sure whether he felt he had succeeded in that quest.

As much as I respected the breadth of knowledge and stern character of Mr. Ōbayashi, I could not help but feel a greater affection for this saké-loving old gentleman before me. I could only hope that his fondest wish would be granted and that he might indeed spend a night with that geisha in Shimbashi before he left this world.

Another individual in the research center was Sam, a nisei college graduate who spoke only English. He was something of an American edition of Mr. Tominaga. He too sported a mustache, wore rumpled clothes to the office, and kept work hours similar to the older man.

"Sam, what are you doing in Tule Lake?" I asked him one day.

"Draft evader," he replied so forthrightly, so openly, that he might almost have been talking about someone else.

"I hate war. But I adore women," he added with no apparent embarrassment, right in front of our female coworkers. I'm not sure what the women thought of him, but I certainly wouldn't have called him handsome.

Sam always had a cheerful twinkle in his eye, but he was a bohemian sort. You never caught him working. He would sit for hours before a mirror on his desk, intently grooming his mustache. When he finished, he would tease the young female typists or sit at his desk reading racy novels. Sam liked his alcohol, too, and after he had had a drink or two he would tell us all about his plans.

"When I get out of here, I'm going to marry a wealthy widow," he would declare.

One day Sam suddenly stopped coming to the office. Rumor had it that he had managed to get himself released from Tule Lake and had gone East. I heard later that he was involved in the labor movement in New York State. There weren't many Japanese Americans in that area then and probably not too many rich widows either. Sam was just naturally an antiestablishment sort of fellow, and I suppose that's how he got himself thrown into the segregation center in the first place.

The group working in that research center was truly an odd selection of characters. Although our ostensible task was to conduct research on Japanese culture, no one but Mr. Ōbayashi submitted reports with any kind of regularity. Mr. Tominaga and Sam, in particular, were never known to put a single piece of paper in Dr. Opler's hands. And Opler did not press them to do so. The anthropologist did ask all new staff members to submit a brief autobiographical essay, though, and it may well be that he was observing in the research workers themselves the effects of evolving conditions in the segregation center. Perhaps Sam and Mr. Tominaga were aware of that. In any case, Dr. Opler was an astute analyst of social psychology, and he certainly did succeed in bringing a cross section of the camp population into his research center where he might observe us at close range.

By now I was heartily regretting my rashness a few months earlier when I had emotionally renounced my citizenship. I now cast about to find someone who could advise me on how to undo what I had done. The people I knew were sympathetic, but no one seemed to have any concrete idea of how to help. Miss Murphy and Miss Allan were people of conscience, but both were in one way or another employees of the WRA, and I did not want to jeopardize their job situations. The same was true of the McCartneys. Tom, on the other hand, did not work for the WRA, and he was certainly a dedicated young man, but I couldn't expect him to know what I should do about a legal problem.

I finally decided I should ask Dr. Opler. Although he was a government employee, he answered directly to the national headquarters and could talk freely with Best. So one day after work I asked if I might discuss a personal matter with him. He listened gravely and did not evidence any particular surprise when I revealed to him that I had refused to answer yes to the loyalty question and, worse, had renounced my citizenship. He responded that the loyalty oath was not in his view anything to worry about.

"That was just something the WRA dreamed up on its own. It has no legal force whatsoever. They won't deport you for that," he assured me. "The problem, though, is your renunciation of American citizenship."

That night I stayed late at the research center, composing under Opler's direction a long letter to United States Attorney General Tom Clark. In it I explained that my renunciation had been an expression of momentary emotional defiance in reaction to years of persecution suffered by myself and other Japanese Americans and, in particular, to the degrading interrogation by the FBI agent at Topaz and being terrorized by the guards and gangs at Tule Lake. In conclusion, I wrote that I had renounced my citizenship under duress, in an atmosphere where I was bereft of any ability to think reasonably. I requested that, for the above reasons, my application to renounce my U.S. citizenship be disregarded by the Department of Justice.

I mailed my letter to Washington the following morning.

U.S. Attorney General Tom Clark was the father of the progressive postwar Attorney General Ramsey Clark. The elder Clark, however, certainly could not be described as progressive. Several weeks after I sent my letter to him, I received a form letter from his office advising me that the Department of Justice had already finished processing my application to renounce my U.S. citizenship. It could not be reversed. Dr. Opler immediately placed a phone call to attorney Wayne Collins on my behalf.

Wayne Collins was a lawyer affiliated with the American Civil Liberties Union (ACLU) and was particularly active in defending the rights of workers in the San Francisco Bay Area. Although never widely known in American society at large, Wayne Collins worked tirelessly all his life to protect the freedom and rights of ordinary American citizens. A stubborn man of Irish descent, he championed the weak and downtrodden in the courts of the land, fearlessly confronting the power elite in the process. Collins defended freedom of speech as the inalienable right of every American citizen, whether in peacetime or in war, and without regard to the person's ideology.

Publications about the internment issued by the government and by the Japanese American Citizens League rarely mention the

name of Wayne Collins. He was a merciless critic of both the
American government and the JACL and also of the WRA and its
chief administrators, the director of the Tule Lake Segregation
Center, and, sometimes, the ACLU with which he himself was affiliated. Each of these parties condemned him in turn as an extremist
in his efforts to protect civil rights. But sometimes the attorney
found that to win his cases in court it was necessary to go to
extremes to demonstrate the pernicious use of coercion by the
United States government. In these cases Collins was challenging
the practices and policies of firmly established government agencies. The victims of those agencies' oppressive practices were
invariably powerless and poor, and Collins not infrequently
defended them without compensation.

Fred Korematsu was one such case. A Japanese American,
Korematsu was arrested for refusing to comply with the army's West
Coast evacuation orders. The evacuation orders themselves were
unconstitutional in that they stripped Japanese Americans of their
freedoms as citizens. At the time, however, anti-Japanese feeling
was at such a high pitch that government officials were determined
to enforce the directives regardless.

Korematsu's case certainly did not have much chance of
being championed by the general American public, for, in the eyes
of the majority of Americans, Korematsu had clearly violated the
law and was a fugitive from justice. Despite Korematsu's unpopular
cause and lack of financial resources, Collins agreed to take his case.
After an initial defeat during the war years, Korematsu at long last
received justice in the courts after the case was reopened in the
1980s. By then Wayne Collins had died, but his successors saw the
case to its completion. It was Collins, however, who was the first to
champion this unpopular cause, actively pushing the case through
the courts, appealing to the American conscience, and calling society's attention to a gross injustice.

Collins also represented the internees who were thrown into
the stockade at the Tule Lake Segregation Center after the imposition of martial law in the camp in the fall of 1943. Although some
of these individuals had resorted to violence, the issue at stake in

their case was the flagrant disregard for due process in their punishment. In the army's attempt to gain control of the situation, many suspects had been rounded up indiscriminately and imprisoned in the stockade, where they were further subjected to physical and psychological abuse. These men continued to be held in the stockade while the administration refused to reveal the exact charges against them or to conduct any investigation.

The legal situation of those of us who renounced our citizenship in the camps was different from both Korematsu's case and that of the prisoners in the stockade at Tule Lake in that we were not accused of violating any law or regulation or of perpetrating any kind of unrest or violence. We were people who had peacefully complied from the beginning with the West Coast exclusion orders (despite their inherent unconstitutionality) and allowed ourselves to be incarcerated without resistance in the WRA camps. Persecuted, pressed to the limit of our endurance after months and years in the camps, we had renounced our U.S. citizenship only as a final symbolic expression of resistance against harsh treatment at the hands of the U.S. government and its agencies. No matter how it was construed, the renunciants were not criminals.

The approximately 5,500 Japanese Americans who renounced their citizenship were predominantly residents of the Tule Lake Segregation Center. Considering that roughly two-thirds of Tule Lake's population of 18,000 were either issei (who had never been granted citizenship) or minors (who were too young to renounce it), that means virtually all of the adult American citizens in the segregation center chose renunciation. This fact in itself speaks volumes about the U.S. government's cruel oppression and abuse of internees at Tule Lake.

The JACL leaders, meanwhile, ever desirous of ingratiating themselves with the majority establishment, refused to touch the issue of renunciation. They utterly ignored and abandoned the renunciants.

Again it was Wayne Collins alone who was willing to help Japanese American renunciants regain their citizenship. Through

Dr. Opler, I requested Collins' help in restoring my status as a U.S. citizen. The litigation initiated by Collins on behalf of myself and the other renunciants challenged the constitutionality of the statute enacted in July 1944 that permitted the voluntary renunciation of U.S. citizenship. In fighting this case, Collins, as always, went to the very heart of the matter, exposing the hypocrisy of an American society that—while professing ideals of freedom and equality—had compiled over the years a pitiful record of racial bias and human rights violations against Japanese Americans and a long history of psychological oppression and physical abuse. Collins made an eloquent and impassioned plea on behalf of the renunciants, thoroughly castigating the American government for its treatment of Japanese Americans.

It was not until August 12, 1955, that the issue of renunciation was finally resolved in the U.S. courts. On that date the Southern Division of the United States District Court for the Northern District of California found in favor of the renunciants. That decision was not just a personal victory for attorney Wayne Collins or for those of us whom he represented. It was a victory for a nation that professes its firm allegiance to freedom for all and the protection of human rights. Wayne Collins fought gallantly on the frontlines of this battle for justice, prodding and appealing to the conscience of the American people. Indeed, Collins defended victims of injustice throughout his career, standing up fearlessly to the power elite time and again, without concern for his own reputation or personal gain. His is a figure that shines brilliantly in the history of the defense of human rights in the United States of America. I am but one of the many beneficiaries of this man's dedication to the American ideal.

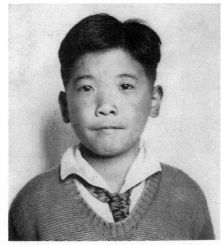

Min's grandfather in the late 1920s.

Min in 1934, at about age ten, just before leaving for Japan.

School yard of Hiratsuka No. 1 Elementary School, where morning exercises were held.

Sixth graders of Hiratsuka No. 1 Elementary School (1935). Min is in the second row, second from the left.

School outing in 1936 to visit the battleship *Mikasa*, which played a vital role in 1905 in the Battle of the Sea of Japan, during the Russo-Japanese War. Min is the second row, third from the right.

Commemorative photo of the victorious San Francisco Kendō Club, April 1940. Min is in the last row, fourth from the right. The trophy banner was a gift from Japanese General Araki—a fact that must have become known to the FBI.

Guard tower at the Tule Lake Segregation Center, ca. 1944.

Dr. Marvin K. Opler, director of the Anthropological and Sociological Research Center at Tule Lake, with staff. Opler is at the far right, next to Min in the back row. The barrack in the background served as the center.

Tule Lake United Christian Church in spring 1945, on the occasion of outside church visitors. Min in white shirt and tie is standing in the third row, third from the right, with Miss Allan the fourth from the right in dark coat and hat. Mr. and Mrs. McCartney are between them, in the back row. Tom Grubbs is seated in the front row, second from the left.

Miss Thomasine Allan in front of the Tule Lake United Christian Church, 1945.

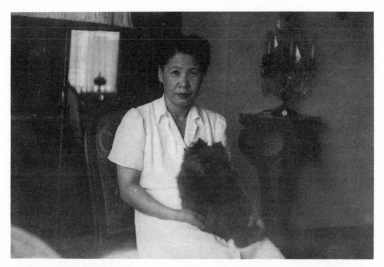

Min's mother, after she was released from Topaz and found work in New York in the summer of 1945.

A wintry Tule Lake, early 1946.

Min beside his dormitory at the College of the Ozarks, spring 1946.

Min with his camera at the College of the Ozarks, 1946.

Min with his grandmother in Hiratsuka, fall 1950.

After landing at an airport near Pusan, Korea, late 1950. Min is sitting atop the steel drum at left.

Camp for Chinese prisoners of war in Korea, summer 1951.

7 Liberation

The war's end on August 15, 1945, did not bring immediate release from internment. Month after month I remained in custody at the Tule Lake Segregation Center along with an assortment of other "dangerous" characters and renunciants. Even though many of us had initiated legal action to have our citizenship restored, that action apparently made no difference to the government. In fact, on November 18, 1945, fifteen hundred Japanese Americans from Tule Lake—"dangerous" issei, along with nisei and kibei renunciants— were loaded onto a ship for deportation to war-devastated Japan. Four months after their departure, in March of 1946—more than half a year after the war's end—I was finally released from the Tule Lake Segregation Center.

I put on my new suit, overcoat, and shoes and gathered my few belongings. Mother had been working in New York City since her release from Topaz in the summer of 1945 and had saved enough money to send me some clothing so that I might return to the world feeling like a human being.

I walked with the other newly freed internees out through the gate and toward the row of buses that stood waiting.

"At last, I'm free!" I rejoiced.

I gulped in the outside air until my lungs almost burst from savoring the sweet taste of freedom. Then I turned and bowed deeply to the people who had come to bid me farewell. My friends from the Tule Lake Christian Church were standing inside the fence waving good-bye. Behind the group of well-wishers, I spotted the tall figure of Dr. Opler in his tattered jacket, standing somewhat apart and watching silently.

How could I ever express my gratitude to all these people who had done so much for me? It was Dr. Opler and the members of that little church who enabled me to survive the hell of internment and to be freed from it at last. The worst part had been the last two years in the segregation center at Tule Lake, but in all I had been imprisoned for four long years for the crime of having Japanese ancestors.

Now I was on my way to Arkansas. With Tom's recommendation, I had been awarded a scholarship to study at the College of the Ozarks, a small, church-related school in the little town of Clarksville, Arkansas.

The bus took us to the train station in nearby Klamath Falls. By the time we boarded the train there, the light was already fading from the early spring sky. I gazed out the window as the train hurried through the darkness, past clusters of lights marking the presence of small towns along the way—a quiet, peaceful nighttime scene.

The passengers inside the train, the newly liberated internees, were quiet as well. This trip was eerily reminiscent of our journey when we were first sent away to the camps. On neither occasion did people make any fuss or commotion. We had not known what to expect at the end of that first trip, but most of my traveling companions were very much aware of what awaited us now—the grim reality of the struggle to eke out a livelihood as an ethnic minority in American society. How would postwar America greet the return of the Japanese Americans? That was the unknown. The one certainty was that we would *not* be welcomed back with much warmth.

My own thoughts were taking a different turn, however. I was meditating on the human cost, on both sides, of the battles for Saipan, Iwo Jima, Okinawa. One after another I envisioned those scenes of carnage. I hated war. I hated the politicians who had led

Japan into the war. But that did not mean that I hated the Japanese friends who had been my schoolmates. How could I hate the Japanese people? Japanese culture was a part of myself.

My thoughts went back to the days at the end of the war, by now several months earlier. When we at Tule Lake received the news of the atomic bombs dropped on Hiroshima and Nagasaki and the vast civilian casualties in those two cities, both Miss Allan and Mrs. McCartney had paled and begun to weep. Mrs. McCartney collapsed in her husband's arms; they had been planning to go to Japan to teach after the war was over. Tom and Pimmy sat with heads bowed, shaking with sobs. Each of these individuals felt a deep love for the Japanese people.

Ironically, at just about this same time, the newsletter of the Japanese American Citizens League was trumpeting the story of the triumphal return and enthusiastic welcome home accorded to a Nebraska-born nisei airman who had participated in the Tokyo air raids. I, for one, could not appreciate what was to be celebrated in that accomplishment.

Someone tapped me on the shoulder, interrupting my somber thoughts. It was Nancy, who apparently had been riding in the following car with her older brothers. She sat down chummily in the empty seat beside me.

Nancy was tall, with dimples that appeared whenever she smiled. In high school she didn't speak up often in class, but she was intelligent and studied hard. She had perhaps been a trifle self-centered in those days, but after she went to work in the research center at Tule Lake she matured into a pleasant young woman with an abundance of good sense. Although there were three or four typists in the office, I always took my reports to Nancy. We walked home together after work since we lived in the same part of the camp, and sometimes I stopped at her place to chat before returning to my own quarters.

Before the war, Nancy's family had owned a large farm in the Sacramento Valley. After the exclusion orders were announced, her father was killed in a tractor accident as he hurried to finish the farm work before leaving. Not long after that, her mother fell ill and died in the concentration camp.

Nancy had two good-natured older brothers. After their father's death it fell to them to settle the family's affairs on the farm. Under pressure to move quickly, they were forced to sell the farm at a ridiculously low price to a Caucasian buyer. It is not hard to understand why these three nisei young people felt so much antipathy toward the United States government that they refused to answer "yes" to the loyalty question. That government was responsible for the loss of the farm their parents had labored so long and hard to build, for the loss of all the property the family had managed to accumulate, and, ultimately, for the loss of both their parents.

Nancy's two brothers often reminisced about their contented life on the farm before the war. They told me about cultivating potatoes, digging them up at harvest time, putting them in gunny sacks, and pitching the heavy 100-pound bags onto a truck. Then, after a hard day's work, their mother would cook them a hearty meal of beef, rice, and fresh vegetables from the farm. For relaxation in the evenings they practiced jūdō. They were athletic young men but also gentlemen who valued the traditional proprieties. It was a pleasure to observe their protective affection for their younger sister. All three were cheerful, positive human beings, but whenever they spoke of their parents their eyes would fill with tears. Certainly these three would never have considered the absurd proposals made by the JACL leaders during the war—that nisei children should spy on their own parents as enemy aliens and report their activities to the United States government or that they should offer their parents to the government as hostages.

Although Nancy and her brothers were originally from the outskirts of Sacramento, they had gone to stay with their mother's relatives in San Francisco after their father died. From there they went to the Tanforan Assembly Center, were moved to Topaz, and then were sent to Tule Lake because of their "disloyalty." Thus, their wanderings during the concentration camp exile had exactly paralleled my own.

"What were you thinking about so intently just now?" Nancy asked.

I flushed, not so much from the question itself as from a young woman striking up an intimate conversation with me in the darkening train car. I was pleased, though.

"Oh, nothing in particular," I replied.

I glanced shyly at her face but looked away when I met her bright, friendly eyes.

Undaunted, Nancy kept talking.

"Min, you know you were pretty gutsy that time in high school at Topaz. I agreed with what you said then, but I didn't have the courage to stand up to the teacher the way you did," she told me.

Her praise embarrassed me more than ever.

"Where are you heading now?" Nancy asked.

"You know, I received a scholarship at that little college in Arkansas. I'm going to make a couple of stops on the East Coast, and then I'll be starting school there."

"You're so lucky. I'd love to go to college, but I can't. I've got to help my brothers get a farm started again."

With all the experiences we had shared, Nancy and I had much to talk about—like that awkward moment at Tanforan when I wouldn't speak to her. For the first time, I apologized to her for my rude behavior that day. She just laughed about it. Then there was the time she had tried to patch things up between me and the social studies teacher at Topaz—I really had appreciated Nancy's concern about me then. We laughed, too, over memories of our days working together in Dr. Opler's research center at Tule Lake. People sitting near us in the train smiled kindly on the two young people obviously having such a good time together. We talked on and on in the dark train car.

"Nancy, it's after midnight! Why don't you come on back to your seat now and get some sleep?" someone said. It was Nancy's eldest brother.

"Oh, Min! It's *you* she's talking to," he said when he recognized me.

Standing in the aisle, he joined our conversation. Nancy told him I was on my way to college and he congratulated me heartily and wished me well. We talked of many other things, and it was nearly one o'clock in the morning by the time the two of them returned to their seats. I leaned my head against the window and dozed off.

A few hours later I was awakened by a quiet bustling in the train. A pale light illuminated the eastern sky and people were busily gathering together their belongings. It was almost 4:30 A.M. In thirty minutes or so Nancy and her brothers would be getting off the train in Sacramento.

Nancy looked sleepy when she came to find me.

"Did you get any sleep at all?" she asked as she sat down beside me again.

"Last night was so much fun," I said. "I wish we could have talked all night."

She dimpled as she smiled at me.

"Well, now I'm going home to the country, where every day is exactly the same as the day before and absolutely nothing ever happens. It's truly boring. You're so lucky—you have new things to look forward to," she said.

"But your brothers are such great people," I objected.

"That's true. I do love them dearly, and that's why I'm going back to help them. Write to me sometimes, won't you?" she asked.

She gave me her temporary address—a hostel for returning internees at a Japanese Buddhist church in Sacramento. Then she went back to her seat to gather her luggage.

Nancy had complained that her life would be dull, but it seemed as though she was really looking forward to it. She had always acted so mature working at the research center, but when you saw her with her two older brothers she was still very much the sheltered little sister.

Now the brothers came to find me. They thanked me for being such a good friend to Nancy.

"Be sure to come and visit us when you're back in California," they urged.

The train slowed gradually and came to a halt. I carried Nancy's bags onto the platform and shook hands with her brothers. Then I held her soft, warm hand in mine for a long moment, reluctant to part. I climbed back onto the train, and as it pulled away I could see Nancy waving her white handkerchief until finally she was no longer visible in the distance.

The other Japanese Americans in my car had also gotten off the train in Sacramento. Alone in the coach, I recalled the conversation I had had with Dr. Opler yesterday before leaving the segregation center. He told me he had received word that our friend Mr. Tominaga passed away on board the U. S. navy ship that was repatriating him to Japan. Apparently he had succumbed to the rigors of that journey across the rough winter seas of the North Pacific. So Mr. Tominaga had not lived after all to see again the hills and valleys of his native land. I mourned the passing of that aristocratic son of the Meiji era, a free spirit who had always lived as he saw fit, without seeking fame or honor.

It was almost 8 A.M. now and the train was approaching San Francisco Bay. The familiar aroma of the seashore drifted through the train windows, awakening all my senses. Opening my window as wide as I could, I filled my lungs with the early morning sea breezes. What a wonderful fragrance, I exulted.

It had been four years since I last saw San Francisco Bay. There was the old Oakland pier with its paddle wheel ferry that I knew so well. And across the bay, glittering, almost dazzling in the morning sun, stood the beautiful city of San Francisco. My beloved city welcomed me home with a clear, fogless view of itself this morning. In that moment, the painful memories of four years of incarceration in the camps began to dim and recede into the background.

I got off the train in Oakland, the end of the line. How I longed to board that ferry and cross the bay to San Francisco, but I could not. The third quarter was already beginning at my new college, and even by the most direct route it was a three-day trip to get there. Besides, I had no money to spare. When I left the segregation center, the administration office had given me a train ticket for my trip to college plus twenty-five dollars cash (coincidentally the same amount given to convicted criminals on their release from prison!).

I had arranged first to visit my mother in New York City. Also the head office of the Japanese American Citizens League in Washington had written to me suggesting that I meet with them before going to college. I figured I would do as they asked, since Washington was on my way from New York to Arkansas.

The train tracks ended at the Oakland pier, where a huge crowd was gathered. A fleet of military ships had apparently just put into port from the Pacific, and the returning military men were everywhere. Pier and train station were festooned with banners of triumph and welcome. Although it was still quite early in the morning, the atmosphere was almost frighteningly electric with emotion.

I had not yet had any breakfast, so I walked into a diner across from the station to get something to eat before my next train. I took a stool at the counter along with four or five marines and several other men who looked like workmen. I sat there for a long time waiting to be served. Finally, the big, balding proprietor in his dirty apron came over.

"What do *you* want here?" he demanded.

"A cup of coffee, please," I said.

"Didn't you see that sign?" he asked menacingly.

Everyone in the diner turned to stare at me. I looked where the man was pointing.

"No Japs Allowed," the sign read.

Turning beet red, I stood quietly, walked to the door, and pushed it open. Just as I stepped outside, though, someone behind me clapped a hand down on my shoulder. It was the young marine who had been sitting next to me at the counter. From the three chevrons on his sleeve I could tell that he was a sergeant. I knew that marines were tough characters and I figured I had just run into a bad one. But the words I heard next were not what I expected.

"Please. Be my guest," the man said.

Truth to tell, I no longer had much of an appetite. I thanked the marine but declined his invitation.

"I'm sorry, but for the sake of the principles I just risked my life for, I would really appreciate it if you would come back in here and sit down again," he insisted.

I had no choice but to go back then, but the situation definitely made me nervous.

"Mister, give this man some ham and eggs and a cup of hot coffee. And be quick about it!" the marine demanded harshly.

The old man hesitated.

"Look. I just came back from this war. You got something against my friend here?" the marine shouted.

Then his friends began yelling at the man as well. Grudgingly, he picked up his spatula and began to cook. The food he set before me was not particularly appealing and I had to wash it down with coffee, but by now I was interested to learn more about this young marine. It turned out his father was president of a large shipping company in San Francisco. A student at Stanford when the war broke out, he had enlisted in the marines and fought in the Pacific. Today was his first day home. I sensed that there was a gentleman of intelligence behind the young marine's rough speech, for I noticed that his lips trembled a bit when he shouted at the old man. It was obvious that he wasn't entirely comfortable yelling at people.

When the marines asked what I was doing and I told them I had just been released from the segregation center, they stared at me in disbelief.

"But . . . but, you're a nisei, aren't you?! You're an American citizen!" they said indignantly.

These men knew the term "nisei." They were natives of the West Coast—home of the most virulent anti-Japanese sentiment. But even *they* could not understand why the U.S. government would treat Japanese Americans as it had.

When I mentioned that I was on my way to begin my studies at a college in Arkansas, one of the other marines pointed to the man who had first insisted I be served.

"You know, he's going back to Stanford University to get a law degree," he told me.

Another marine took up the conversation.

"War is such hell. I still can't see why you went and enlisted in the marines when you didn't have to," he said to the first man. "Me, I was out of work. I didn't have any choice."

Another chimed in: "Yeah, if I'd been you, I'd have listened to my old man and stayed in school. Then I'd have got me a wife and a law practice and had an easy life of it!"

Still, behind all the banter and loud laughter, there was no doubt that every one of these men was proud to be a U.S. Marine.

The time came for me to catch my train. I told the marines good-bye and thanked them warmly for their kindness. As I went out the door, I thought I heard a ripping sound behind me. Glancing back over my shoulder, I could see that one of the men had just torn the "No Japs Allowed" sign off the wall.

The war was clearly over for those guys.

Leaving California, my train passed through the desolate deserts of Nevada and Utah, over the rugged Rocky Mountains, and on through the fertile plains of the Middle West, finally arriving on the third day in Chicago. With no particular business in that brutal city, I settled into my seat for the remaining two-day journey to New York. As the train traveled eastward, we passed through the industrial cities that I had fancied as my destination when I was plotting my escape from Topaz.

In New York City, I found my mother doing well but longing to return to the Pacific coast. The East Coast was alien territory to her, and she told me that she planned to return to California as soon as the anti-Japanese feeling began to die down out there.

Mother did not ask for details about what I had gone through at Tule Lake. Nor did I volunteer the information. There was no need—she could imagine it all too well. At any rate, we both realized that the difficult part was yet to come. She tried to give me three hundred dollars to help with my school expenses, but I refused to take the money. I was well aware that my small scholarship would not cover all my living expenses at college, but I planned to get a job to supplement the scholarship. Besides, I had graduated from high school and did not want to be a burden on my mother any longer. Because of the war and the internment she had lost everything she had managed to accumulate until then. And returning to San

Francisco without any savings would be fairly risky—I did not want her to do that.

The following morning I bade Mother farewell and headed for Washington, D.C., and the JACL headquarters. There I met with an officer of the Japanese American Citizens League.

"Min—welcome!" the man said. "Congratulations on your college scholarship. I want you to remember now that you were awarded that scholarship as a Japanese American, so you have a responsibility to act as an ambassador for all Japanese Americans at your new college. As a Japanese American, you must excel academically. As a Japanese American, you must earn the highest honors."

I reflected to myself that this certainly was an odd way of thinking and I replied, "The way I see it, I have a responsibility as an individual. I do intend to excel academically, as an individual. As an individual, I will indeed earn the highest honors."

It was clear that this JACL official and I did not see eye to eye. His concern was for the future of Japanese Americans as a group, for raising the social position of Japanese Americans as a community. I honestly could not have cared less. I wanted no part of the Japanese American community. I intended to live in a much broader world than that, a new world, where the cultures of East and West would meet and engage one another directly.

The JACL official was palpably disappointed.

"Uh, well, what do you plan to be?" he asked.

"An educator," I replied.

"Ah, that's good. That's good. And what will you study?"

"First Western philosophy, then Eastern philosophy," I told him.

"Wait a minute now. You can't teach philosophy in high school!" he objected.

"I don't plan to teach high school. I plan to teach in a college," I told him.

"Forget it! You think they'd actually hire a Japanese American college professor? You've got to be crazy! Even if they did, who in America would want to study Asian philosophy anyway? You'd better be a little more realistic and prepare yourself as a high school teacher," he insisted.

I had to smile when I saw the similarity between this exchange and the conversations about my future with Grandfather in Hiratsuka years earlier. But Grandfather was an old-fashioned Meiji era Japanese. This JACL official had been born and bred in modern-day America and was a well-educated man. But he was so caught up in being realistic in the present moment that he had no vision, no dreams. How pitiful, I thought to myself.

"I plan to do exactly what you say is impossible to do!" I declared as I left his office.

That visit to the JACL headquarters lasted no more than twenty minutes, but it proved extremely beneficial to me as a provocation and a stimulus. Then and there I determined to do precisely what that JACL official declared was impossible, to become exactly what he said I could not be.

I set off on the final leg of my journey to college in high spirits, with renewed aspirations. Just another day and a half on the train and I would be there!

When my train pulled into the station in St. Louis, I noticed more black people there than I had seen anywhere else in the country. A number of them boarded the car I was in and sat down quietly at the other end. After a while a white conductor came through. He passed by me once, and then immediately retraced his steps.

"Excuse me, sir. We are in the South now. You should move to the car ahead, if you would please," he said.

Puzzled by the conductor's excessively polite instructions, I looked up at him uncomprehendingly.

"This is the colored car," the man explained.

I still didn't get it. I certainly wasn't black. But neither was I white. However, I didn't want to complicate matters unnecessarily by asking too many questions, so I did as I was told and moved forward to the white car.

I gazed in fascination as we passed through the southern towns. Every train station seemed to have separate restrooms and waiting rooms for whites and blacks. Even the drinking fountains were designated by race. And the blacks I saw appeared to be acting so submissively toward the whites, so humble and polite. Is *this* what generations of oppression had done to them? I wondered.

I will *never* submit, I vowed to myself.

It was almost noon the following day when we arrived in Little Rock, Arkansas, where I changed to a train with a coal-fired engine. It pulled out of the station and began to move tranquilly across the Arkansas countryside, trailing clouds of black smoke in its wake, its deliberate pace fitting perfectly with the sedate tempo of the South. About two hours out of Little Rock the train brought me to the town of Clarksville, home of the College of the Ozarks. In the station I asked the clerk for directions to the college.

"Oh, you just walk east a ways along this street out front of the station till you come to the corner. Then go on up the hill to the north and you'll see the college right there, on top of the hill. Won't take you more'n about ten minutes," the old man said in a soft, unhurried cadence.

I started off with my suitcase in the direction the station clerk indicated, but a few moments later he came hurrying after me.

"Young man, you're in luck. Someone just came down from the college to pick up some baggage. I'll see if you can't get a ride on back up the hill with him."

What a kind old man, I thought.

The driver of the small truck was a student worker. He appeared perfectly happy to give me a lift and started up the hill, whistling as he drove. He had the gas pedal pressed all the way to the floor, but even so that old truck barely managed to chug up the steep incline. To my surprise, the young man evidenced not the slightest bit of curiosity about me. He just chattered on in a monologue about this and that—his girlfriend, bits of gossip about various professors at the college. I nodded politely in response, not knowing exactly how to reply. Then we began to see attractive coeds walking along the sidewalk. My driver would greet each young woman with a facetious remark, toss her a kiss, and then tell me her name. I smiled.

When we reached the college, the student pointed out the administration building and I started off in that direction. It was a

small college with fewer than a thousand students, and since not
many GIs had yet returned to school after the war, the great majority of students on campus were women. Every few paces a pretty,
healthy looking southern coed would turn to look at me with interest, honoring me with a smile. As I returned their smiles, I began to
feel my initial tension slipping away.

The campus was small, with only a few buildings, but it was
beautiful. Green lawns extended in every direction. Magnolia trees
blossomed luxuriantly here and there, and many of the young
women had pinned the fragrant blossoms in their hair. Across the
campus I could see a trim, medieval-style chapel building.

"Let me show you the way," a voice said. It was a petite
blonde coed, who began walking importantly beside me.

"You were really late getting here. Everyone was afraid you
might not come after all," she said.

"Everyone? Who's everyone?" I asked, taken aback.

"Oh, everyone in school knows about you. I mean, you're the
first Japanese ever to come to this college."

She didn't appear to feel any hatred or bias toward me
because I looked Japanese. I guess she was just curious because I was
different. Well, I could be satisfied with that. It would certainly be
pleasanter to be surrounded by beautiful young coeds and supervised
by book-toting professors than by barbed wire fences and bayonet-
toting soldiers! I was genuinely glad now that I had come to this
small southern college.

The young woman led me to the door of the registrar's office.
To express my gratitude, I took from my pocket a pretty pin that Mr.
Tominaga had made at Tule Lake, from shells he dug up and polished to a fine luster. When I presented it to her, she was delighted
and asked me to meet her for dinner. Then she hurried off down the
corridor, stopping en route to show her new pin to her friends. Mr.
Tominaga was always so fond of the ladies that I felt sure he would
have been pleased to know that I had bestowed his creation upon
this attractive young woman.

The registrar was not in, but his secretary processed my registration. I had corresponded from Tule Lake with Miss King about

my admission to the college, so I felt as though I knew her already. She was somewhat older than the students and had a firm, no-nonsense manner. But she also had an air of composure and a ready smile that made me feel reassured whenever I spoke with her.

By the time I got settled in my assigned dormitory room it was almost the dinner hour, and I started across the campus toward the dining hall.

At last I was beginning the college life that I had so often dreamed of during my four years of imprisonment.

8 A Higher Education: Of Head and Heart

The College of the Ozarks, affiliated with the Presbyterian Church, has a long tradition in Arkansas educational history. Its predecessor, Cane Hill College, was established in 1834 as the first institution of higher education in the state. During the Civil War all the buildings on campus were burned, but the college was rebuilt soon after the war ended and has served the people of Arkansas ever since as a center for learning and the cultivation of human talent. In 1920 Cane Hill College changed its name to the College of the Ozarks. The president while I was there was a Dr. Hurie—a portly man, small in stature, who smiled perpetually. He had a long tenure as college president, from 1920 until the late 1940s. This small college very likely had never had an Asian student before. Certainly I was the first Japanese American to attend.

I had not been to a barber for months, so during my first week at college I headed downtown as soon as I found time between classes. I entered the barbershop with some trepidation but was immediately invited to take a seat in a huge, old-fashioned iron chair. The barber, a man in his mid-fifties, proceeded to cut my hair, regaling me with one entertaining tale after another. I learned that he had been barbering in the same shop with the same barber chair for over thirty years. This man seemed entirely oblivious to any racial difference between us. He even took it as a matter of course that I spoke English.

There was a black man in the shop, too, but not to get his hair cut. He was down on his knees, polishing the shoes of the barber's white patrons.

"That fella's been working here ever since he was a boy," the barber informed me.

My eye was caught by a yellowed calendar hanging on the wall. The year printed on it was 1923.

"Why do you have such an old calendar over there?" I asked the barber with curiosity.

The man grinned and replied, "Well, I was young once, too, you know. Just take a look at that picture. Isn't she a beauty?"

Indeed, the faded calendar did boast the portrait of a young woman, although she certainly did not fit my standards of beauty in 1946. This man seemed to have no sense of the passage of time. But then, what is time anyway? I wasn't so sure. I realized that in any case it was all relative.

While I sat there having my hair cut and thinking these thoughts, the black man was humming a tune and polishing the shoes of two patrons. When I turned to leave the shop after paying the barber for his services, the man shining shoes spoke to me.

"Sir, we would surely be pleased to do your laundry for you, if you'd like. I could send my grandson over to your dormitory to pick it up," he offered.

I agreed to have him do this. Sure enough, two or three days later a child appeared outside my dormitory, calling out, "Mr. Japan! Mr. Japan!" Appealing dark eyes twinkled in his brown face.

"My grandpa told me to come and get your laundry," he said.

"Are *you* going to wash my clothes?" I asked him, smiling.

"No, sir. My mama'll do it," he replied earnestly.

"Where do you live?"

"Over in the woods, out behind the college."

"All right. You take these and get them washed for me, okay?" I said.

Arms full of clothes to be laundered, the little boy ran off barefoot toward home. He reminded me of myself as a child, going along with my mother when she worked in the homes of white people.

Now that I was finally in college, I launched into my studies with feverish intensity. I suppose I was attempting to satisfy the thirst for learning that had been building up for so long during those years in the concentration camps. At the beginning of each new term I pored over the course catalog, greedily selecting the classes that interested me the most. Every term I enrolled in German, French, math, chemistry, and philosophy classes. I also audited courses in Western history, the classics, and English literature. Between classes I did yard work at professors' homes or worked in Miss King's office.

Alcohol was not allowed on the campus of this Christian college, nor were bars and liquor stores to be found in Clarksville, a so-called dry town. In the dormitory room next to mine lived an unmarried, middle-aged German professor. He was a slim, quiet man named Bohm. It soon became obvious to me that, despite the college prohibition on alcohol, Professor Bohm had the custom of enjoying a bit of whiskey or brandy in his room in the evenings. Every Saturday afternoon I would see him leaving his room, gingerly carrying a bulging bag. No matter how careful he was, I could hear the sound of empty bottles clanking together as he descended the stairs. Late Sunday night he would return carrying the same bag. He must have traveled to another town every weekend to replenish his supply of alcoholic beverages for the following week.

Professor Bohm's fondness for alcohol was certainly no secret among the students and very likely the administration knew about it as well. It was even doubtful whether this instructor considered himself a Christian—a shocking idea at a church college in the 1940s. He did attend the required chapel services regularly, but he was known to criticize Christianity quite harshly in his lectures. Probably the college administration chose to overlook these aberrations in Professor Bohm's case, however, because he was without a doubt the most distinguished scholar on campus. He not only was a language teacher and widely read in German, French, and other European languages but also was an insightful thinker. He was particularly well-informed in history, philosophy, and literature and quite astute in his comments on contemporary issues. Even the political science professors had to defer to his opinions.

Professor Bohm took extra trouble with students who were bright but mercilessly flunked those who could not do the work. Students both liked and feared him. His teaching methods were definitely unorthodox. In the second-term German class he required us to memorize the lyrics of German songs. He would sing the song two or three times over in his hoarse voice and then we were to commit the words to memory, referring to dictionaries to decipher their meaning. Invariably, these turned out to be drinking songs. At the end of the exercise, the whole class would join in singing the entire song with great gusto. A most refreshing approach to language teaching!

There were many extracurricular activities at the college, including sports, chorus, and Bible study. I decided to join the Debate Club, primarily because Professor Bohm was its adviser. The role of club adviser in this case was not just a nominal one. Bohm actively critiqued both the method and the content of our arguments and occasionally participated in a debate himself.

The Debate Club held periodic competitions with other colleges around the state. The topics for debate—usually political or social issues—were determined by student representatives from the participating colleges. In preparation for the debates the students gathered relevant material, researching and analyzing the questions and receiving merciless criticism from Professor Bohm.

One day when there was a debate on our campus, the other club members, as a prank, assigned Professor Bohm to be my opponent. I arrived at the debate entirely unaware of this plot. The topic that day was "Should the United Nations be transformed into a world federation?" It was only after the debates began that I realized who was to be my debating partner. I was rather taken aback but resolved to go through with it.

The United Nations was created after World War II by the Allies who had fought the Axis countries of Japan, Germany, and Italy. A declaration of intent to form the United Nations was first announced by twenty-six nations in Washington, D.C., on January 1, 1942, and the organization was established by representatives of fifty countries just before the end of the Pacific War in 1945. The

U.N. was an international confederation that recognized the right of member nations to govern themselves; it was a supranational political structure placed over them. A world federal government, by contrast, would have given each country regional administrative powers but no recognition of national sovereignty. That is the difference between a confederation and a federation.

In my argument, I demonstrated how the rise of nationalism in the modern period had been the cause of war. I advocated the consequent necessity of establishing a world federation that would transcend national sovereignty so that warfare might be eradicated.

In his rebuttal, Professor Bohm emphasized the realities of international politics:

> As Min has pointed out, the role of nationalism in international politics cannot be ignored. It is for this very reason, however, that the establishment of a world federation is impossible. Why? In a federation there is no effective police power. An international organization with no effective police power has no effective means of controlling nationalism when it turns into aggression. This is the case with the United Nations. There is no point in converting a United Nations that has no effective police power into a world federal government that likewise has no effective police power. So long as individual nations refuse to surrender their sovereignty, no effective power of enforcement will ever exist. And no country, no matter how progressive, is going to voluntarily surrender its own sovereignty. Indeed, the more powerful a nation, the more it will resist that. The same is true in the economic sphere: the more affluent a country, the less likely it is to give up its sovereignty.
>
> The idea of establishing a world federal government is just an idealist's dream. The United Nations is by no means a perfect international political body, but given the realities of the international situation we cannot expect anything more.

With this argument, Professor Bohm effectively defeated me in the debate. But the important part for me was his conclusion.

> In countering Min's position, I have stressed a realistic perspective. However, unless young people pursue their dreams, they cannot look forward to any progress in their own time. College should give young people dreams that transcend reality, equip them with a skeptical mind, refine their thinking, and offer them the knowledge they need to see reality clearly. In that regard, I must express my respect for Min's dream.

As he finished, Professor Bohm glanced over at me with a smile. This man may have enjoyed his whiskey and taught his students drinking songs, but he worked tirelessly, encouraging his students to think, preparing them to be members of a postwar generation equipped to respond to the challenges of a new era. Professor Bohm was a great educator.

Another professor, Dr. McDavid, was a lovely but stern and unsmiling woman in her thirties. A divorcée, she lived with her child, a cute girl of five or six, in a trim white house at the edge of campus. All the students would fall silent when Professor McDavid walked into a classroom. She was a gifted classicist with a keen mind and an incisive manner of speaking. Reading English translations of Greek classics like *The Odyssey* and *The Iliad* under her direction, I developed a great fascination with this ancient literature.

Then there was Miss Crump, a lecturer in modern English literature. She was a single, middle-aged woman who had worked as a missionary in the Philippines for many years. Although in her fifties, Miss Crump was working diligently to complete her doctoral degree, living in New York every summer to take courses at Columbia University. In every way this teacher exuded a youthful air that belied her age.

Miss Crump had been captured and interned by the Japanese military in the Philippines during the war, but I never heard her express the slightest hostility toward the Japanese people. Indeed, she was more than ordinarily solicitous toward me.

In private she would say to me, "I understand Asians better than anyone else in this college."

And in the classroom, she would almost gush in her praise of the Japanese. "The world will be astonished at how fast the Japanese will recover once they turn their mental and physical energies from destructive activities to constructive ones. Japan will be a world economic power within twenty years," she predicted.

Miss Crump never hesitated to introduce topics other than English literature into her classes, and frequently she talked of Asia. One day in class she spoke for almost an hour about the forty-seven samurai who avenged the wrongful death of their master and were forced to commit suicide as their punishment. She told this classic tale to illustrate to her students the admirable Japanese qualities of self-sacrifice, loyalty, and dedication. I wondered how on earth this could be the same woman who had endured a Japanese Army internment camp during the war. I found it amazing that she was able to transcend her own harsh experiences as a prisoner of war and look toward the future as she did.

Since this was a church-affiliated college, Scripture was a required course. I thoroughly hated this class. I had already done a systematic reading of both the Old and New Testaments with Tom at Tule Lake, so I was not altogether ignorant of the Bible. My problem with this class was the teacher—a local man of the cloth. Incapable of offering students anything substantial to think about, he ended up essentially giving sermons in his classes. The way the preacher dressed bothered me, too. I rather preferred Professor Bohm's appearance—I don't think he had polished his shoes since the day he bought them. And he always wore the same stained necktie, carelessly thrown on in the morning with a suit that was old and unfashionable. Nor was there any evidence that he ever combed what hair remained on his balding head. He probably just ran his fingers through it when he got up in the morning. Far more important than Professor Bohm's external appearance, though, was what was on the inside—his scholarship. By contrast, the minister always wore a seemingly expensive suit with a neat, stylish necktie, shiny black shoes, and pomade in his perfectly parted hair. There was never a flaw in his appearance—but his head was full of them. I found him thoroughly detestable, and flunked his course for skipping so many classes.

One evening as I was walking across the campus with Professor McDavid, I happened to confess to her with a rueful grin that I had failed the Scripture course. It was the first time I ever saw her smile. Apparently, she had no use for ministers. But what surprised me most was not her opinion of the clergy. It was Professor McDavid herself—I had discovered that she could smile. I realized then that her stern demeanor was simply a defensive facade, constructed to conceal her pain from others. It dawned on me that scholars are human beings, too, people who have troubles just like anyone else, and I began to feel a new warmth toward this professor.

After I confessed to Professor McDavid my particular interest in Indian philosophy, she offered a class in Vedic literature the following term. Occasionally she invited me to her house to lend me reference works on Indian literature. Her bookshelves were lined with Greek and Sanskrit books. When I envisioned her engrossed in her research there in her little house, I had a sense of loneliness, but also of strength. She could never have succeeded in her work without that kind of strength, for the academic world was still very much a male preserve. It could not have been easy for her to make her way alone in that world, teaching, doing research, and caring for her little girl.

Professor Bohm was a progressive, contemporary scholar. Professor McDavid was a contemplative, classical scholar. Both had depth and character and commanded my sincere respect. Although Miss Crump was not such an outstanding academic as Professors Bohm and McDavid, she was in her own way a fine educator. And she had the ability, despite her experience of persecution under the Japanese military, to look perceptively at Japan and foretell its future.

Among the students, I became friends with a number of GIs, who began to return to school after the war. Like myself, they were older than most other students, had clear goals, and were serious about their studies. With the help of the GI bill, they were able to devote themselves fully to their college work. One such man was Simmons. Since he was also a philosophy major, the two of us often spent time together discussing the books we were reading or studying our German.

The College of the Ozarks' gift to me was more than an intellectual one. The scars of the persecution I endured in the concentration camps did not immediately heal, but the friendship extended to me by the students at this college did much to assuage the pain I still felt. The young women especially were a delight to know. These were not sophisticated city women but they were gentle and sincere. After the ice of winter melted, the campus was carpeted with new green grass and the young women shed their layers of winter attire, revealing their soft, fair skin. In the spring on the tennis courts or in the summer by the pool, they readily and unaffectedly posed for photographs. And they were always happy to accept an invitation to dine at one of the local restaurants. I derived boundless pleasure from our conversations over dinner. Southern women are the most beautiful of all, I thought—in body and in soul. And they were in no sense inferior intellectually to their counterparts at first-rate colleges on the East and West Coasts.

Quite frequently, I walked the narrow sidewalk that ran along the edge of campus and down the hill into town. Often I would encounter black people coming up the walk in the opposite direction, but always before we met they would automatically jump off the sidewalk out into the broad street. One time I leapt into the street first, yielding the sidewalk to them. They just stared at me with puzzled expressions. After that incident, I began to think that I would like to visit the black settlement in the woods. I said nothing of my intentions to my white friends of course, for I sensed that the "Negro problem" was a taboo subject.

One day when the little boy came to pick up my laundry, I asked if he would take me to visit the settlement where he lived. He hesitated, but I reassured him.

"I'm not white, you know," I said.

A big smile creased the boy's face.

"Okay," he agreed.

Twenty or so dwellings comprised the gloomy, clammy little settlement in the woods. It had no sewer system. Inside the dilapidated wooden houses, broken-down furniture stood on dirt floors. A common lavatory and a well were at the center of the settlement, and next to these a tumbledown structure served as a combination school, church, and community meetinghouse. A foul odor hung in the air. Every dwelling appeared to be brimming over with small children.

The little boy introduced me to the minister who apparently served as the community's spokesman. He was a humble old gentleman but wary of outsiders, and I found it difficult to talk with him. I was not, after all, black. From the black point of view, anyone who was not black was white. And in point of fact I was a student at a white college, a college that did not admit black students.

I returned to campus, shaken by what I had seen. The settlement was so much more impoverished than I had ever imagined. And there was such profound wariness toward outsiders, that sense of perversity and inferiority that is so common among the oppressed. I began to have rash notions of doing something for this community if ever I had the opportunity.

Every Sunday evening a group of fourteen or fifteen college students, committed Christians, met at a church in town. I attended occasionally. One evening the discussion topic was Christianity and Social Action. Thinking that this would surely be a receptive group, I described in some detail what I had observed at the black settlement behind the college. The other students listened to me with fascination. Some had not even known about the existence of that settlement. After discussing it for a while, the group—mostly young women—reached the consensus that they should do something to help the black community.

Leading the group that evening was Anne, a senior at the college. She was a young woman I frequently took to dinner on the weekends. In fact, I had come to this evening's gathering at her urging after the two of us had dinner at a restaurant in town. Anne was from Clarksville, an outstanding student who was listed in *Who's Who of American Colleges*. She was fair skinned, with a gentle, quiet nature and a strong sense of justice. She would be graduating from college with a major in French in just another month.

Anne made the wise suggestion that we first arrange a joint worship service for blacks and whites and afterwards talk with representatives of the black community. The others agreed. Anne and I were charged with making the arrangements. The two of us remained at the church for about thirty minutes after the meeting to formulate our plans.

By the time we finished it was dark, so I decided I should walk Anne home. Her house was quite a distance away, beyond the campus on the opposite side from the black settlement. She lived at home with her parents and her sister, who was a sophomore at the college.

Anne began to talk as we walked along.

"You know, I've always lived here. I've been raised with segregation and all the traditions that go with it, so I know very well that this isn't a problem that will be quick or easy to solve. But I'm glad you came here and actually went to visit the colored settlement to see for yourself the miserable conditions there. I was really moved by what you told us about it tonight. You've made me determined to do something."

"Anne, I only went there out of curiosity, you know. An outsider like me can't really do much. The only way is for concerned people like you who live here to solve the problems. But I *am* willing to do what I can to help," I assured her.

"Min, I want to tell you something. I don't think there's anybody else I could say this to. I was born into a Christian family and I've been a Christian all my life, but now that I'm about to graduate from college, I really am beginning to have serious doubts about Christianity. I mean, here is this miserable colored settlement right in the same town with a Christian college and all kinds of Christian churches. And neither the college nor the churches pay any attention to such things. But tonight your courage revived my faith. Even if our plan isn't realized by the time I graduate, I do hope we can at least get something started," she said.

For a quiet young woman who rarely asserted herself on campus, Anne held surprisingly strong convictions, I realized.

Then Anne began to ask me questions about my past. I really did not want to tell her about it, for I didn't feel I had anything in particular to be proud of. But when I evaded her queries she only became more curious. Luckily for me, we had reached her house by this time, so I was able to stall by promising to tell her about myself later. I bade her good-night and walked back to my dormitory.

Early the following morning I was startled out of my sleep by a loud banging on my door. I opened my eyes and glanced over at the clock on my desk. It was only six A.M. When I got out of bed and opened the door, the local minister who taught the Scripture class and the college chaplain barged in. Both men launched into me at once.

"Min, what on earth do you think you were doing last night, proposing such a preposterous thing?!" they demanded.

"What thing?" I asked.

I knew very well what they were talking about, but I sat down casually on the edge of my bed in my pajamas, rubbed my eyes, and gazed at them with a blank expression. If truth be told, I didn't particularly care for either of these ministers of the gospel. And they became even more infuriated when they saw my disdainful attitude. The chaplain rolled his eyes to the ceiling and turned purple with rage.

"You are an outsider here!" he roared. "You know nothing about the traditions and customs of people who have always lived here. I am going to tell you something, and you had better listen: you just try and get a Negro to set one foot inside a church in this town and you will be lynched as a nigger-lover!" he fumed.

Next the town minister took up the attack: "You'll be thrown into jail for inciting a riot! If you want peace and order in this town you must promise right this minute to keep your hands off the Negro problem!" he commanded.

I'd had plenty of experience being yelled at by authority figures, so being shouted at by a couple of country parsons didn't
bother me in the slightest. With my back to the two ministers, I
deliberately set about removing my pajamas and putting on my
clothes. I needed some time to collect my thoughts. In fact, we all
needed some time.

The chaplain began to talk a little more calmly. "Min, we
haven't mentioned this incident yet to the president of the college.
Depending upon what you have to say, we could just pretend that
this whole incident never took place," he suggested.

So—now it was an "incident." They were softening their
accusations, attempting a compromise.

Smiling sardonically to myself I thought, you know, I kind of
wish they *would* tell the college president. I'd like to see that ever-
smiling face of his looking anxious for once. On the other hand, the
president can expel a student. Oh well, if I were expelled, I would
just transfer to another college. If this "incident" became a big issue
in town and things got too bad, I could leave. But Anne couldn't
leave—she lived here. She was supposed to be graduating in another
month, and it would be especially rough on her if things got out of
hand. For all her brilliance as a student, I knew she was pretty innocent about the ways of the world.

After thinking all this through, I knew what I had to do. I
finished getting dressed and slowly turned to face the two ministers.
There they stood waiting for my response with their mouths open
like so many dogs anticipating a bone.

"All right. I will try to do as you wish. Anne and I will come
and see you at the church this evening," I assured them.

When I got to my German class that morning, Anne's
younger sister Jeanne, who was in the same class, was anxiously
waiting for me. She told me that Anne wanted me to meet her
behind the chapel after the second class period.

When I arrived, Anne was nervously waiting in a secluded
spot by the chapel, her eyes red and swollen.

"I just don't believe it! What those ministers say and what
they do are two entirely different things! I am so sick of hearing

them talk about the love of God and the equality of all people and being of service to humanity!" she proclaimed indignantly.

She was so upset that she was on the verge of tears. The ministers' hypocrisy was blatant indeed—for although they had said they would speak of the "incident" to no one, clearly they had already gone to Anne's house. They must have told her parents about it in order to put pressure on her. No doubt they had already told everyone else in town, too.

"Anne, the only thing those ministers are telling people is that we had a very sensible idea—to improve understanding between blacks and whites by having a worship service together. So something good came out of their anger after all. But you can't put a good idea like that into action unless the environment is ready for it. There's nothing wrong with our plan—it's just not time for it yet. I'm really sorry I made so much trouble for you with all my rash ideas.

"Look, you're going to graduate in just another month. Please don't let anything stand in the way of that," I begged, resting my hands lightly on her shoulders to calm her. "Anne, you should have seen those two preachers this morning. They came to my room at six o'clock to yell at me! They were so panicked, it was hilarious."

That finally brought a smile to Anne's lips, and she dabbed at her tears with her handkerchief. The chapel bell rang and the two of us walked slowly together toward the front door for the required weekly service. Ironically, the preacher for the day was the same local minister, and his sermon was on "Love thy neighbor." I squeezed Anne's hand and the two of us exchanged wry smiles.

That evening Anne and I went to the church and solemnly promised the two ministers that we would not agitate the black community, that we would abandon our proposal of a joint worship service for blacks and whites, and that we would have nothing more to do with this incident. It was all over in ten minutes.

Anne and I left the church and started walking along the narrow sidewalk up the hill toward the college. About halfway up the hill I noticed two figures lurking in the shadow of some trees ahead. Sensing something strange in their manner, I took Anne's hand and moved out into the center of the wide street. The men likewise stepped into the street. I could see the hard rubber clubs in their hands and sense their menace. They began to approach us. I pushed Anne behind me. As we came up to them, one of the men raised his club in the air. Without a second's hesitation I leapt at him, chopped his right wrist with my right hand, then grabbed it with my left. Then, with my right hand, I scooped him up, twisted my body around, and threw him. Just as the other man was about to jump me, I whirled around and kicked him in the thigh, throwing my whole weight against him. He fell to the ground.

I grabbed Anne's hand and ran as fast as I could up the hill, pulling her along with me. Only when we reached the top did I look back to make sure the two men had not followed. Anne collapsed, gasping for breath. I picked her up and carried her home.

Apparently, the so-called "incident" was by now common knowledge among the locals. There was no doubt that the two men were townspeople. I realized that my ideas had brought on this violence.

I walked back to campus greatly relieved that Anne had not been hurt. When I got to my dorm room, I found Simmons waiting for me. That young man had been very wise when he first came to this college. He had taken one look at the local situation and determined not to get drawn into matters he figured had nothing to do with him.

"Simmons, this is my second year here," I said. "I've decided to go back to California after this term is over. I do like this college. I like the professors and the students. But I've decided I want to go somewhere now where there is more intellectual stimulation."

"You're scared," he shot back.

So—Simmons had heard about the incident, too.

"I know," he went on. "You want to go somewhere that's not so religious, where there aren't so many hypocrites, not so much prejudice, somewhere freer."

Simmons began to roar with laughter. His guffaws were so infectious that I finally had to laugh, too. It was impossible not to like this fellow.

After our laughter subsided, I confessed: "Simmons, two guys jumped Anne and me tonight."

He was alarmed at that. "You'd better report that to the police!" he said.

"Forget it. I don't want this to get blown up any bigger than it already is. I just promised those two preachers I wouldn't have anything more to do with the whole business. Besides, the police are locals, so naturally they're going to side with other townspeople on something like this. Please don't tell anyone else about it," I said.

Simmons understood and readily agreed. I knew I could count on him to keep it quiet.

"Min, you know what? The reason I came to your room tonight was to tell you I'm planning to transfer to California, too. To UCLA. Where are you going?" he asked.

"UC Berkeley."

"Well, let's travel together as far as Los Angeles," he suggested.

A few weeks later, I attended the commencement ceremonies to see Anne receive her college degree. Afterwards, I presented her with a graduation gift—a small compact. She was delighted. But when I told her that I would be leaving for California to finish college, she could not hide her dismay. She laid her head on my shoulder and wept, heedless of what people around us might think.

The College of the Ozarks had given me my first taste of real freedom after my release from the segregation center. It had given me a warm welcome. The Caucasian students who had befriended me without prejudice and included me in their activities, Professor Bohm with his keen intellect and sense of humor, the solitary Professor McDavid—I would miss them all.

The next day I boarded the train with Simmons and headed west. But the picture of Anne remaining behind at the Clarksville station stayed with me for a very long time.

I arrived back in San Francisco early in the summer of 1947. By this time my mother had already returned to the West Coast from New York and was hard at work. She had found a place to live on Steiner Street, a little ways from the old Japan Town. That part of the city had changed a great deal with urban renewal during the past few years. Mother had readied a room for me in her apartment. I found a part-time job working in the nearby university hospital from 7 to 11 P.M., pulling charts for the following day. My earnings there would cover my tuition, transportation, and spending money. I had two more years to complete my college education. I planned to concentrate entirely on philosophy.

I discovered that the University of California, Berkeley was very different from the College of the Ozarks. It wasn't just that it was bigger. For one thing, in such a large university interaction among students was more limited. The many Japanese American students in particular tended to keep to themselves. Of course, UC Berkeley was then as now one of the most distinguished universities in the country, with a world-class faculty offering outstanding lectures. But there wasn't the same opportunity as at the College of the Ozarks for a student to have a personal conversation with a professor while strolling across the campus, to receive a teacher's guidance in such a leisurely, comfortable atmosphere.

My days back in San Francisco consisted of a repetitious cycle of going to class, coming home, and going to work. But I reveled in the chance to bury myself in study and research among the well-stocked shelves of the university library.

Two years after transferring to UC Berkeley, I submitted my graduation thesis on German existential philosophy. It was accepted by the faculty and I was assured of graduating at the end of that term. I had long planned to shift my focus at this point to Asian philosophy. Specifically, I wanted to study Indian philosophy with an emphasis on Buddhism. But I was faced with a problem here—no university in America offered a degree in Buddhist philosophy. That actually made the subject all the more intriguing to me. I knew I could study such subjects in Japan, but I lacked the funds to get there. And even if I did manage to get to Japan, I couldn't see how I would possibly be able to support myself as a student in a country that was still so devastated from its wartime defeat.

There was one possibility, though. I had noticed on the bulletin board in the university placement office an announcement

from U.S. Air Force Intelligence. They were recruiting college graduates who were fluent in both Japanese and English. I could apply
for that, I thought, and if the job took me to Japan I wouldn't need
to find the money to get there. Maybe I could work for the air force
for a few years and save money to study at a Japanese university. I
was confident that my Japanese would be good enough to handle
the work.

I was considering these questions as I lay sprawled on the
grass under the campanile on the Berkeley campus, when I caught
sight of a young Japanese American woman hurrying by with several
thick tomes in her arms. She looked vaguely familiar. I was sure I
remembered her from somewhere. Then it came to me.

"Nancy! It's Nancy!" I shouted her name and ran to catch up
with her.

She looked around. "Min!" she exclaimed, rushing back
excitedly to greet me.

"How *are* you? Oh, I want to talk to you so much, Min, but
I'm on my way to my last final exam. Could I see you tonight? Come
and pick me up at five o'clock. All right? Five," she reiterated, as she
told me her address and hurried off to her exam.

My discouraged thoughts about the future did a sudden
about-face. It had been almost four years since I'd parted from
Nancy after our release from Tule Lake. I'd sent her Christmas cards
from college in Arkansas, but after that we had lost touch with one
another. This was Friday and the hospital clinic would be closed
over the weekend. I could go in on Sunday to pull the charts for
Monday. Tonight I would take Nancy to San Francisco for a night
on the town. We had so much to catch up on.

I had two hours until it was time to pick up Nancy. In the
interval, I went to the university placement office, got an application form for the air force job, and carefully filled it out, checking
U.S. citizen in the appropriate box. The renunciation issue was still
under adjudication, but until the courts ruled otherwise I considered
myself an American citizen—I certainly wasn't anything else.

Somehow I had the feeling that I would get that job. Today
was my lucky day.

I located Nancy's apartment near the campus in Berkeley.

"You're late! I'm tired of waiting for you," she said accusingly.

I was glad to see that Nancy was the same assertive young woman as ever.

"Hey, it's not even five yet," I protested. "How about I take you to San Francisco tonight?"

"Sure. Anywhere's fine. I'm starved!" she declared.

"It'll be cool in San Francisco, you know. You'd better take a coat. And dress up, because I'm going to take you someplace very elegant. You've got to wear makeup and everything," I demanded.

Assertive as she usually was, Nancy meekly assented, clearly delighted at the prospect. It was only a one-room apartment, so she began to change her clothes with me right there in the same room. Feeling a bit awkward, I strolled over to the window and looked out. But I told myself that Nancy and I were old friends and we shouldn't have to stand on ceremony or be self-conscious with one another. My heart was dancing—I was graduating from college, I had a feeling I was going to get a job that would take me to Japan, and I had run into Nancy again.

"Min, what do you think?" she asked.

She'd been quick. I turned around and took a good look at her. Nancy was tall, and in her makeup and dressy clothes she no longer looked the student. She was a young woman.

"Hey, you're beautiful!"

Nancy smiled with pleasure.

"You know, I've been at Berkeley a whole year and I've never yet gone into San Francisco," she confessed. "I guess I'm really just a country girl."

This country girl was fine with me. I felt honored to walk down the street with such a lovely woman.

We could ride the train that crossed the Bay Bridge into San Francisco, but that seemed too ordinary, so I decided we should take the more leisurely ferry across the bay to the city. It was a quiet ride with only a few people on board. There was just a bit of fog on the bay. The ferry's horn made its lugubrious plaint over the powerful noise of churning paddle wheels on either side of the boat. The vessel sent up a fine spray as it pulled away from the pier and into the bay.

Nancy and I leaned against the railing at the bow on the top deck, gazing in companionable silence at the twilight skyline of San Francisco. Both of us were occupied with similar recollections. Many were the times we had strolled together at dusk along the dusty roads of Tule Lake on our way home after a day's work at the research center. That time of day had offered us something of a respite from the cruelly oppressive atmosphere of the segregation center. As we crossed the bay, both Nancy and I were thinking about the painful past we shared.

She moved closer and I pulled her to me, saying, "Hey, you're cold! Do you want to go inside?"

She didn't answer.

It was a brief voyage, but pleasant.

After the ferry landed, we boarded the streetcar on Market Street, changing to a cable car at Powell, one of the busiest streets in San Francisco.

At last Nancy spoke.

"The cable car's so cute!" she murmured in a small voice.

Within ten minutes the little cable car brought us to the top of Nob Hill, where we got off. I led Nancy to the revolving rooftop bar of the Mark Hopkins Hotel. She looked around in surprise and delight at the luxurious surroundings. We sat down and ordered wine at Nancy's request.

"Nancy, tonight is to be a celebration of our reunion. And to express my gratitude to you for introducing me to Dr. Opler. And to thank you for that wonderful night on the train to Sacramento. Here's to you!" I said, raising my glass.

"My, you've gotten so eloquent, Min," she teased.

Perhaps I had done some growing up, too.

"Look out there, Nancy. See the patches of fog racing by the window? If you look between them, you can glimpse the city. Can you see the cable cars down below? Isn't it beautiful? This is *my* city, the place I was always dreaming about when we were in Tule Lake."

"Min, you're such a romantic. I never knew!"

"What have you been doing since I saw you last, Nancy? What are you studying?" I asked.

"Min, I'm really hungry. What with my exam today, I haven't eaten a thing since breakfast this morning. I think I'm just a bit tipsy, too. Do you suppose we could talk over dinner? Let's eat Chinese. First-rate Chinese. All we ever get in that dining hall is American food."

We left the Mark Hopkins hand in hand. The fine ladies and gentlemen in the lobby and outside on the street smiled benignly on our happiness. San Francisco's Chinatown was not far away. With more Chinese establishments in one place than anywhere else in America, we had our pick of first-rate restaurants.

I encouraged Nancy to order her favorite dishes. Then she settled back in her chair.

"Now. We can talk. You wanted to know what I've been doing. Well, for three years I worked with my brothers, helping them to get their farm going. Then I told them I really wanted to go to college, and they were willing to support me so I could do that. I've just finished my first year of undergraduate work. After I graduate, I plan to go on to med school and specialize in psychiatry. I have approximately ten more years of school to go—it will be a long haul."

"Boy, you sure don't pick the easy route, do you?" I commented.

"Thanks to you. You're the one who got me interested in studying, you know. But I don't just chase after dreams like you do."

She threw an impish grin in my direction. Then she got serious.

"I mean, you're always talking about religion and the love of God and all that kind of thing. But you can't study things like that objectively or scientifically," she said.

"So, you're going to be a doctor?" I asked.

"Well, not really. I'm not like you—I don't especially like people. I mean people who talk about helping other people and all that—as often as not they turn out to be hypocrites. I don't like people like that. I want to hole up in my study and do research. Of course, my research will involve clinical work, too."

"You say you don't like people, but you do plan to get married someday, don't you?" I asked her.

"Maybe. If I meet the right person. But, right now I'm more interested in the research I want to do. I'm fascinated with the fact that a human being isn't simply the product of a relationship between one man and one woman. You have to take into account all those other things that you're so interested in—history and society and culture. Psychiatry is the study from a medical point of view of the emotional problems of people born and raised with that social and cultural background."

Nancy did love her wine. She was drinking it with dinner, and she had had a glass earlier on an empty stomach at the Mark Hopkins. Flushed and loquacious, she talked on and on.

"So—what are your plans, Min?" she asked.

"Nancy, I'm not a Christian. I never was. But I do have a kind of existential interest in Christianity. What I've been studying is Western existential philosophy. Now I want to go to Japan and study Buddhist existential philosophy. You see, I want to do comparative research on the philosophical systems that produced two such different cultures. You can't study anything like that in America right now, but I think that by the time I finish my degree in Japan there'll be an interest in such things in this country— because there's bound to be more and more cultural interchange between Japan and the United States. I want to prepare myself to play a part in that."

"You always have had a unique way of looking at things, Min. You like to do things no one else is doing, don't you?" she said.

"I suppose it's because of everything I've been through, and because I'm so aware of all the contradictions in myself. I'd be great material for your clinical research," I told her.

"I don't know about material for my research, but I would love it if we could collaborate on our work some day," Nancy said.

At this break in our talk of matters intellectual, Nancy suddenly demanded, "Tell me about Arkansas!"

She laughed and laughed when I told her about the "incident." This woman was so much like Simmons: She was smart. She was a hard worker. And she always had a stimulating response to what I said.

It was after ten o'clock. Nancy refused to let me see her all the way back to Berkeley, so I took her as far as the train station and we made plans to meet again. What a delightful evening it had been. Nancy had matured into an intelligent young woman—and that pleased me more than anything.

N orth of San Francisco's Golden Gate Bridge is San Anselmo, a lovely, quiet little town adorned with multicolored flowers. Atop one of its hills stands a tall, majestic building with a facade reminiscent of a medieval rampart. This is the San Francisco Theological Seminary. Not long after my reunion with Nancy, I received word that, thanks to the recommendation of the minister at the church I'd attended in San Francisco, I had been awarded a fellowship to attend this seminary.

Despite my reservations about Christianity, seminary study did hold a certain appeal for me, for these were the days of the existential theology of Paul Tillich and Reinhold Niebuhr. I still did not know whether I would be able to get to Japan, so I decided that for the time being I would accept the fellowship and enter the seminary.

I moved onto the campus as required, but after I got there, I found that on weekends I would be expected as a seminarian to preach at a Japanese American church south of San Francisco. I was to hold services in both Japanese and English, for issei and nisei members of the congregation. The very thought sent chills down my spine. Moreover, my roommate in the seminary dormitory turned out to be a plump Caucasian fellow whom I did not much care for.

One day this roommate confided his future plans to me. "After I'm ordained, I think I'll try to get a rich church in a big city," he said. "If that doesn't work out, though, maybe I'll go to Africa as a missionary."

He paused ever so slightly, then looking at me pointedly he added, "Or maybe I'll go to Japan."

The seminary seemed to be full of hypocrites like this fellow, people who were smugly confident of white superiority.

In June of 1950 the Korean War began with the North Korean Army's invasion of the South. Within a few months I received notice from the U.S. Air Force that I had been given a job with them and should proceed immediately to Washington, D.C., to attend a one-month orientation course. Disappointed as I was with my experience in the seminary, I was happy to have a reason to leave. I gladly terminated my studies there and headed for the nation's capital as directed.

I was doubly pleased at this turn of events, for I had heard that Anne was working in Washington, in the French documents section of the Library of Congress. I wanted very much to see her again before I left for Japan. Thus, at the end of my month's stay in the capital, on the last day of my course, I went to the Library of Congress. There I found her in the corner of a reading room, diligently poring over some documents.

"Hello, Anne," I said, coming up behind her as she worked.

She gave a start and whirled around.

"Min!"

People in the reading room glared at us accusingly. We went out into the corridor.

"Oh, Min, it's *so* good to see you! It's been *two* years! And you only wrote to me twice that whole time. Let's have dinner together tonight. Wait for me here while I finish up and get my coat. I'll just be ten minutes."

At this point I began to regret not staying in touch with Anne more during the past two years.

Anne knew very little about things Asian, but her friendship with me had sparked her interest. Tonight she said she'd like to go somewhere Japanese, but we couldn't find a single Japanese restaurant in Washington. As the next best thing, I took her to a Cantonese restaurant on F Street near the Capitol Theater. It was in a basement, atmospheric with dim lights and candlelit tables.

"We'll have to make do with this for now, Anne, but next time I'll take you to Chinatown in San Francisco," I told her.

Then I thought to myself, now what have I said? First I lose her trust by not writing, and then I go and make an empty promise like that!

Not surprisingly, Anne said nothing. She just gazed at me reproachfully. I averted my eyes, looking down and silently begging her forgiveness. But she showed no sign of losing her composure.

"Min, when we were in college you said you were planning to go to seminary. Did you?" she asked.

"Yes, I did, but I left the seminary, and I don't have any plans to go back. To tell you the truth, Anne, the reason I'm in Washington now is because I've been training here for the past month for a civilian job with the air force. Tomorrow I'll be leaving for Japan. I'm going to work there for three or four years, and then I plan to stay for a few years after that, to do graduate work. I'm not exactly sure how long it will be before I get back to the States, and I wanted to see you again before I leave."

Silence.

This was not going well at all.

Weakly, I said, "Well, tell me about yourself since I saw you last."

A few more moments passed before Anne spoke again.

"Well, after college I got my teacher certification and taught French in the high school in Clarksville for a while."

At that moment our dinner arrived—abalone soup, roast duck with peanuts, shrimp and vegetable stir-fry. Our conversation lapsed while the waiter served us. I thought about how much I'd like to have a cold beer with my meal, but I couldn't bring myself to order one in front of Anne. Finally the waiter ladled out our soup, bowed, and left.

Anne looked lovelier than ever in the candlelight, I thought.

"I've received a proposal of marriage," she said.

My spoon stopped in midair, halfway to my mouth.

After a long pause, I finally blurted out, "Well, congratulations, Anne."

I meant it, sincerely.

"I really *am* glad for you. I'm just a little surprised, I guess. It's kind of sudden, you know. Who's the lucky guy? Anybody I know?"

For the first time, she smiled. I had no idea how to interpret that.

"Min, I said I *received* a proposal. I didn't say I'd accepted it. Of course it's someone you know, very well," she said.

I pondered that one for a minute. If it was someone I knew well, then it had to be someone from college.

"It's Bob," she volunteered. "Bob McGill."

"Oh. Bob." I could hardly get out the words.

I hadn't been particularly close friends with Bob, but he was in the Debate Club with me and we had worked together on club activities. I recalled that he was a local boy who was planning to be a lawyer. He was much taller than I, sociable and athletic, always popular with the women. Academically, he was perhaps a bit above average.

Bob's father owned a bank in town, and I remembered people saying that he also owned an enormous amount of real estate in the area. He was a pillar of the community and made substantial contributions to the college every year. I had heard, too, that Bob's family had a second home in Florida. Anne's father, on the other hand, had a small orchard, and her mother was an elementary school teacher. As far as I could see, Anne and Bob had nothing at all in common, in terms of personality or of family background.

"Bob has changed a lot since he graduated, Min. He didn't go on to law school, but he does have a lot of sense. I know he played around quite a bit in college, but he's settled down now. He's working for his father," she said.

"So why did you come to Washington?" I asked.

"Well, that's just it. Oh, it's not that I don't care for him. We grew up in the same town and went to school together all the way from grade school through college, so we certainly know each other well. It's just that Bob and his dad are both so completely absorbed in their business that they have no dreams. I could be perfectly happy with a simple, quiet life, so long as I have some kind of dream.

I just don't know if I could get used to being around the kind of harsh business world that Bob deals in all the time. That's what I'm worried about. So I came to Washington to think it over by myself for a while. Bob calls me faithfully every weekend, though."

I knew this last remark was a touch of sarcasm aimed right at me.

"You're lucky, Anne. Bob's a good man. He's a businessman with a future. You'll get used to his world in time and you two can be happy together. Why are you making him wait so long?" I asked.

"Min, what are *you* thinking about marriage?" she asked.

"Me? I'm in no position even to think about it yet. I have so many more years of study ahead of me," I replied.

"You're lucky. At least you have your dreams," she murmured. Then after a moment she asked, "Min, why didn't you write to me?"

I looked down again. I didn't know what to say.

"You know, you were at the College of the Ozarks for two years, so you know all about me," she said. "And the college is in Clarksville, so you even know the town I grew up in. But you've never told me anything about yourself. Every time it came up, you always changed the subject. I think you know *my* feelings very well, but you've never told me what yours are. Tell me about yourself tonight, Min. Tell me about your past and your dreams. Tell me why you didn't write to me more often, and why you came to see me today. *Do* you love me, Min? Tell me!"

On the verge of tears, she pressed me almost fiercely. Trembling and hesitant, I looked up at her. Her steady gaze demanded an answer. Several moments of silence followed, until finally I knew that I had to reveal the feelings I had managed to keep to myself for so long.

"Anne, I didn't want to tell you about my past before, because it was just too painful for me. I was very deeply wounded by the government's persecution during the war, and those wounds were still pretty raw when I first came to college. You see, when things were especially bad for me in the camps, I refused to declare my loyalty to the U.S. government, because the only thing I felt toward it at that point was bitterness. My experiences at college in Arkansas did help to soften those bitter feelings a bit, but I still feel a tremendous need to prove to myself that there is something more in life than just loyalty or disloyalty to a government—because I don't think those things have anything to do with the true measure of a person's human worth.

"Maybe I should explain myself better. You see, because of all the people who were so good to me at the college—especially you, Anne—I began to have an understanding and love for Americans. And I love the Japanese, too, because I went to school in Japan as a child. So I'm very much aware that the crucial thing is for people to understand each other. That's the foundation for peace. But understanding between two countries can only happen if each one learns about the other's culture. That's the reason I want to study in Japan. I want to prepare myself to teach in a college or university when I come back. That's my dream. I feel certain that within the next ten years, political and economic relations between Japan and the United States are going to open up, and if those relations are going to go smoothly, there has to be some cultural understanding between the two countries. I want to make a contribution to that understanding, because that is something that goes way beyond issues of loyalty or disloyalty.

"But, Anne, this dream of mine is going to take at least ten more years to realize, because first of all I have to work and save the money to study in Japan. And even after I work and study all those years, I'm not absolutely certain that my dream will be realized—maybe it's too idealistic. So I'm taking a big risk. But I'm willing to take that risk because I have to prove—I'm *determined* to prove—that I was right when I refused to swear my loyalty to the U.S. government in the camps. And I'll never be at peace with myself unless I do realize that dream. World War II is still going on inside me, Anne, and I don't know when it will ever end. And any woman who married a man who's carrying around so much turmoil inside of himself is bound to be unhappy.

"But that doesn't mean I don't love you, Anne. Do you remember that night when those two guys jumped us in Clarksville?

I was terrified when I saw them waiting in the shadows with clubs in their hands, but I decided right then that there was absolutely no way I was going to let them hurt you—even if they killed me. I fought them for everything I was worth, and then I picked you up and carried you home. I did that because . . . because I love you, Anne. I couldn't tell you then, though.

"Anne, those times in Clarksville when the two of us went out to dinner together—those were the happiest times in my life. I don't think I'll ever have that kind of happiness again. And the most painful thing I've ever done was telling you good-bye at the Clarksville station when I left. I don't want to feel that kind of pain again, either. If I'd written to you more often these past two years, we would only have become closer, and that would have just meant more pain in the end. And my first priority right now has to be studying in Japan. So that's why I didn't stay in touch with you, Anne.

"I've been in Washington for a month now. I've been thinking about you and wanting so much to see you. But at the same time I was afraid that if I did see you, the pain of parting again would be so unbearable I wouldn't be able to leave you. But then I realized that tomorrow I'll be going to Japan and I don't know when I'll ever see you again. I agonized over what I should do, and finally I thought maybe I could just come by and see you for a little while and say good-bye sort of casually.

"Do you understand what I've been saying, Anne? About my past and my dream? About how difficult it will be to realize that dream? Do you understand how determined I am to pursue it, even so? And that if I don't realize it, I will never have any peace? Can you understand now why I didn't write to you? And how desperate I was to see you, even though I did wait until today?"

Tears were streaming down Anne's face when I finally finished talking, but she just sat there gazing at me silently, almost in a trance, not wiping away the tears.

We left the restaurant, Anne clinging fiercely to my arm as I walked her home. When she started to say something, I covered her warm lips with mine.

"Don't say it," I pleaded. "It will only make it harder."

There was so much that I had to accomplish in the next ten years. And even at that I hadn't told Anne everything. It wasn't just a matter of accumulating the funds to do graduate work in Japan—I had legal problems as well. I was in the midst of a long court battle to regain my citizenship. If I lost that lawsuit while I was in Japan, the U. S. government would not have to "repatriate" me. I would be exiled there. Not only that, I would be stateless, with neither American nor Japanese citizenship. I'd be stranded with no possibility of getting a job. Even if I did win the lawsuit, it could take years. In the meantime, the American military's security agencies were bound to unearth the facts about my past. Either way, the Japanese police would probably eventually arrest me for illegal entry. It seemed that the trail of persecution from Tule Lake would follow me forever. World War II certainly had not yet ended for me, and I did not want to get Anne involved in a predicament for which I alone was responsible. I would just have to resign myself to a solitary journey.

The College of the Ozarks had been a paradise of happiness for me when I was a student there, but now that paradise was the source of an even greater sorrow. Tenderly I pulled Anne to me. With the warmth of her body in my arms, I was overwhelmed by all the precious memories. My tears fell on her face. Gently, Anne wiped them away with her handkerchief.

The following day I boarded a plane for the trip from Washington to Tokyo, the vision of Anne's face engraved upon my soul.

9 U.S. Intelligence, Far East Air Force

By mid-October 1950, World War II had been over for five years and the Allied occupation of Japan had another year and a half to go.

The military plane I boarded in Washington took me to Travis Airbase near Sacramento, California. I had no time to visit my mother in San Francisco before departing for Japan on a C-54 air force transport plane early the following morning. En route, the four-engine World War II prop plane set down for refueling in Hawaii and Wake Island. Wake was still littered with the remains of the Japanese Army's small tanks and mortar shells, and its beaches were strewn with the sun-bleached bones of Japanese soldiers.

Fifty-four hours after leaving California we landed at the U.S. airbase at Haneda Airport on the outskirts of Tokyo. There we were greeted by the stench of raw sewage that flowed into the water near the shore. The medical officer gave a long list of warnings to the newly arrived young soldiers traveling with me.

"Do not eat raw fish. Avoid uncooked vegetables. And *always* protect yourself when you sleep with a Japanese woman!" he said emphatically.

We boarded a military bus and started toward Tokyo, bouncing over a highway full of potholes. One sleazy bar after another lined the road near the American base, with "ladies of the night" loitering about even at midday. Beyond this was wasteland. As we came closer to the city, around Kamata, we began to see the steel skeletons of burned-out buildings and some impoverished dwellings.

Eventually we came to the center of Tokyo. I was to live in the Nomura Securities Building at Nihonbashi. That structure had been requisitioned by the occupation forces and designated as living quarters for occupation personnel, who promptly rechristened it Riverview Hotel. Though small steamboats actually puffed up and down along the river, it was nothing but a giant sewer—complete with the characteristic odor.

The intelligence sections of both air force and army were headquartered in the commandeered Japan Mail Line Building in Marunouchi, Tokyo's business section. In the great, high-ceilinged room on the first floor hung framed pictures of the Pacific route passenger liners whose forms were so familiar to me from my childhood. There was the *Taiyō Maru*, which brought me to Japan as a young boy; the *Chichibu Maru*, which carried Mother back to the States; and the *Kamakura Maru*, which returned us to America together in 1938. Every one of these vessels now rested silently on the floor of the Pacific Ocean.

The old Marunouchi Building still stood intact next door to our headquarters. For some reason, it had escaped requisitioning by the occupation. Hundreds of logs floated in the large pond across from it, destined to serve as construction material for the New Marunouchi Building. Tokyo was gradually embarking upon the road to recovery.

Arriving at the front entrance of the U.S. military intelligence headquarters to report for my first day of work, I saw an armed nisei guard by the gate yelling at a middle-aged Japanese man whom he accused of being late for work. Never mind that the man had just traveled two hours to get there, he was three minutes late, and this guard was deriving evident satisfaction from sending him away for this infraction. Meanwhile, a bunch of sleepy-eyed American employees, including myself, were arriving for work equally late after a leisurely ten-minute ride from our quarters in a military bus.

My job with Air Force Intelligence was to interrogate, day after day, demobilized Japanese soldiers who had only recently returned from prisoner of war camps in Siberia, where they had been detained by the Soviets for several years after the end of World War II. The American military was intent on learning as much as possible from these men about Siberia's industrial zones—its factories, air fields, new railway lines, and steel bridges. I, however, did not stop at seeking such strategic information in my interrogation of these men. I probed for details about their personal experiences. They told me of being cruelly forced to construct railroads near Bratsk, to labor in factories in Chita, and to build sewers and roads in mid-winter in the frigid city of Khabarovsk. I listened with particular fascination, smiling ruefully to myself, when some men described attempts to escape from their captors.

For the most part, the hatred of the demobilized Japanese soldiers toward the Soviets was so intense that they were happy to provide the Americans with information. Among the noncommissioned officers in particular, a number of men had significant information to offer. I was impressed with their keen powers of observation and their retentive memories.

Those who had the most detailed information, though, were some men in their late twenties and early thirties who had become Communist sympathizers, for they had been allowed a certain amount of freedom of movement in Siberia. No doubt these men had been made to dance to the tune of the Japanese militarists when they were young, so that in their disillusionment after Japan's wartime defeat they became easy converts to communism. And most of these converts were passionately convinced of their new ideology. Though these men did possess valuable information, they would not give it up easily. Some of the American interrogators tried threatening them, but that was not effective. Personally, I thought it would be much more productive to take them down to the Shinjuku entertainment quarter for an evening, ply them with good food and plenty of drinks, and offer them some female companionship. Sooner or later they would have spilled everything. I thought that would have been a creative use of excess funds that otherwise just went to waste. But the self-important, unimaginative functionaries I worked with would never understand such tactics.

One of the first things I wanted to do after arriving in Japan was visit my grandparents, so during the weekend I went to Tokyo Station to find a train to Hiratsuka. Overwhelmed by the sea of humanity filling the station, it took some time to locate the bank of ticket windows, which had long lines of people waiting in front of them. I took my place at the end of one line and at last worked my way up to the window, where I asked for a ticket to Hiratsuka. The clerk just sat arrogantly behind his desk and muttered inaudibly in response to my request. When I put my ear to the tiny aperture in the glass to hear what he was saying, he yelled rudely, "Go over there!"

Exasperated after my long wait, I shouted back at him, "I don't have any idea where to go! I'm with the American military, and I just arrived in Japan!"

The transformation in the man's attitude was instantaneous. At the words "American military," the mousy clerk jumped up, bowed deeply, and hurried out of his office to guide me to the proper ticket window for the Shōnan train that would stop in Hiratsuka. From there, he personally led me through the wicket, up a special passageway, and found me a seat in the car for occupation forces. He even remained to bow and doff his cap as the train pulled out of the station. I purposely ignored this last performance, for the man reminded me altogether too much of the bureaucrats I had encountered at the Consulate General of Imperial Japan in San Francisco as a child. Japan's political system may have changed after its defeat in the war. What had not changed in the least was the feudalistic mentality that made people grovel to superiors and lord it over their inferiors in the rigid social hierarchy.

The Shōnan train passed through stations whose names I remembered from my childhood—Kawasaki, Yokohama, and Ōfuna—but nothing in the scene outside the window looked in the least bit familiar. That whole stretch had been laid waste by the war. Finally, when we came to the familiar Banyū River, I could see Mount Kōrai and Mount Ōyama sitting calmly in the distance just as they always had. These landmarks took me back to my childhood. Then I spied my old fishing spot on the Banyū River and the single pine tree rising from the summit of Mount Kōrai. There was the field where we stole watermelons. And the empty lots where my friends and I had played. Because of my refusal to swear my loyalty to the U.S. government during the war, I had managed to get through those years without taking up arms against my old childhood comrades. I had suffered cruel repression in return, but now I was glad that I would be able to meet those friends again without any feeling of shame.

I wondered whether old Yassan the vegetable man and Tora-san the bamboo craftsman were still alive and well. Where was Toyoko, the neighbor girl who had been sold as a geisha, and what was she doing now? I was sure she would be delighted to see how I had grown up. It was more than fifteen years since she had rescued me from that humiliating fight in the school yard. I hoped against hope that all those friends, who had been so dear to me, had come through the war safely.

The train pulled into Hiratsuka Station. Nothing here was the same—the city was a burned-out wasteland. Hiratsuka, with its naval powder depot, had been a prime target for B-29 bombing raids.

I left the station and crossed the wide Tōkaidō Road, walking through streets where I had played as a boy. I came to the spot where Hiratsuka No. 1 Elementary School had been and found the building burned to the ground. For a few moments I stood in the center of the yard where we had had our opening exercises every morning, performing calisthenics to the directions of a radio announcer. I remembered the exact spot where the boys had pulled my hair and yanked my necktie on that first day of school. I stood there, trying to recall my emotions on that day. The anger and resentment I had felt toward my classmates had long since evaporated. I wondered what had become of my old friends who had bowed so politely after the teacher handed each a chocolate kiss from the box of candy my mother had sent from the States.

"Let them be alive," I breathed.

I walked to what used to be the backyard of the old school. It was quiet and deserted, as it always had been. I felt sure I would hear Toyoko's voice calling to me any moment now. But the swings where she had stood that day were no longer there.

My grandparents' large house had been near the school, but when I walked out of the school yard in that direction, all I could see was an open field with several little shanties in its midst. The rambling two-story house where I had lived with Grandmother and Grandfather was no more. Even the huge oak tree I had scrambled up to escape from Grandmother's scoldings was gone.

I found my grandparents eking out an existence in three little hovels built of board and tin and patched with cardboard. They were living separately in two of these huts, barely managing to survive by renting out the third. Much of their land had been requisitioned by the wartime government to widen the road. All they had left was a piece of property about two hundred yards square on which their three little huts were standing.

Neither of my grandparents had the characteristic energy that I remembered. It wasn't merely that they had aged; it was the effect of the war. The bombings here had been intense. They had had to flee from constant air raids and had barely escaped with their lives.

Grandfather introduced me with some embarrassment to a much younger woman who was living with him in his hut. He muttered a few words of explanation about how she had been a great help to him during and after the war. But his relationship with her had very likely begun long before that. Grandmother complained to me tearfully of her plight, accusing Grandfather of hardheartedness.

When I asked Grandfather about Tora-san the bamboo craftsman, I learned that an incendiary bomb had made a direct hit on his house across the street and that everyone inside had perished. His daughter Toyoko was the only one of the family who had survived, for she had been in Tokyo at the time. Grandfather told me that she was still working as a geisha in the Mukōjima district in the city.

I gave my grandparents the presents I had brought for them from my mother and myself and then took my leave. I feared that I had not done a very good job of concealing my surprise and dismay at their drastically changed circumstances. As I left, I went around to the old back garden to look for the paulownia tree where Pooch was buried. It too was gone.

Before leaving Hiratsuka I tracked down my old school chums Toshi-chan and Dekun. Both were well and greeted me warmly. I found it impossible, however, to talk with them about my painful experiences because of my stand on the loyalty question, or about my cherished dreams for the future. Somehow I sensed that such abstract ideas were not within their intellectual sphere. Inevitably, the conversation reverted to nostalgic reminiscences of our boyhood together. History would flow inexorably onward, but it was not within these men to grasp the direction it was taking or to exert themselves in contemplation of the new world that was then being shaped.

Gantetsu had died of disease at the front, so they told me, and Gakera had been killed in action in the South Pacific. I lighted a stick of incense for each of these old childhood comrades and said a prayer for their eternal repose. I was reminded once again of the truth of the Buddhist teaching that the winds of impermanence blow without ceasing.

I made my way back toward the station. The autumn rain fell bleakly on the wooden vaulting horses in the school yard. I had found no one here in my Japanese hometown to whom I could confide what was in my heart. It seemed to me that, at least in this time and place, anyone with visions of a new world would be pushed aside to lead a solitary existence. I returned to Tokyo that night with unsettled thoughts.

I was battling against time, for I had no idea when the air force would dredge up the loyalty and renunciation issues and dismiss me from my job. I was anxious to save as much money as possible within the time left to me. Then I learned of a good opportunity to increase my earnings—it was announced that those who volunteered for service in Korea would be given a bonus of 25 percent over and above their present salary. I wasted no time in submitting my application to go and was told that I would receive my orders in three weeks.

I did want to locate my old neighbor Toyoko, however, before I left for Korea. Grandfather had known only that she was working as a geisha in the Mukōjima district of Tokyo. If I went looking for her in the evening at the establishment where she worked, then they would think I was a client, so one Saturday afternoon I drove to

Mukōjima in a borrowed jeep. Not knowing what name Toyoko might be using professionally made it especially difficult to track her down. The young patrolman in the police box by the bank of the Sumida River regarded me warily at first when I approached in an American military vehicle, but when I explained why I was there he kindly directed me to two or three geisha residences in the neighbor-hood. At last I located the place where Toyoko lived and found the woman in charge of the house. She looked somber when I asked to see Toyoko.

"Toyoko has tuberculosis," she informed me tersely. "She has been in the hospital at Tokyo Women's Medical College for the past three months."

"Ma'am, I have known Toyoko since we were both children. I just arrived from the States and I wanted to see her again," I explained.

At that, the woman visibly relaxed and began to tell me more about Toyoko.

"Oh, I'm so glad you've come. I've looked after Toyoko ever since she came to Tokyo. She was such a sweet, pretty young girl. You know, she was so loyal to her parents that before the war began she sent home every bit of money she could save from her earnings. And she's such a warm-hearted young woman that she's always had a large following among our clients. But now that she's ill, there's no one but me to go visit her in the hospital—when I can find the time. I'm really very worried about her. I think she's just lost all desire to go on living. And it's so sad—she's only thirty years old," the woman sighed.

I got back into the jeep and hurried directly to the hospital in Kawada-chō. I drove quickly through the empty, burned-out streets of Tokyo, arriving in just under thirty minutes. The hospital itself had escaped the bombing, but inside it was dark and depress-ing. The patients with communicable diseases were housed together in a basement ward that reeked of disinfectant.

When I found her, Toyoko was lying in bed pale and still, her eyes closed as though asleep. I could see nothing of the young girl I had known in that face on the pillow, so ravaged with pain and exhaustion. But as I approached the bed, she opened her eyes and I could see that they were indeed Toyoko's eyes, their clarity just a bit dimmed. These were the lovely eyes of the young Toyoko I remembered. She looked up at me suspiciously.

"Toyoko-neesan," I said softly.

She stared. I had not used her professional name—I had called her "older sister" as I did when we were children together.

"It's Minoru, Toyoko—Minoru from the house across the street in Hiratsuka."

"Ah! Botchan!" she exclaimed. Weak though it was, her voice was full of joy and affection.

Toyoko tried to sit up, but I laid my hand on her shoulder, restraining her gently.

"Oh, Botchan. You're all grown up! You're such a fine young man!" she marveled.

"Toyoko, I have never forgotten what you did for me when I was a boy."

I had no need to say more than that; she would know what I meant. For just a few moments she became that young girl again. Tears began to stream down her face. I knelt beside her bed and wiped them away with my handkerchief. I didn't care if she had tuberculosis. This was Toyoko and she was a gentle, brave, pure-hearted human being. She had always been good to me, and now she was so unfortunate. I didn't care what her profession was, I just knew that I had to do whatever I could for her.

"Botchan, it's so good to see you. I can't believe you remembered me after all these years." She spoke with difficulty as the tears continued to stream down her face. But then, without warning, she pushed my hand away and spoke sharply.

"I do appreciate your coming today, Botchan, but please don't come here again. You mustn't ever come again. I am an unclean woman, unclean in every way. I am not the Toyoko you remember. I do not want to see you again," she repeated and turned her face to the wall.

I just stood there, speechless with astonishment.

"Please go," she said again.

I left the room and found the nurse in the corridor. I questioned her about Toyoko's condition.

"She's suffering from syphilis in addition to the tuberculosis. I'm afraid she hasn't long to live," she told me.

I described Toyoko's sudden radical change in attitude toward me, thinking the nurse might be able to explain it. She just inclined her head in puzzlement.

I sought out the attending physician to ask whether there wasn't some sort of medication that would help Toyoko. He replied that he had heard that streptomycin and penicillin—both of which had been developed in the States—would be effective, but there were no such medications available in Japan at this point. That evening, I placed a call to the United States and ordered streptomycin and penicillin airmailed to me in Japan. (These "wonder drugs" could be purchased then without prescription.)

My orders to report to Korea arrived sooner than I expected—less then two weeks after I submitted my application. I was to leave Japan in two days. Fortunately, the medications for Toyoko arrived that day, so in the evening I went back to the hospital. When I started to enter the basement ward, though, I was intercepted by the same nurse who had been on duty at the time of my previous visit.

"Toyoko has been adamant that you should not be allowed in to see her. Did something happen last time?" she asked.

"I have no idea what happened," I told her. "I'm going to be leaving for Korea day after tomorrow, though, and I've brought some medicines for Toyoko. I ordered them from the States and they just arrived today. Would you please give them to her doctor and ask him to treat her? Also, here is a little present for Toyoko from the States. Please give it to her for me, along with this money. I want her to buy whatever she would like with it. I'm afraid I won't be able to come back for quite some time."

I left the hospital and went back to the jeep I had parked on the street. Then the nurse came running out.

"Sir, are you a relative of Toyoko's?" she asked.

"No, but we were neighbors when we were children, and she always looked out for me. I hadn't seen her in fifteen years," I said.

"I think I understand now—about her not wanting to see you. Only another woman could really understand it," she said with an air of importance. "Toyoko was a beautiful woman, but she's wasting away now, little by little, just waiting to die. She doesn't want you to see her in that state. She wants you to remember her as the young girl you once knew. After you left last time, she cried all night."

I got out of the jeep and bowed in silent gratitude to this perceptive nurse. As I drove away from the hospital I could not help but pray, "Let the medicine work a miracle. Toyoko, please live."

With the southward advance of the North Korean Army, the U.S. forces were obliged to fall back temporarily to a position near Pusan, on the southeastern tip of the Korean peninsula. Then, under the command of General Douglas MacArthur, the Allied troops surprised the enemy with an amphibious landing at Inch'ŏn, just a hundred miles below the 38th parallel, and proceeded to drive the North Koreans back to the border between North Korea and Manchuria. However, on November 26, 1950, Chinese Communist troops massed along the Yalu River began to advance in a "human wave" that forced Allied troops to retreat southward once again. The American troops who had landed on the east coast of the Korean peninsula were then trapped behind enemy lines. Only some were rescued, and with great difficulty, by the navy. Meanwhile, the Chinese Communist and North Korean armies recaptured the present North Korean capital of P'yŏngyang and continued their advance toward Seoul.

I was attached to a unit of the Far East Air Force Intelligence Squadron on the front lines. We were stationed in a small village at the southern end of the Chonho Bridge over the Han-gang, the broad river that divides the city of Seoul into north and south. The commander of our unit was Captain Wilson, a big, heavy man who had risen from the ranks. He commanded about thirty U.S. Air Force officers and men, plus sixty South Korean soldiers.

Captain Wilson's speech and actions were somewhat coarse, so the college-educated American officers regarded him with a certain amount of condescension, exchanging derogatory remarks about him behind his back. He no doubt was aware of that, for he tended to surround himself with the Korean soldiers rather than the American officers. For some strange reason, though, when I arrived he offered me the room next to his and invited me to take meals with him in his quarters rather than going to the mess hall. As we ate together he would divulge his plans to me, fine-tuning them as he talked. He was basically a shy man, but when he felt comfortable he could hold forth at great length.

The original mission of our unit was to capture enemy agents and to send South Korean agents across the lines into North Korea. Now that the situation had changed, however, there was no time for these leisurely activities. Seoul was already within range of enemy artillery fire, its residents evacuated, and the U.S. Army had begun to pull back in the face of the enemy advance.

Captain Wilson meanwhile had his men working around the clock on shifts, tracking the progress of the American withdrawal and the enemy advance. He required that his men report to him every detail they learned, while to all appearances he himself just took it easy at unit headquarters. Finally, he got the report that the entire U.S. Army had completed its retreat from Seoul. By this time the advance units of the enemy were already closing in to within thirty miles of the city. Now the captain swiftly mobilized his entire unit and personally led his troops back into Seoul under cover of night. Dividing into several smaller parties, we proceeded to scour the abandoned U.S. Army quarters for any materials left behind—trucks, jeeps, parts, gasoline, food, arms, and ammunition. Wilson ordered us to carry as much as we could back across the bridge and out of the city. Meanwhile, he loaded several boxes of hand grenades onto a jeep, and, driving with the headlights off, he did a final round of Allied quarters, using the hand grenades to explode all remaining ammunition after his troops had taken everything we could.

Just as Wilson was doing his last rounds, enemy troops appeared at the street corner. He whirled his jeep swiftly around and headed as fast as he could toward the bridge with the enemy in hot pursuit. It was pitch-dark, and from the opposite bank of the river we could not distinguish between friend and foe, so that when the captain finally got to the bridge we did not see him. All we could discern were the headlights of the trucks full of enemy troops following him, so we quickly lit the charge and blew up the bridge. Wilson was stranded now on the other side with no alternative but to destroy his jeep and leap into the river. He grabbed a log floating near the bank and began to swim like crazy. Only when the jeep exploded did we realize his position, and then some of the men sped across the river in a motorboat to rescue him. When at last the captain was pulled out of the water, he was nearly frozen. Nevertheless, the moment he climbed onto the other bank, drenched and shaking, he started yelling at us.

"Goddamn you guys! Why the hell did you have to go and blow up that bridge so quick?!" he demanded.

Then he caught sight of his burning jeep on the other side of the river. He just stared at it with his mouth open, full of regret, like a child whose favorite toy had been snatched away. Then, urged on by the other officers, trembling in the cold with nothing but three army blankets wrapped around his naked body, Wilson finally mustered the troops and ordered us to follow after the main body of American forces with our booty. It was daybreak, January 4, 1951.

Under pressure of the advancing Chinese, the U.S. Army had retreated to a point seventy-five miles below the 38th parallel, the second retreat since the beginning of the conflict. But Allied aerial bombing campaigns succeeded in checking the Communist advance, and, as supply routes were reestablished, Allied forces began to make plans for the recapture of Seoul. By this time it was mid-March.

Captain Wilson had already sent ahead dozens of South Korean agents to infiltrate the city of Seoul and was receiving daily reports from them. American infantry units were within striking distance of the city and closing in. At this point, the captain personally took several of his men and parachuted from a small plane into an area near Seoul's Kimp'o Airport, there to await the beginning of the battle to retake the city. Thus, as the Allied forces began their move back into Seoul, a fierce secondary battle broke out near the airport, keeping the enemy busy on two fronts.

This time, Captain Wilson's maneuver positioned our unit to seize the leavings of the enemy as they retreated. By the time Seoul was again fully occupied by the Allies, we had reequipped our unit with large quantities of the enemy's weapons, ammunition, trucks, jeeps, and gasoline. Soon thereafter, we settled into our previous quarters on the south side of the city and from that base resumed our operations behind enemy lines.

The intelligence unit was always at the very bottom of the quartermaster's priority list for distribution of trucks, jeeps, weapons, and ammunition, so the equipment that our unit scrounged for itself as the enemy left the city provided us with more than we would otherwise have had for our activities. Captain Wilson may have been an uneducated boor, but with his skills as a looter he was extremely effective in accomplishing his unit's mission.

Off the west coast of the Korean peninsula are scattered numerous small islands. Because the U.S. military had been able to achieve naval supremacy early in the conflict, they succeeded in securing these islands even as they retreated southward on land. The islands had no direct bearing on the battle for control of the peninsula, but from the enemy's point of view they no doubt presented the disconcerting specter of a row of steppingstones leading right to the peninsula itself. Indeed, the enemy had several battalions dug in on the coast just opposite these islands.

In any case, when the war reached a stalemate the islands were useful as bases for spy operations. Agents were sent from the islands into enemy territory to make contact with friendly guerrilla forces in the mountains on the peninsula. Also, if an Allied plane were hit by enemy fire, then its crew might be saved if it could get close to the islands. It was only a chance, for the ocean waters in that area were frigid, and crash survivors had to be rescued within ten minutes.

One of these small islands was called Cho-do, defended by just a few hundred U.S. Marines. It was strategically located a mere fifty miles from the North Korean capital of P'yŏngyang and only five miles across the water from North Korean territory. The island was close enough to the peninsula to be hit occasionally by ninety-millimeter shells from the other side, and with a pair of binoculars we could clearly monitor from there the movements of enemy soldiers on the peninsula.

Captain Wilson ordered 1st. Lt. Burns and me to take up a position on this island. We reached it via seaplane in the early summer after the recapture of Seoul. Our mission was to take charge of the several dozen Korean soldiers and the score of Korean agents who were now based on the island.

When I first landed on Cho-do, the Korean soldiers gathered around and looked me over with great suspicion.

"He's a Japanese soldier!" one of them spat out disgustedly, speaking in Japanese.

Most Korean soldiers could speak the Japanese language as a result of Japan's occupation of their country for several decades before World War II. The Koreans, however, were reflexively anti-Japanese and understandably so. It was not just that they had been oppressed by the Japanese military during the war. Korean resentment against Japan had a long history, beginning in the Middle Ages when Japanese pirates plundered the Korean coastline and continuing into the modern period when Japan annexed Korea and forced the emigration of many Koreans to Japan to supplement the labor force. Most Japanese—who were the oppressors in this instance—do not seem to regard these events as particularly significant, but the victims in such cases are not so quick to forget. In light of my own past as a victim of oppression, I could not blame the Koreans for their feelings toward the Japanese. Indeed, I sympathized with them. I decided the best course was to bide my time and hope to win their confidence in the long term.

My hopes were realized sooner than I anticipated. I had known Lt. Burns since our days together in the Air Force Intelligence Squadron in Tokyo. A big man and a college-educated Easterner, he had always acted the perfect gentleman there. But people's personalities can change on the front line of a war—the tension causes them to lose their rational faculties. That happened to Lt. Burns when we got to our island outpost—he entirely lost his self-control. He became violent and abusive toward the Koreans, screaming obscenities and beating them. Thus it was that the

Korean soldiers who had mistrusted the "Japanese soldier" so much when we first arrived began to turn to me with a much friendlier attitude. It was probably a matter of language, too, for the lieutenant and the Koreans had no common tongue between them, while I could communicate both with him in English and with the Korean soldiers in Japanese.

Every morning I ate breakfast with Burns, not out of courtesy but because I wanted my morning coffee. I had lunch and dinner with the Koreans, however. Again, I wasn't trying to be polite—I simply preferred their food because they had rice with their meals. I felt a bit sorry for Lt. Burns as he ate his nutritious army C ration of canned meat all by himself, but personally I couldn't stand the stuff. If I ate it three days running, the smell of it alone would make me nauseous. Burns either was very stoic or had absolutely no sense of taste—I suspected the latter. It was amazing how uncomplainingly, indeed with what gusto, he would dig his spoon into the canned rations day after day, eating his meals in solitary splendor.

The food eaten by the Korean soldiers (brown rice, kimchee, dried fish) was undoubtedly considered primitive by American nutritional standards at the time. I, however, greatly enjoyed sharing the Koreans' meals—which both surprised and delighted them. Army C rations might fill your stomach, but I found Korean Army food to be far more satisfying. Content as I was with the food situation, I felt somehow liberated and able to work with zest on that island—despite the tension of being on the front line of a war.

But there did remain a few difficulties with our basic food supplies: we lacked potable water, fresh vegetables, and salt. The water on the island was full of parasites and thus was extremely dangerous for outsiders, who lacked the necessary immunities. Captain Wilson, having a great taste for alcoholic beverages himself, was very considerate in solving our water problem—he ordered the troops to airdrop one hundred cans of beer onto the island for us each week. So, I brushed my teeth and quenched my thirst with beer every day, with the result that the time on that island passed quite pleasantly indeed.

Captain Wilson also had large bags of fresh vegetables airdropped to us, but by the time we retrieved them the greens—

packaged in tightly sealed plastic bags—were hopelessly wilted in the summer's heat. There was no safe water in which to wash them in any case, so we ended up throwing them out. In their place, the Korean soldiers gathered mountain grasses to stir-fry. It took a while to chew these, but they were certainly tastier than wilted vegetables.

Once our kimchee supply was exhausted we had no salt at all and could not survive without it. Finally we discovered some rock salt on the island and broke it into small pieces to lick. It is impossible to imagine how good salt can taste unless you have had the experience of being deprived of it for a long period of time.

We also came upon a real treat—eggs! Eggs could not be air-dropped, of course, but we found that by climbing a steep promontory near the shore we could obtain large sea gull eggs. They were a trifle gamy but quite tasty once we got used to them. They certainly could not have been any fresher! I now appreciated the Korean name for this place—Bird Island.

Little by little, as we shared our meals together, I won the trust of the Korean soldiers. Burns, no doubt aware of this trust, turned over to me all responsibility for overseeing them and giving them their orders. He himself, meanwhile, spent his days chatting on the wireless to unit headquarters or, when there was nothing else to do, listening to jazz on the shortwave radio. Before long, he developed an unsightly paunch from his lack of activity. Burns had been quite the gentleman at the Tokyo Officers Club, but a gentleman officer with no knack for supervising people is useless on the front. Thus it was that I ended up directing all the covert operations from Cho-do Island. Under cover of night we would drop agents into the mountains on the peninsula from a helicopter or send them over to the mainland quietly by boat. None of these agents, however, were known to return to the island. Many no doubt were double agents, as there was good money in it for them. I certainly was in no position to fault them. After all, I was essentially doing the same thing there—working for money.

Despite the fact that our agents never returned to the island, we kept on sending them in, for those were our orders. I figured, somewhat cynically perhaps, that our operations from the island were merely one piece in the overall psychological strategy, so I was not overly concerned about the double agent issue. I just kept on drinking my beer and lightheartedly enjoying my work.

One day I had to go to Inch'ŏn on official business and there I encountered a fascinating character by the name of Choi. A man in his late twenties, he had been apprehended on the street by American military police who accused him of heading a smuggling operation. He refused to confess even when they inflicted a good deal of pain on him. I identified myself to the military police as an American intelligence agent and asked them to turn the man over to me. They promptly agreed. In questioning Choi I learned that, although he was Korean, he had been born in Manchuria and spent the war years in Tokyo. After the war he attended Meiji University and got his college degree before returning to Korea. Somehow he had obtained some drugs and candidly admitted to me that he was selling them. He was perfectly nonchalant about the whole thing and did not try to escape.

As I was talking with him, about a dozen tough-looking fellows surrounded us. Suspecting that they had come to free Choi, I tensed and instinctively laid my hand on my gun.

Choi laughed. "These are my men. Why don't you help them out, too? Let us work for you. I promise we'll do a good job."

Burns was none too pleased when I returned to the island with these new recruits. He immediately contacted Captain Wilson.

The captain, however, was delighted. "We don't have nearly enough men. Use them. If they're smugglers, they ought to be real good at this work," he replied to Burns' urgent message.

Now there was a sensible man. I breathed a sigh of relief. But Burns was on his guard. He slept every night with a .38-caliber pistol by his side and spread pots and pans in front of his door to ensure he would not be caught by surprise if they tried to sneak into his room at night. Meanwhile, I slept soundly next door without any precautions at all. I didn't even keep bullets in my pistol, because I knew I could never bring myself to shoot anyone.

Choi and his men were indeed good workers. Whenever a U.S. military reconnaissance plane was downed, Choi would issue brisk orders to his men and they would go swiftly to the rescue. I learned a great deal from this man.

One day I took Choi out on the Yellow Sea in an armed speedboat. Before we knew it, we had gone deep into North Korean territory and were spotted by a Chinese Communist Coast Guard vessel. We made a swift U-turn to get away, but the coast guard boat was faster. It was just beginning to catch up to us when a U.S. Air Force F-86 appeared, chased the Communist vessel, and sank it.

"Hey, Min, you're amazing at decoy tactics!" Choi exclaimed.

The heck I was. I had been running for my life. But I was not exactly honest, because I never did admit it to Choi. He thought I was a master tactician, and I had no intention of destroying his absolute faith in me. I made very sure never to venture into the Yellow Sea again, though.

One day Choi came to see me.

"Min, you're our commander, and you know that we would do anything for you. I have just one favor to ask of you in return. My mother is still in Manchuria, and I want to go and get her out of there. I want you to come with us."

I was astounded at this reckless plan.

"Choi, I have no desire to throw my life away for your mother. Besides, we'd never get permission from headquarters to go on a private mission like that!" I told him.

Early the following morning I was awakened by the Korean soldiers pounding on my door.

"Choi and his men took off in the night with our speedboat. They took weapons and ammunition and all kinds of supplies!"

Choi had surprised me again. Burns turned on me with a sour I-told-you-so expression.

The following morning we received a wireless message from some friendly guerrilla fighters that Choi and his men had been intercepted by North Korean troops and shot on the beach. Thus ended the life of one hot-blooded young character in the tumult of the Korean War. I have no doubt whatsoever that he would have chosen to die just that way, too—in the daring attempt to rescue his mother. He was one of a kind.

By this time Burns and I were on such bad terms that we were no longer able to work together. I decided that I should take responsibility for the situation, so I volunteered to return to unit headquarters. When the Korean soldiers learned that I was leaving the island, they presented me with a valuable piece of pottery. These men were extremely poor, but we had developed a good relationship after they became convinced of my sincerity. Korea is a Confucian country. Once a good relationship is established between a leader and his men, the men will place their absolute trust in him and show every possible form of courtesy. I felt honored to have earned the confidence of these Korean soldiers.

After I returned to headquarters on the peninsula, I found that Captain Wilson had heard all about Choi's desertion, but he just laughed it off.

Around that time, the number of Chinese Communist prisoners of war increased dramatically, and I was sent to Seoul with a group of nisei colleagues to interrogate them. I was supplied with a Korean interpreter who could speak both Chinese and Japanese. One group of wounded Chinese soldiers exuded a strange odor—they must have been wounded by napalm bombs. Among them was a self-professed platoon leader about eighteen years old who had a bandaged head and festering hand. When the Korean soldiers interrogated him, this youth just bit his lip and kept his silence. Even when they struck him and knocked him down, he would not break. Then they began kicking him. At this point, unable to watch any longer, I intervened and had the prisoner returned to the stockade. After that, I noticed the young man standing near the gate when I arrived at the prison camp in the mornings. Pretty soon we started to smile at one another, and I would bring him slices of bread and oranges from the staff dining room.

One day, an American sergeant announced with a smile that I had a visitor and ushered the Chinese soldier into the interrogation room to see me. The youth stood at attention and saluted. I motioned him to a chair, but he sat down on the floor instead, a surprisingly traditional gesture for a Communist. I called in my Korean interpreter.

"I've been fighting because I believe the revolution of the proletariat is justified," the young man told me. "I was willing to give up my life for what I believed. But tell me about this American democracy. Was I all wrong?"

Here was a sincere man whose earnestness surely transcended any national boundaries. I could not help but think back to my own troubled youth when I was about his age.

"You'd better stick with your own ideas," I replied, "because I'm not so sure what this American democracy is all about either."

After my own experiences in concentration camps in the United States, I was no apologist for American democracy. The Korean interpreter gazed at me in disbelief. Laying my hand on the young prisoner's shoulder, I led him out of the room. American and Korean soldiers alike were staring in mute amazement at the whole strange scene.

Around this same time, I had a very unpleasant experience with my nisei colleagues. I had brought to Korea several Japanese books on Buddhist philosophy and was reading them in the evenings to prepare for graduate school in Japan. Many of my nisei colleagues, however, preferred to spend their evenings either playing poker and drinking beer or making the rounds of Korean houses of prostitution. Apparently it annoyed them to see me reading my books instead of joining in their fun.

One evening as I lay reading on my bed, one of the guys grabbed my feet and yanked me out of bed onto the floor. At that point I had to make a choice. I could let this creep get away with it and endure the humiliation. Or I could respond to his challenge and get both of us arrested by military police, interrogated, and suspended from our jobs. I knew very well that such an incident would hopelessly complicate my plans to stay in Japan to continue my education. So I swallowed my rage and did nothing. But that night I said to myself, I've had it with this job!

While I was still on Cho-do Island, I had received a letter from the nurse at the hospital in Tokyo, informing me that Toyoko had passed away. I had been thinking that if it looked as though she were going to pull through, I would like to take a leave and visit her. Now that she was gone I had no particular reason to hurry back to Tokyo. Still, I had been in Korea longer than I had ever planned. Besides, the nurse wrote that Toyoko had left something for me, and I kept wondering about that.

An armistice was concluded on the Korean peninsula in July 1953. This was as good a time as any to go back to Japan, I thought. But it was autumn before I had concluded my obligations and was able to bid a final farewell to Korea with its many memories and return to Tokyo.

By the time I arrived at Yokota Air Force Base it had been more than two years since I had left Japan. That country was now a haven of peace compared with Korea. Brown leaves skittered along the pavement in Tokyo and autumn aromas filled the air. The trim little houses looked settled and comfortable and the women walking along the streets were lovely.

I returned to my old lodgings in Nihonbashi and found a letter waiting there for me from Anne. I tore open the envelope excitedly and found a wedding announcement. Anne had married Bob after all. No other message was enclosed.

Bob must have persisted until Anne finally agreed to marry him. She did keep him waiting three years, though, I consoled myself. I couldn't say that I didn't mind, but I still had so much more to do. I had only just begun the work to realize my dream. I told myself not to waste time with useless regrets.

I suppose I should write and send Anne and Bob my congratulations, I thought.

Still wondering what it was that Toyoko had left for me, I telephoned the hospital the following morning and spoke with the nurse who had written to me in Korea. I told her that I would stop by that evening. She was not scheduled to be on duty that night but kindly agreed to remain at the hospital until I got there.

When I found the nurse, she told me about Toyoko's last days.

"She died peacefully. She refused to take the new medicine you brought, though, no matter how much the doctor urged her. She just had no desire to live. She would not accept the present or the money you left for her either, so I'll return those to you. But she did leave you this letter," the nurse said, handing me an envelope.

I tore it open and read Toyoko's farewell message:

Botchan, thank you so much for not forgetting me and for coming to visit me in the hospital. I am afraid that I spoke to you more harshly than I ever intended that day—please forgive me. And thank you so much for the medicine, for the present from America and the money. But I don't need these things now. Please give them to someone else who can use them, and allow me to accept only the kind feelings with which you gave them to me.

I was so glad to see you again. It reminded me of the old days when we were children. That was a peaceful, happy time, wasn't it?

Botchan, you are such a fine young man now. I will be praying for your success and happiness always from that distant world.

In her letter Toyoko had enclosed a photograph of herself as a young girl.

I asked the nurse—in accord with Toyoko's wishes—to give the medicine, the gift, and the money to another patient. Then, thanking her for her many kindnesses, I left the hospital.

After I returned to my quarters, I kept thinking about Toyoko. She had been so young when she allowed her father to sell her as a "pillow" geisha to help support their impoverished family. Because of her profession, she had contracted syphilis and tuberculosis and endured all manner of physical and mental torment—but never did she utter a word of resentment toward anyone. She had died all alone, with memories of happier times in the past her only consolation, even asking that everything I had tried to give her be passed along to someone else.

I gazed at the photograph she left for me and realized that what the nurse told me before I went to Korea was true: Toyoko wanted me to remember her as the young girl I had known in my childhood. She had lived with grace and beauty and died in the same manner. She may have had only a grammar school education, but she was a woman who exemplified the traditional Japanese sense of beauty.

These were deeply melancholy days for me. I had cared so much for Anne, but now that was over—she had married Bob after all. And I could not get the memory of dear Toyoko out of my head. I would have paid any price to make her well again. How I wished I might see her healthy and hear her gentle voice once more.

I found it harder and harder to concentrate on my work during the day and even lost all motivation to read in the evenings. One night after dinner I walked out the front door of my lodgings at Nihonbashi. I looked right and then left. The road to my left led to the bustling streets of the Ginza and Kyōbashi, with their specialty stores and high-class restaurants. To my right was the way to Kanda, with its used bookstores, cheap bars, and coffee shops. I turned right and began to walk. After about thirty minutes I passed Mitsukoshi Department Store and then came to the overpass at Kanda Station. I went a little farther until I noticed a small establishment identified in glowing neon as the Fuji Bar. I entered. Inside were only a few customers. I took a seat, and a bar hostess in heavy makeup sat down beside me. Another, decked out in cheap earrings, necklace, and bracelets, sat in the chair across from me. Neither was particularly attractive.

I ordered a beer. Then, looking around, I noticed another bar hostess across the room. She was wearing very little makeup and no jewelry at all and was gulping down whiskey and water. Somehow the woman looked familiar to me. In fact, she looked almost like Cindy, the girl I'd encountered outside the little church at Tule Lake, the girl who had come out to fill the coal bucket and invited me in. I had heard that Cindy had been deported to Japan with her parents, so I knew she was in the country somewhere. But Cindy was a committed Christian—surely *she* would never be in a place like this. Besides, the young woman had such a hard expression on her face, it couldn't be Cindy. And yet she looked so much like her.

"Hey, why do you keep staring over there?" the woman beside me asked, leaning closer to start a conversation.

"Do you know the name of that girl sitting over there?" I asked her.

"That's Yumi," she said.

So, I was wrong. On the other hand . . . women working in places like this rarely used their real names. I got up as if to go to the men's room.

"Cindy?" I said in a soft voice as I walked by her.

She reacted, glancing up at me with suspicion.

"What are you doing here?" I asked her in English.

"Min!"

But quickly she lowered her eyes and, turning to the customer beside her, made a clumsy show of continuing their conversation. There must be some reason Cindy is here, I thought. I'm going to find out.

I stayed in the bar until closing time, then went outside and waited on the street. Before long Cindy came out, clearly expecting to find me there.

"Come on over to my place," she said. "I'm living in Suda-chō. It's not far from here."

Cindy began to talk as we walked to her apartment. Her parents had been devout Christians who originally came from a rural area in Wakayama Prefecture. They went back there after their repatriation from the States. Both, however, died of illness soon after their return to Japan. Food was scarce right after the war and there was no medicine to be had. But that may not have been all there was to it, I thought—perhaps they were discouraged and disillusioned when they did not discover the old homeland of their dreams.

Cindy's apartment was a mess. She threw her coat down and went to get some drinks. While we drank, we continued our conversation.

"You've changed, Cindy," I told her.

"Min, I'm not the Cindy you knew before. That Cindy never could have survived in this kind of world."

She took a drink of her whiskey.

"At first I stayed with my uncle and his family in the country. He'd built the house they lived in with money my father sent him from the States before the war. But as soon as my father died, my uncle started treating me like a maid, like I was just in the way."

Cindy became more and more agitated as she told me about her uncle and how he had treated her. She made no attempt to conceal her intense hatred for the man. After a while she went to make herself another drink, but when she came back I gently removed the glass from her hand.

"Stop now, Cindy," I urged.

She complied without objection.

"Cindy, have you been in touch with Tom or Miss Allan at all?" I asked.

"I'm not a Christian anymore, Min. If I had anything for those people, I wouldn't mind seeing them. But I don't want to see them right now. I don't want their sympathy," she said.

I could easily understand her feelings. I knew very well that some "religious" people will extend the warm hand of friendship so long as they think you accept their religion, but as soon as they suspect you have abandoned the faith they will turn around and denounce you. Something like that happened to me when I stopped by my old church in San Francisco before going to Washington for the air force orientation. When I told the nisei minister that I had quit seminary to work for the U.S. military in Japan and that I had plans to study Buddhism over there, he launched into a regular tirade. He denounced Buddhism as the religion of the devil and declared that anyone who studied it was sure to go to hell. So I knew very well that there were such fools in this world, but I also knew that Tom and Miss Allan were not narrow-minded people. They were above such religious biases—they were individuals who sincerely cared about others.

We talked for a long while, but finally Cindy collapsed in a drunken stupor. I picked her up and carried her over to her bed. It suddenly occurred to me that she might be addicted to stimulants, because she was so changed from the Cindy I had known before. Her emotional highs and lows seemed so extreme.

"Poor girl—she's had a lot to deal with. She's not at all like the innocent young Cindy I knew at Tule Lake," I murmured, gazing down at her sleeping face.

I covered her with a quilt, went outside, and hailed a taxi to return to my lodgings. By this time it was four in the morning.

Two days later Cindy called me on the telephone.

"Come over Saturday night, won't you, Min? I want to talk to you. You're the only person who could possibly understand. I'm going to take the night off and cook dinner for you, so come around seven," she said.

That night Cindy's apartment was so tidy I hardly recognized it. This was the Cindy who had grown up in America, the Cindy I had met at the church in Tule Lake. The table was attractively set, the salad all made, and the aroma of roasting chicken filled the room. I presented my hostess with a bouquet of flowers and kissed her lightly on the cheek. For the first time since I had found her at the bar the other evening, Cindy smiled.

But then she began to drink again. This time it was straight whiskey. I took the glass away from her.

"Cindy, I did not come here to put you to bed again. You said you had something you wanted to talk to me about, so I came to hear what it is," I said.

All the softness went out of her smile then and her expression hardened. We began to eat in silence. Suddenly, Cindy started yelling furiously.

"Damn those Americans all to hell! They just used the war with Japan as an excuse to rob my father of everything he owned, to throw us all into those horrid concentration camps. I was so young I didn't even understand what was going on. But they drove me out of the United States and sent me over here to this godforsaken, bombed-out country. After my parents died I had no idea what to do. I came to Tokyo and went to the U.S. Embassy for help, because I had no way of surviving in this country. I just wanted to go home—I wanted to go back to the only home I ever knew, the country where I was born. But as soon as they found out at the embassy that I'd been at Tule Lake, they wouldn't even listen to me any more. I cried and begged, but they just called the guards, who literally picked me up and threw me out the front door. By that time I had no money left and nowhere to go, so I just wandered around the streets of Tokyo all night and ended up getting raped by a *yakuza* gangster. *That's* how I ended up where I am now!"

She flung herself on the table, sobbing. I rose from where I was sitting and walked around the table. I stood behind her, rubbing her back, trying to soothe her. I could certainly understand her bitter hatred for the United States.

Suddenly Cindy leaped up and threw her arms around me, sobbing. I held her lightly in my arms for several minutes. Finally, she spoke again, her voice more subdued.

"Do you know what, Min? *Now* the U.S. Embassy says they'll let me go back to the States. But it's too late. I'm totally degenerate now. I live on stimulants. The only reason I work is to get my drugs. Anyway, I still have some pride. After all this time I refuse to humiliate myself by going back to that embassy and groveling to those people again. I'll go to my death hating the United States.

"But don't you pity me, Min. I think it's you nisei who should be pitied—because you just keep on trying every way you can to be 'good' Americans. You tell the world every chance you get what a loyal American you are, what a good citizen you are. What a waste! If you were *real* Americans, you wouldn't have to do that. I feel so sorry for the poor nisei, because they're never quite sure they're going to be accepted unless they keep on saying those things, over and over.

"I had a chance to work for the occupation, you know, but I turned it down. Everywhere you looked there were nisei. And I don't like nisei. They wear American-style clothes and eat American-style food and drive around in fancy American cars, as if to say, 'Look at me, I'm an American!' I despise their attitude. No matter how hard they try, nisei are never going to change the way they look, so they're always going to be second-class Americans. That's why they go around acting so high and mighty here in Japan—they don't get a chance to do that back in the States. But you are a little bit different from the rest, aren't you, Min? There's always been something more Japanese about you."

The intensity of Cindy's hatred of Americans and her disdain for the nisei were certainly understandable given the cruel things that had happened to her. But her experience was so limited that she was incapable of seeing the larger picture and taking a more balanced view. However that might be, I sensed that if things continued on their present course, Cindy would almost certainly try to take her own life. Her harsh attack this evening sounded to me like a clear warning signal from a suicidal individual. And even if she didn't intentionally try to kill herself, she was dangerously addicted to amphetamines. I thought perhaps I could talk the problem over with that thoughtful nurse I had met at the hospital when I visited Toyoko.

During the week that followed my dinner with Cindy, I was swamped with work, putting together my report on the mission in Korea. I made arrangements to take some time off the next week, though, so I could go over to the hospital and ask the nurse's advice about Cindy's addiction. But the day after I had resolved to do that, a police officer appeared at the office looking for me. The police had seen my name and address on a slip of paper in Cindy's apartment. The officer informed me that Cindy had been found dead from an overdose of sleeping pills.

So the war was not over yet. The persecution at Tule Lake still had its repercussions even here, even now, nearly a decade later. I realized how very lucky I had been to remain in the States after the war ended, leisurely getting my college education in the country that was the victor in that conflict. The situation Cindy faced in Japan had been radically different. Young and unprepared, she had been deported to a country she knew nothing about, a country that was war-ravaged and desperately impoverished. And there she was left to cope alone after her parents died.

The U.S. Embassy's treatment of Cindy when she went there to appeal for help had been cold and cruel. Probably the bureaucrats in the embassy were not even conscious of just how cruel their treat-ment was. But then, that is the nature of bureaucrats. Cindy was younger than I, so she could not possibly have been old enough to renounce her citizenship at Tule Lake. There should have been no question on that point, and the U.S. Embassy should have checked the facts the first time she went there. Well, it was all over now.

The law does not exist only to judge people, I reflected. It should protect their rights as well. But the law is administered by human beings, and human beings are the problem. In Tokyo there was no fearless defender of justice like Wayne Collins, and that was Cindy's bad luck. She had been unlucky in every conceivable way.

Cindy left behind no suicide note, but it was not likely that she would have done so. She had said everything she had to say to me that last time we met. In fact, she had prepared her own farewell banquet that night—a feast for two. Well, that is all right, I told myself. The fewer people struggling on with wounds from the persecution at Tule Lake the better. I knew there were many, though, who still lived with scars from that experience, and I wished them well.

Not long after I returned to Japan from Korea, the Far East Air Force Intelligence Squadron pulled its operations out of Tokyo and moved to Shiroi Airbase near the small city of Matsudo in Chiba Prefecture northeast of Tokyo. Here I worked with Mr. Itō, a cultural anthropologist trained at Tokyo University. He possessed extensive knowledge about the peoples and cultures of China, Mongolia, and Southeast Asia and was employing that knowledge to compile a handbook of emergency information for American pilots to use if downed in enemy territory—an evasion and survival manual. For the first time since being employed by Air Force Intelligence, my job involved something intellectual. However, this interesting work was not to continue for long.

The event I had feared and expected for almost four years finally came to pass. On July 12, 1954, Colonel Cook, chief of the Shiroi Airbase Intelligence Squadron, stalked up to my desk and thrust a letter of discharge into my face. Reason for discharge: False statements on application submitted in spring of 1950 for employment with the U.S. Air Force (that is, the crime of concealing that I had refused to declare my loyalty to the United States and that I had renounced my American citizenship). This was a grave charge. I was taken by an air force officer to the headquarters of American Military Security at Shinagawa in Tokyo.

Nothing had changed. Their methods of interrogation were exactly as they always had been. A fat, cigar-puffing civilian official sat with his feet propped on the desk, his shoes practically in my face. When he tired of that position, he paced around and around like a caged tiger, yelling at me, flinging questions at me. I remained unperturbed. When I had been grilled by the FBI agent at Topaz, I was still a youth not yet out of high school. That much, at least, was different now.

To the charges directed against me, I replied that the loyalty oath had been demanded behind barbed wire fences where I was forcibly detained without due process of law. The Renunciation Act, furthermore, was implemented under duress, and that issue was still being decided by the courts. I considered myself an American citizen so long as that litigation continued. I maintained that the manner in which I had filled out the employment application for the air force job therefore did not constitute a case of falsification.

After about half an hour of heated discussion, I spat out, "You have no call to treat me like a criminal. I am going to get up now and walk out of here. If you want to arrest me, show me a warrant specifying the charges."

After that, the interrogator's attitude softened slightly, and at length he released me.

The next day when I reported for work at the Air Force Intelligence office, however, Colonel Cook informed me that I was to be discharged from my position after all. A few days later I drew up a written protest of my discharge and sent it to Colonel Cook. I received no reply from him.

I was curious why an investigation of my status had not occurred before this. Fortunately for me, anyway, I had managed to continue working in what was quite a sensitive position for almost four years before they finally caught up with me.

Then came a letter from the American Embassy in Tokyo: "You are requested to bring your passport to the Embassy of the United States for inspection."

I went down to the embassy in Toranomon and met with the official in charge.

"Show me your passport," he demanded sharply.

I held out the document for him to take a look.

"You have no right to this passport!" he declared, snatching it out of my hand and heading toward the back office.

The bastard! Determined to get my passport back from him, I jumped over the counter and grabbed the man's lapels. I knew full well that without that passport I could neither go home to the United States nor register as an alien resident in Japan. This bureaucrat should know that. How could he be so callous and unfeeling? At this point, two guards came running over. They grabbed me by the arms, literally dragged me to the front entrance and threw me out the door—precisely on the spot where they had thrown Cindy, no doubt.

I was now stateless, stranded in Japan.

10 Beyond Loyalty

After I was dismissed from my job with the air force and stripped of my U. S. passport, I concluded that there was no use fretting over the situation. I decided that until I received formal notification of the courts' decision on the renunciation issue and got my passport back from the embassy, I would just go ahead and audit classes. I would study on my own to prepare for entrance exams to the graduate school of Tokyo University.

That fall, I met with Professor Hanayama Shinshō, head of the Department of Indian Philosophy (and also, incidentally, chaplain to General Tojō Hideki during his war crimes trial and until he went to the gallows). I received Professor Hanayama's permission to begin attending lectures in his department as an auditor. Luckily, he did not ask to see my passport.

All winter I audited classes and in March I sat for the entrance examination for the Department of Indian Philosophy. I was formally admitted to Tokyo University as a graduate student at the beginning of the Japanese academic year in April.

The spring day was overcast but warm. I strode through the "Red Gate" onto the campus of Tokyo University, a feeling of triumph surging through me as I arrived for my first day of classes as a registered graduate student in Indian philosophy. Relishing that long-anticipated moment, I made my way beneath the stately rows of trees and along the gravel path bordering Sanshirō Pond. I recalled that I had read about that very pond in Natsume Sōseki's novel while still a young teenager in San Francisco.

A tremendous explosion suddenly violated this peaceful campus scene. Something flew over my head and landed on the branch of a tree overhanging the path. I looked up to see a bloody chunk of human flesh. Another fell at my feet. A disappointed young man had just lit a stick of dynamite to end his life—another casualty of the tough entrance exams of Tokyo University.

A few days later, I visited the scene of the suicide. By now the scattered remains of the body had been removed, but a boulder by the edge of the pond was marked by a pattern of fresh blood-stains. Apparently, the young man had lain face down on this rock with the stick of dynamite wedged beneath him. A slight fissure in the rock indicated where the explosion had occurred.

I stood by that boulder for several long moments and reflected on the course of my own life. Had I not succeeded in reaching this point, I might well have ended up just like this devastated young student. I knew from my own experience what it meant to gamble your whole life on obtaining an education.

"May he rest in peace," I breathed.

It was after I had matriculated in the graduate school at Tokyo University that I received official word that the Renunciation Act had been declared "null, void, and without legal effect" by the U.S. courts, effective August 12, 1955. It was not until June 13, 1956, some ten months later, however, that I was finally informed of my reinstatement in my former position with the United States Air Force.

I decided to accept reinstatement in that job, for I wished to establish without any doubt the injustice of my discharge from Air Force Intelligence. The timing worked out well in any case, since summer vacation at the university was about to begin. I worked all summer, and then, just before the start of fall term at the university, I handed my letter of resignation to Colonel Cook. I no longer had any need to participate in the unproductive work of that agency. When the colonel read my letter, he turned beet red and started yelling at me. Ignoring his tirade, I turned on my heel and walked out the door. What a tremendous relief it was to be liberated at last from that corrupt, bureaucratic world. It signified to me that I was another step closer to the realization of my dream.

Eventually the U. S. Embassy even deigned to return my passport. To my great relief, they sent it to me through the mail. I certainly had no desire to go back to the embassy and pick it up in person. I felt just as Cindy had on that point.

In the past few years I had crossed some treacherous bridges. I had left the United States before the final judgment in the lawsuit to regain my citizenship. I had taken a job with Air Force Intelligence, where I was constantly concerned about dismissal. And I had voluntarily walked into the tumult of the Korean War to earn the money to continue my education. But now these dangerous bridges were behind me. The Renunciation Act had at long last been declared null and void, I had gotten back my documentation as an American citizen, and I had demonstrated the injustice of my discharge from Air Force Intelligence.

Now I was free to devote myself without distraction to the study of Buddhist philosophy at Tokyo University, the most prestigious university in Japan.

After three years of graduate work, I completed my master's degree and was accepted into the doctoral course at Tokyo University. At that point I received a letter from the Japanese Ministry of Education notifying me of my selection as a government-sponsored foreign student. As such I would receive a grant in support of my continued studies at Tokyo University. Perseverance *did* have its reward after all, it seemed. But I was aware that perseverance by itself would have been useless had I not had the support of my teachers. I was overjoyed to accept the fellowship, for up to that point I had been scraping by on scant resources.

I worked diligently at the university for eight years in all, my study of Buddhist philosophy nourishing mind and soul alike. The day when at last I submitted my doctoral dissertation, I recalled the words of the mother of that nisei youth with whom I had argued over the loyalty issue at Topaz.

"Minoru-san, you are still young. You are too idealistic," she had told me.

But the real and the ideal are two sides of the same coin. Without reality, there can be no ideal. Without the ideal, reality becomes hollow and meaningless. A painful reality had made me an idealist, had made me search for a realm beyond political loyalty and disloyalty.

That nisei soldier's mother had been correct on one point, though: "When this war is over, we'll see who was right," she had told me.

Well, now my war was finally over. I was now confident in the knowledge that there is indeed a realm beyond the narrow concept of loyalty versus disloyalty, a world without boundaries—the world of free intellectual inquiry. In that broad perspective, loyalty to any one nation state is peripheral. This point is crucial, for we have now mastered the technology to destroy humankind in ever greater numbers, more swiftly and efficiently than ever before. The existence of humanity itself will be threatened if we do not abandon such narrow thinking.

I recalled something else, something that the official of the Japanese American Citizens League had asked me doubtfully when I visited JACL headquarters in Washington, D.C., on my way to college in Arkansas: "You think they'd actually hire a Japanese American college professor? Who in America would want to study Asian philosophy anyway?"

I had crossed all those treacherous bridges in the past few years with the purpose of challenging this nisei's obsequious attitude toward Anglo culture. And now the new era I was anticipating had at last arrived: I had just been appointed assistant professor in the newly established Buddhist Studies Program at the University of Wisconsin-Madison. The creation of this new academic field at a prominent American university represented an effort to look at Asian culture from a new perspective.

Now I *will* be in a position to teach about the spiritual heritage of Asia, I thought. And to vindicate my own actions during the war. Finally, I have won the battle! But it never was a matter of justifying my actions to convince others I was right. The point was to justify my actions to myself. The battle I had won never was a battle against anyone else. It was always a battle within me.

A Buddhist scripture speaks of "the two rivers and the white path." This expression refers to the way humankind travels through life—along a narrow path that runs between a river of water and a river of fire, with a pack of bandits and wild beasts bearing down upon us from behind. The river of water symbolizes greed and hatred; the river of fire symbolizes anger and envy; and the gang of bandits and beasts symbolizes the evil passions within us. We human beings must scurry swiftly along that narrow path without succumbing to either fire or water and without being overtaken by that wild pack pursuing us from behind.

I reflected on the pain I had experienced along the path I had traveled. For eighteen years—ever since I refused to affirm my loyalty to the U.S. government at Topaz—I had been fighting a battle. When I was humiliated and degraded by the FBI interrogator's treatment of me, I was so filled with rage and hatred that I would gladly have killed the man then and there, regardless of the consequences for my future. When I saw other nisei young people being released from the camps to continue their education, I was so envious that the pain I felt was almost like being physically knifed in the back. When I dragged myself to the administration office at Tule Lake to beg for their help, I was cursed and shot at by the guards, and back in the camp I was attacked and beaten by violent pro-Japan thugs. I resolved then that I would never forget my anger. In Tokyo, when the official at the U.S. Embassy grabbed my passport and the guards threw me out the front door for trying to get it back, I was infuriated. But now at last the hatred, the jealousy, the resentment, and the fury were all behind me.

I would not, however, forget the compassion that so many individuals had shown to me as I traveled along the narrow white path of my life. It seemed there had been Christians helping me ever since I was a young boy. In San Francisco when I had been so lost, so naive about life, it was the wise and gentle Mrs. Sano who gave me a dream to hold onto. Her voice still echoed in my mind, saying, "Minoru-san, we must do what we can for the world, for other people." And at Tule Lake, when I had reached the very end of my

rope, it was Tom and Miss Allan and the McCartneys who comforted me and renewed my hope and courage. I would always
remember their friendship and admire these pacifist Christians who
so courageously challenged the power of the state and worked
unstintingly for the oppressed, with no thought of accumulating the
goods of this world for themselves.

There were others, too. That I had ever been able to escape
from the hell of Tule Lake was due to the efforts of Dr. Marvin
Opler and attorney Wayne Collins. My encounter with these men
of high principle had made me keenly aware of the sense of justice
that ideally *does* exist in a democratic society.

The faculty and students at the College of the Ozarks had
welcomed me warmly and opened to me new worlds of the mind and
heart. And my professors at Tokyo University exposed me to the
strict scholarly discipline that enabled me to explore new realms of
knowledge and, in the end, to vindicate my actions during the war.

Still, that narrow white path stretches on ahead without
end. Life is forever a matter of rushing along that path pursued by
the pack of thieves and wild beasts that dwells within oneself.

Before returning to the United States, at my mother's direction
and equipped with an envelope of money she had sent for the purpose, I went to visit the graves of my grandparents at Bodaiji, the
Buddhist temple near Hiratsuka with which my family had always
been affiliated.

The current priest in charge of the temple was the grandson
of the old Rinzai priest whom I remembered from my boyhood. I
could still envision that old clergyman as he went about his duties,
his figure bent over the handle of the baby carriage that he pushed
along for support. As often as not, he would go off and forget the
offering envelope Grandmother had prepared for him. But this
young priest, his grandson, did not hesitate a moment to accept the
money I offered him.

What's more, he pulled himself up importantly and
announced: "Since a family living in America cannot very well look
after its own graves, the temple is obliged to perform that service for

you. For this purpose we will require one million yen. Otherwise, your ancestors will become *muenbotoke* (lost souls), unable to attain salvation. And you know of course that families who allow their ancestors to become *muenbotoke* will only accumulate bad karma for themselves."

I informed that greedy priest on the spot that if that were the case he could just go ahead and let my ancestors become *muenbotoke*.

Ironically, history records that the Buddha Sakyamuni, before departing this life, admonished his disciples, saying: "Leave the world's rites for the dead to the *brahmins* to perform. Buddhist monks should preach the *dharma* to living human beings." If Sakyamuni is watching this temple from the far shore of nirvana, he must be sorely disappointed, I thought. And the old priest must be turning over in his grave in rage at his grandson's behavior.

Karma means impulsive action. It is not a curse. There are no curses in Buddhism. Karma is one of the central themes of all major religions and all great literatures of the world. Life is predestined inasmuch as it is shaped by karma, but karma is also shaped by the individual—a relationship that creates an existential paradox. Hence, the Buddhist conceives of life, shaped by karma to be sure, as a challenge.

Grandfather and Grandmother had both passed on by this time. Grandfather died first. One day after his death, when Grandmother was still living, I took her to visit the cemetery. When we came to the family tomb, Grandmother turned around, rolled up her long red under-kimono, and paid her respects to Grandfather by showing her bare buttocks to the grave. It was a truly comic scene. But she was dead serious. This was the only way she had left to express her deep-seated resentment toward her husband. Women are surely tough—it almost seemed as though Grandmother had outlived her husband just so that she could give him this final insult.

Still, I found it difficult to blame Grandfather. He certainly had not had an easy time, caught between two women as he was for a good part of his life. No doubt the course of his own past life—the concatenation of all his own actions—resulted in his complicated situation. But as impulsive as his life had been, as misguided as he was, he never criticized others while he lived and it seemed that he had died a satisfied man.

Åbout two months before I was to return to the United States, I was surprised to receive a letter from Nancy.

> Congratulations, Min! I just read in the campus
> newspaper that you're going to start teaching here at UW
> starting next semester. I finished my degree last year at
> Berkeley and now I'm doing research in the medical
> school here, working day and night in the lab. Can you
> believe it's been ten years since that time you took me out
> to dinner in Chinatown? There's so much I want to
> discuss with you. Remember, it's my turn to treat you this
> time. I'm very much looking forward to your arrival.

I had not thought about Nancy for a long time, but the vivid memories came crowding back—Nancy's cheerful, dimpled smile, the time I had snubbed and angered her at Tanforan, her hard work in Dr. Opler's research center at Tule Lake, our pleasant walks home from work, the emotion-charged night on the train to Sacramento after we were liberated, the pleasure of that embrace on the ferry in San Francisco Bay, her delighted smile at the view from the revolving bar atop the Mark Hopkins, the confidence with which she had described her ambitions over dinner in Chinatown.

Nancy had also been studying for the last ten years to earn her degree. She was a hard worker. We shared the same history of persecution in America during the war, and she had reacted to that persecution much as I had, by taking it as a motivation to seek a new world. There was no doubt that we would have much to talk about. Nancy always said whatever came into her head, but she was positive, upbeat, and never harbored a bit of ill will toward others.

Nancy's note was followed within weeks by another unexpected epistle from the States—this time from Anne's husband Bob. He was coming alone to Tokyo and had something he wanted to discuss with me. I met him at the Imperial Hotel soon after his arrival.

"Min, how are you doing? It's been ages. I'm living in Los Angeles now, you know—I've set up a new business there, exporting southern cotton to Japan. It's going extremely well, and I want to ask your help. You see, there's a real future in trade with Japan right now, so I'm planning to set up an office in Tokyo. Since you know Japan so well, I want you to be the manager. Just name your salary," he said.

"Bob, I'm no businessman. Besides, I just handed in my dissertation and I'm waiting to hear if it's been accepted. I already have a job lined up back in the States. I'm sorry, but I really can't help you," I told him.

"Well, how about coming in as a partner? Half the profits are yours. You can't say no to that, can you?" he insisted.

"Are you crazy? You know I don't have any money to put into a business. Besides, I told you, I'm just not a businessman!" I repeated.

"I'm not asking you to put any money into it—I need you, Min. The business is growing fast and it's more than I can handle all by myself. I really need someone who can speak both Japanese and English, someone I can count on. You won't make any kind of money as an academic. You know that."

"It's not a matter of money, Bob. I'm telling you I'm just not cut out for business. Give it up, would you? I'm not interested in your offer," I said again.

Bob looked dejected.

"I guess Anne knows you better than I do. She said it was no use asking. She swore you'd never agree to be a partner in this business," he said.

"How *is* Anne?" I asked.

For a moment Bob seemed to be at a loss for words, but then he started speaking again, more slowly this time, his voice subdued.

"You know, I bought a big house for Anne. It had a huge yard and a swimming pool. I even hired a maid for her. I've given her a good life, Min. But listen to this, would you? One time when I took her up to San Francisco, I wanted to show her Chinatown. But she refused to go. Do you know why?" he asked.

I could guess what was coming next.

"She said, 'Min promised *he'd* take me to Chinatown someday.'"

Bob suddenly burst out in loud, boisterous laughter. It was a scornful laugh but revealed his own hurt at being scorned.

"A few years ago I was planning to bring Anne with me on a trip to Japan. I had some business negotiations to take care of, which I thought we could combine with a pleasure trip. She wouldn't hear of that either. I told her we'd look you up, but she told me you'd never agree to see us. Is that true?" he asked.

I evaded that one.

"Things are going okay with you two, aren't they?" I asked.

"Well, actually, that's the other reason I wanted to talk to you, Min. Anne seems very lonely. She's always talking about you. Do you still love her?"

"Bob, don't ask me a thing like that. Anne is your wife. You're a successful businessman—you should have more confidence in yourself," I told him.

"Actually, Min, when I get back to L.A., Anne won't be there. She did three years of graduate work at UCLA and now she's going off to France to study for a couple more years. She told me she just wanted to get away from the States for a while, but I know it was really me she wanted to get away from. You probably didn't know all this. Anne says she doesn't write to you because it would distract you from your studies and you wouldn't appreciate that. But let me tell you the truth of the matter," he said.

Bob bit his lip, paused, and went on in a quiet voice, "She's convinced that you hate her for marrying me. She's afraid to write to you. It's ridiculous. She just doesn't understand a man's feelings. Not that I understand hers! But I do know this—Anne is waiting for you to come back. If you let her know you're returning to the States, she'll come flying home from Europe in a minute. I just wanted to tell you that for her sake—maybe for your sake, too."

Bob may not be much of a thinker, but he is a good-hearted guy, I thought.

He had more to say. "This goes back a ways, but do you remember giving Anne a compact when she graduated from college? Well, she still carries that darn thing around with her everywhere she goes. Min, I've pretty much given up on our marriage. I guess my business is more important to me anyway."

I had a sense that I could understand how Anne had grown away from this man. She had been an honor student in college—she was much more of an intellectual than Bob. She was fluent in French, and the night I had seen her in Washington she told me she wanted to do research on the nineteenth-century French romantic author Chateaubriand. Somehow romantic literature fit Anne's personality. She always had been a dreamer who valued creative expression, a literary spirit who rebelled against modern rationalism. Like me, she just wasn't cut out for the business world. And she wasn't the sort of woman who would jump for joy at a swimming pool, a big house, and a maid. Bob would probably never have an appreciation for her literary interests. He just didn't have those kinds of sensibilities.

I felt for Anne. She was a woman who would bear her pain without ever speaking of it to anyone else. At the same time she was acutely sensitive to other people's feelings. And I had never done a thing but make her life more difficult. It seemed as though every time I saw her, I had to apologize for something, and she always forgave me without a murmur. As Bob talked, I couldn't help but recall the evening I had spent with Anne in Washington, D.C., more than ten years ago now.

Bob stayed a week in Japan, and then, in fine fettle, he reported that all had gone well in the negotiations with his Japanese business contacts and that he was returning to Los Angeles. I went to the airport to see him off. Bob climbed the steps jauntily and, waving like a boy in high spirits, disappeared into the airplane.

Not long after that, I returned to Haneda Airport for my own departure from Japan.

"Minoru, I know you'll do your best."

How I treasured those parting words of encouragement from Professor Yuki Reimon. He had been my teacher in Buddhist philosophy at Tokyo University as well as the kendō master under whom I continued my training in Tokyo. I was humbled that he had come out to the airport on a chilly winter's night to see me off on my journey back to the United States. There is a term in Japanese— *onshi*—a teacher and mentor to whom one is so deeply indebted that repayment is altogether impossible. This single word carries the fragrance of thousands of years of Asian culture and conveys the quality of human compassion that finally enabled me, the rebellious kibei, to prevail in the bitter struggle that raged within me for eighteen long years. Scholarship that is devoid of this quality of compassion is hollow indeed.

The sparkling lights of the Tokyo night bade me farewell as the plane lifted into the sky and turned eastward to cross the Pacific Ocean.

It was January 1962.

Reflections

I would like to acknowledge with deep gratitude those people who did so much to enable me to overcome the confusion of my youth and the desperation and bitterness of the internment years, those who offered their friendship and guidance: Mrs. Sano, the young Christian teacher of Japanese literature in San Francisco's Japan Town, who gave me a dream to hold onto as I struggled with questions of my identity; the Christian pacifists at Tule Lake, who showed me another dimension in life, one that transcends issues of political loyalty; Dr. Marvin K. Opler and attorney Wayne M. Collins, whose championship of the oppressed restored my faith in the American system of justice and fair play; the students and faculty members at the College of the Ozarks, who helped to heal the wounds of mental anguish from my four years of incarceration; and Professor Yuki Reimon of Tokyo University, whose scholarly and personal guidance enabled me to achieve a kind of rebirth during my period of graduate study in Japan.

I do not know what happened to Mrs. Sano after the war began, but I am confident that whatever circumstances she faced she continued to live a full life, exhibiting compassion toward all humankind. Among that small community of pacifists who worked in the Tule Lake Segregation Center, Tom Grubbs studied Japanese at UC Berkeley after the war, then went to Japan as a missionary. Following his return to California he worked among Japanese Americans for a time and later among African

Americans. He is now retired and living in San Mateo, California, where he continues his efforts on behalf of the disadvantaged. Miss Thomasine Allan returned to Japan after the war, to the place she considered home, a small fishing village in Iwate Prefecture. She has since passed on, but I hear from a colleague that a women's college has been named in Miss Allan's honor in her Japanese hometown. Miss Allan not only taught the Christian gospel as a missionary but had a deep commitment to improving education, particularly the education of women in Japan. The McCartneys also went to Japan after the war, to Kyūshū, teaching English in secondary schools and the Bible in their home. Eventually they returned to their native Minnesota, where Mrs. McCartney passed away. She had received a master's degree in English from Columbia University and was a prolific writer, leaving behind a number of books, including *In the Gray Rain* (1955), a story of women in postwar Japan overcoming severe economic hardships to face life again with hope and expectation. Mrs. McCartney, like Miss Allan, loved the Japanese people and dedicated her life to them. Mr. McCartney also passed away in St. Paul in early 1995. I do not know what became of Ruthevelyn Pim or Miss Murphy after the war; I would assume, though, that they too continued to live meaningful lives.

Opler and Collins have passed on, Opler leaving behind works in psychological anthropology that command the respect of scholars, and Collins endowing a legacy that has had considerable impact upon civil liberties in this country. Professor Yuki, my mentor at Tokyo University, enjoyed a quiet retirement in central Japan, reading books on Buddhist history and philosophy. He passed away in 1992.

I was extremely fortunate to encounter so many individuals of high principle, people of tolerance, understanding, and a vision that transcends national and ethnic boundaries. These human values—as exemplified by the people named here—had a great influence upon my life. They instilled in me the notion that Americanization—the goal of most Japanese Americans—does not mean conforming or submitting to the norms of the dominant

Anglo culture, but rather entails stimulating and developing this country's culture by introducing to it an "alien" tradition.

I was not alone, of course, in experiencing the tragedy of the Pacific War and the internment. Other Japanese Americans faced this same situation and responded differently. The reaction of many of them was to affirm their loyalty to the U.S. government and to strive to enhance the social status of Japanese Americans as a group. Although the experiences of these men and women are not the subject of this book, I would be remiss to highlight my situation alone while ignoring their accomplishments.

The central issue in any case is *not* whether one pledged unconditional loyalty to the United States government while in the internment camps or even whether the decision one made then was the right one. For at times of tremendous confusion and uncertainty such a judgment is meaningless. Whether one made a commitment to the government's cause and defended it from its enemies or instead challenged that government for its injustices and in consequence was consigned to the segregation center, the crucial issue was one of personal integrity. Circumstances forced me to choose the second alternative. But in all fairness, the validity of the other option needs to be acknowledged. For this reason, I would like to touch briefly upon the self-sacrificing accomplishments of the nisei soldiers in World War II and to reflect on this society's treatment of these loyal Americans and their conscientious, hardworking issei parents.

Early in 1943, shortly before the loyalty/disloyalty discussion began in the internment camps, the War Department announced plans to form an all-nisei combat team. Two army units comprised entirely of nisei enlisted men were subsequently formed—the 100th Infantry Battalion from Hawaii and later the 442nd Regimental Combat Team (with which the 100th merged in 1944). Most nisei troops were trained at Mississippi's dilapidated Camp Shelby and Wisconsin's Camp McCoy, while those who could speak any Japanese trained for intelligence work at Minnesota's Camp Savage before assignment to the Pacific front. In Europe, the nisei army units were deployed first to North Africa and Italy and then to the French front, where the Axis powers had drawn a strong line of defense. The nisei units succeeded without exception in liberating every region they were ordered into in the European theater. Especially noteworthy is the record of the 442nd on the French front. In the episode of the "Lost Battalion," they extricated over two hundred Texans of the 36th Division, who were surrounded by German troops in the Vosges Mountains. With fierce fighting, the nisei of the 442nd managed to break through the enemy's encirclement to free their compatriots, but only at great cost to themselves. The destruction of regimental records by enemy fire and the necessity for constant reinforcements make the figures difficult to determine, but it is said that the rescuers of those two hundred and some Texans sustained eight hundred casualties.

The nisei units garnered more medals than any other combat units of comparable size in the U.S. Army during World War II (more than eighteen thousand individual decorations and seven Presidential Distinguished Unit Citations), and they sustained large numbers of casualties. Ironically, the medals earned by nisei soldiers who gave their lives in the war were often presented to their issei parents in concentration camps back home, where the parents were being held prisoner by the United States government.

What made the nisei fight so fiercely and with so much sacrifice? Treatises written since the war have sometimes attributed this phenomenon to the soldiers' "samurai spirit"—a romantic notion that reveals a total lack of understanding of Japanese Americans. One overpowering motive drove these young men to fight and gamble with death on the battlefields of World War II: their desire to prove to the American public that they were loyal Americans. This common goal created a powerful bond of solidarity within the nisei units. The "Go for broke!" motto of Japanese American soldiers from Hawaii expressed the fierce determination that characterized all nisei soldiers during the war.

When survivors of the nisei army units returned victorious to the United States, they marched proudly down the broad avenues of the nation's capital, greeted by the president, his cabinet, and members of Congress and hailed by people from all walks of life who lined the streets of Washington. The tears glistening on those soldiers' faces as they paraded before their fellow Americans were by no means the tears of Japanese samurai. These were the tears of American soldiers who were relieved to be recognized at last as true Americans by their fellow citizens.

But even the sacrifices made by these nisei soldiers did not immediately improve the situation on the home front. Indeed, while nisei regiments were performing heroic deeds on the battlefields, and even after their triumphal return, bias against Japanese Americans continued to flourish in American society. Chester Gannon, a California state legislator from Sacramento, for example, was in the forefront of an effort to prevent Japanese Americans from ever returning to the state of California. When someone sent him a newspaper clipping regarding three Sacramento area nisei who had been killed on the front lines in Italy, Gannon returned the article to its sender with the words "Glory! Hallelujah! Hallelujah! Hallelujah!" penciled in the margin.

Certainly the tears shed by government officials who welcomed the gallant nisei troops home from the front were about as genuine as the proverbial crocodile tears, as was made vividly clear by the actions and attitudes of these same politicians and bureaucrats throughout the war. Most seemed unable or unwilling to recognize that the majority of the people they had interned in concentration camps were without question citizens of the United States by birth. Indeed, these officials assiduously avoided using the word *citizen* in referring to Japanese Americans. FBI chief J. Edgar Hoover, for instance, called the nisei "non-alien Japanese," while Dillon S. Myer, national director of the WRA, termed them "American-born Japanese."

Regardless of the official celebrations in their honor and the numerous military decorations on their uniforms, the nisei veterans returned to a racist society. Racial prejudice is not, of course, suddenly erased by members of a minority enlisting in the armed forces and fighting for their country. Daniel Inouye, who later became a

United States senator from Hawaii, was one of the courageous young soldiers of the 442nd. He survived the war but lost an arm in combat. En route home to Hawaii immediately after the war ended, and still wearing his army uniform, he walked into a West Coast barbershop to get a haircut—only to be met with the proprietor's curt statement: "We don't serve Japs here."

One veteran of the 442nd was blocked from buying a home in Texas when the neighbors voiced objections. However, after he made this incident known to local newspapers, many people rallied to his cause—particularly members of the Texas unit that had been rescued by the 442nd—and ultimately the man was able to purchase the house. At least this Japanese American soldier received a concrete reward for risking his life for his countrymen. Later, Texas recognized members of the 442nd as honorary citizens of that state. It is cause for celebration that there were at least some Americans of good sense even in those biased times.

Most repugnant of all the racist sentiments expressed in that period were the violent words uttered in the U.S. Congress by Representative Jed Johnson of Oklahoma. He demanded the sterilization of all Japanese Americans who were imprisoned in the concentration camps. This was no official of Nazi Germany speaking. He was a member of the Congress of the United States, an elected official of a democratic nation.

Even twenty-five years after the war ended, former WRA chief Myer showed not the slightest indication of regret at the government's wartime treatment of Japanese Americans. Indeed, he went so far as to write with great pride of his own actions as head of the WRA. According to Myer, many of the internees "never had it so good."* How insulting! Whatever their economic situation, Japanese Americans—issei and nisei alike—were leading meaningful and productive lives before the war. They devoted themselves to their work and their studies, knowing full well that only their own

---

* Dillon S. Myer, *Uprooted Americans: The Japanese Americans and the War Relocation Authority During World War II* (Tucson: University of Arizona Press, 1971), 291–292.

unrelenting efforts would bring them any approximation of social equality in this country. Despite the adverse conditions in which they lived and labored, the Japanese American community produced virtually no criminals, for they considered it shameful to break the law. And elderly issei consistently refused government assistance or welfare, no matter how desperate their situation, for they regarded dependence on government aid a personal disgrace.

Myer's implication that Japanese Americans welcomed the easy life of his WRA camps is an insult to the personal dignity of every Japanese American, and such a statement only emphasizes the WRA chief's own ignorance of the people whose lives he controlled during World War II. The very existence of concentration camps for Japanese Americans constituted an officially sanctioned violation of civil rights, but it was a double tragedy that the administrator of the entire undertaking was incompetent. Myer was entirely uninformed about the history of hardworking Japanese Americans. He had no understanding of their aspirations and no appreciation of their strong sense of morality. No Japanese American, not even the most ingratiating nisei, would have agreed with him that the Japanese Americans "never had it so good" as in the internment camps.

The Japanese American Citizens League, moreover, did nothing but play into the hands of these same biased, ignorant bureaucrats and politicians. For example, soon after the beginning of the war, one JACL officer urged other nisei to serve as informants to the government, reporting any "anti-American" activities of their issei parents. Another officer declared with no apparent sense of shame that "nisei should leave their issei parents as hostages in the hands of the U.S. government, and form a suicide squad to fight the Japanese Army."* In their rush to accommodate the currents of the time, these JACL leaders would abandon even the traditional Japanese virtue of filial piety in order to prove their loyalty to the

---

* Cited in Richard Drinnon, *Keeper of Concentration Camps: Dillon S. Myer and American Racism* (Berkeley: University of California Press, 1987), 67.

United States. Ingratiating human beings possess no sense of independence. People without a sense of independence will exploit even their own parents. People who are willing to exploit their parents have no integrity whatsoever.

The officers of the JACL euphorically trumpeted the accomplishments of nisei soldiers as they continued their efforts to curry favor with the establishment. But with the end of the war, the organization's impact, even on the promotion of civil liberties for Japanese Americans, diminished. Although the long-delayed rights of naturalization and property ownership were finally granted to the issei in the mid-1950s, this had become possible primarily because times had changed. Having played a major role in ending the war, the United States was forced to assume global responsibility and world leadership and, as a result, began to develop a more cosmopolitan attitude among its citizens and a more progressive social consciousness. These historical forces made possible the granting of civil liberties to Japanese Americans in the 1950s.

But by that point in time, what could it possibly have meant to elderly issei men and women in their seventies and eighties—after all they had suffered before and during the war—to stand before a judge and the American flag, solemnly placing their hands over their hearts and swearing to defend and uphold the Constitution of the United States? Should they feel pleased and honored? Allowing the issei to take American citizenship at that late date had meaning merely as a symbol that America had finally, belatedly, agreed to extend the most basic of civil rights and to grant U.S. citizenship even to racially different Asian immigrants—the very same privileges it had always extended to white immigrants from European countries.

Very few issei applied for citizenship when they were at long last allowed to become naturalized in the 1950s. The question for them was whether or not they could ever develop a physical and spiritual sense of belonging to this society. It is doubtful that the mere granting of citizenship could ever engender that sense of belonging in people who had suffered so much persecution at the hands of American society. It is true that to feel a sense of belonging requires an effort on the part of the individual, but if not acknowledged and accepted by the surrounding social milieu, that effort is futile. When these issei were younger, such a receptive environment simply did not exist in the United States.

The ownership of property can give people a material sense of belonging to a society, but when the issei were forcibly removed from their West Coast homes and imprisoned in 1942, most of them lost whatever possessions they had been able, with difficulty, to accumulate in the years before the war. This property was never restored to them, nor did they receive any comprehensive reimbursement for it. Thus, in a sense the war never ended for the issei. The Civil Liberties Act of 1988 did mandate $20,000 in restitution to be paid to each Japanese American incarcerated in the relocation centers during World War II. But by 1988, most surviving members of the first generation were spending their days in nursing homes with little but death before them. In any case, $20,000 could not begin to replace the property and opportunities that were taken from the older generation almost five decades earlier. The majority of these people had set out for America in their youth full of hope and a determination to succeed that inspired them to work tirelessly year in and year out at the sacrifice of every personal luxury. Then the war came, and the internment, and all their hopes and aspirations were extinguished.

But the younger generations of Japanese Americans, the children, grandchildren, and great-grandchildren of these issei—who inherited from their elders the virtues of hard work and thrift and a sense of shame associated with any violation of the law—constitute one of the most successful ethnic minorities in the United States today. Many are proud of their ethnic heritage and, because they are, they have become successful Americans.

This fact should be weighed seriously in light of a remarkable statement made in 1942 by Earl Warren (then attorney general of California and later governor of California and chief justice of the United States Supreme Court), not long after the promulgation of the Japanese American exclusion order: "We believe that when we are dealing with the Caucasian race, we have methods that will test the loyalty of them. . . . But when we deal with the Japanese, we are in an entirely different field and we cannot form any opinion that we believe to be sound."* In essence, Warren was declaring that an entirely different standard of judgment is required when dealing with people of Japanese ancestry. If nothing else, the internment experience should have demonstrated clearly that a standard of judgment that is not universal inevitably results in bias and injustice.

---

* As quoted in Richard Drinnon, *Keeper of Concentration Camps: Dillon S. Myer and American Racism* (Berkeley: University of California Press, 1987), 32.

Afterword

Forty-three years after the end of World War II, the United States Congress passed the Civil Liberties Act of 1988 (Public Law No. 100–383), which acknowledged that the wholesale incarceration of West Coast Japanese Americans in 1942 was an unconstitutional violation of their fundamental human rights.

The legislation contained an apology from the United States government to Japanese American internees and a commitment to institute educational measures designed to ensure that this country would never again take such illegal actions against its own citizens. The 1988 law further stipulated that restitution in the amount of $20,000 was to be paid to each Japanese American detained in the World War II "relocation centers." Needless to say, $20,000 did not begin to compensate for the businesses, personal assets, and opportunities lost by Japanese Americans when they were hastily rounded up and locked behind barbed wire fences in the spring of 1942. Nor could this sum ever repay them for the pain and indignity of being treated like criminals simply because of race and ethnic origin. Nonetheless, it was important, even at that late date, to receive the U.S. government's acknowledgment of its mistake.

I have chosen to write here of my personal experiences as a Japanese American who was interned while a teenager, because although documentary studies can relate the facts of the event, they can never adequately convey the frustration and anxiety, the fear and uncertainty, the hope and aspirations of an individual who is subjected to government-sponsored harassment and injustice.

My hope is that this book demonstrates how extreme and unreasonable government demands designed to ensure the absolute and unquestioning loyalty of citizens causes tremendous anguish and suffering for many people. In every nation, the individual is vulnerable to the power of the state, and any government—democratic or otherwise—that would abrogate the human rights of its own citizens is guilty of oppression.

I have taken some liberty with the details of my story, selecting and extracting events in which I participated. I have used fictional names to protect the privacy of certain individuals, but those whose privacy would not be violated are identifiable in real life.

Appendix

Government Files

In 1987 I obtained through the Freedom of Information Act the files that were kept on me by the Department of Justice (including the FBI) and other government agencies during and after World War II. Below are some excerpts from those files that I found particularly interesting, along with my comments.

The FBI interrogation at Topaz: A document states that: "Provost Marshal's memorandum notes FBI report, June 23, 1943, that subject preferred to be repatriated and live in Japan, refused to serve in the U.S. Army and to forswear allegiance to the Japanese emperor." Perhaps I did say such things in the heat of the moment. But if I did, it was in response to the FBI agent's provoking interrogation. Looking back, had it not been for this FBI interrogation, I would gladly have served in the U.S. military. But this is pure speculation. The fact remains that this encounter with the FBI agent decisively shaped the course of the life I was to lead for the next eighteen years.

The nisei meeting in Topaz about registration: According to the Provost Marshal's memorandum, I spoke "at a block meeting opposing registration [that is, completing the WRA questionnaire that contained the loyalty question]." This bit of information is interesting, and I'm curious who reported it. I did speak at the meeting, but I do not recall opposing registration. I did in fact register.

My release from Tule Lake in March 1946: I am grateful to those whose letters were instrumental in effecting my release: Gordon K. Chapman, executive secretary of the Board of National Mission; Haruo Ishimaru, then a graduate student at the University of Chicago, who once worked for the National Council of the YM-YWCA and National Japanese American Student Relocation Council; Dave Tatsuno, my YMCA leader in San Francisco when I was a youngster; and, of course, the members of the Tule Lake Union Church—Thomasine Allan, Lillian Bristow, Tom Grubbs, Mr. and Mrs. McCartney, Ruthevelyn Pim ("Pimmy"), and others.

I discovered one unexpected letter in the Department of Justice file, a letter from the principal of Lowell High School in San Francisco, upon which the Justice Department comments:

> . . . a letter from a high school principal in San Francisco
> commends subject highly personally. But the writer, a
> veteran of the First World War, expresses extreme bitterness
> at all Japanese, indicating he never wants to see another
> one in California. Another letter from this principal
> indicates that he thinks subject is an exceptional case.

Of all my letters of recommendation, this perhaps was the most effective.

By this time Justice Department officials seem to have taken a more sympathetic attitude toward me. The file says, "Subject is of high character. He has never belonged to any camp organization. Dr. Opler appeared as a witness for him"; "The record indicates that this Japanese is unusually intelligent"; and so on. These statements might seem to contradict the actions I took at the time—conduct that might appear irrational. In this respect, it is important to take into account that in an atmosphere tense with violence, fear, and uncertainty, one's reasoning powers are curbed and one reacts in strange, unexpected ways.

I do not remember precisely what I said to the official conducting the renunciation procedure, but I was interested to note the following comment penciled in on the form the official handled: "He's an idealist." I have been called that by many people on many occasions. Actually, I do not know what the term means, because my view is that sheer realism is idealism and vice versa.

Finally, the file says, "Subject had a fight with Hōshi Dan member because he was not sympathetic with their views." I wonder how the administration obtained this information. It is frightening to speculate.

Aside from the record of the FBI interview—a record whose accuracy I doubt—there is nothing in the Department of Justice file to suggest that I ever posed a threat to the internal security of the United States of America.

My dismissal from Air Force Intelligence: This issue was clarified for me when I obtained my U. S. Air Force file. According to those documents, the USAF headquarters in Washington, D.C., already knew of the ongoing litigation regarding the restoration of citizenship but was reluctant to inform its Tokyo office about this. Hence, when the Tokyo office strongly requested a security decision in my case, headquarters simply informed it of my refusal to answer the loyalty question satisfactorily and my renunciation of citizenship in the camp. Headquarters neither supplied the Tokyo office with details of the continuing litigation nor instructed it to put me on hold until litigation was resolved. I doubt very much, however, that it would have made any difference even had headquarters supplied the Tokyo office with more detail.

My resignation from the USAF Intelligence position after reinstatement: It was fortunate for all concerned that I resigned from my post in the air force when I did, for Colonel Cook—notwithstanding the fact that I had been legally cleared and had the right to return to my former position—was assiduously making plans to fire me. According to a document in the USAF file, Colonel Cook forwarded the following memo to the chief, DAFC (Department of Air Force Civilian) Division, Central Civilian Personnel Office:

> 1. This headquarters desires to process (subject) as
> a security risk under the provisions of AFR 40–12.
> An SF 52 is attached requesting that you prepare the

correspondence necessary to suspend (subject) under
provisions of paragraph 16f, AFR 40–12.

2. In our conversations yesterday it was assumed
that (subject) would be returned to duty, and then
resuspended. There is a question that would the return to
duty clear him completely of the charges of falsification
now against him. If so, perhaps he should not be returned
to duty, but concurrently and independently suspended
under AFR 40–12.

Interestingly, the reply from the personnel office, handwrit-
ten in red over the cover letter forwarded from Cook's office, states,
"No Action." Sometimes the law works surprisingly in one's favor.

Civilian Exclusion Order No. 5

WESTERN DEFENSE COMMAND AND FOURTH ARMY
WARTIME CIVIL CONTROL ADMINISTRATION

Presidio of San Francisco, California
April 1, 1942

INSTRUCTIONS
TO ALL PERSONS OF
JAPANESE
ANCESTRY

LIVING IN THE FOLLOWING AREA:

All that portion of the City and County of San Francisco, State of California, lying generally west of the north-south line established by Junipero Serra Boulevard, Worchester Avenue, and Nineteenth Avenue, and lying generally north of the east-west line established by California Street, to the intersection of Market Street, and thence on Market Street to San Francisco Bay.

All Japanese persons, both alien and non-alien, will be evacuated from the above designated area by 12:00 o'clock noon, Tuesday, April 7, 1942.

No Japanese person will be permitted to enter or leave the above described area after 8:00 a.m., Thursday, April 2, 1942, without obtaining special permission from the Provost Marshal at the Civil Control Station located at:

1701 Van Ness Avenue
San Francisco, California

The Civil Control Station is equipped to assist the Japanese population affected by this evacuation in the following ways:

1. Give advice and instructions on the evacuation.

2. Provide services with respect to the management, leasing, sale, storage or other disposition of most kinds of property including: real estate, business and professional equipment, buildings, household goods, boats, automobiles, livestock, etc.

3. Provide temporary residence elsewhere for all Japanese in family groups.

4. Transport persons and a limited amount of clothing and equipment to their new residence, as specified below.

THE FOLLOWING INSTRUCTIONS MUST BE OBSERVED:

1.   A responsible member of each family, preferably the head of the family, or the person in whose name most of the property is held, and each individual living alone, will report to the Civil Control Station to receive further instructions. This must be done between 8:00 a.m. and 5:00 p.m., Thursday, April 2, 1942, or between 8:00 a.m. and 5:00 p.m., Friday, April 3, 1942.

2.   Evacuees must carry with them on departure for the Reception Center, the following property:
   (a)   Bedding and linens (no mattress) for each member of the family;
   (b)   Toilet articles for each member of the family;
   (c)   Extra clothing for each member of the family;
   (d)   Sufficient knives, forks, spoons, plates, bowls and cups for each member of the family;
   (e)   Essential personal effects for each member of the family.

All items carried will be securely packaged, tied and plainly marked with the name of the owner and numbered in accordance with instructions received at the Civil Control Station.

The size and number of packages is limited to that which can be carried by the individual or family group.

No contraband items as described in paragraph 6, Public Proclamation No. 3, Headquarters Western Defense Command and Fourth Army, dated March 24, 1942, will be carried.

3.   The United States Government through its agencies will provide for the storage at the sole risk of the owner of the more substantial household items, such as iceboxes, washing machines, pianos and other heavy furniture. Cooking utensils and other small items will be accepted if crated, packed and plainly marked with the name and address of the owner. Only one name and address will be used by a given family.

4.   Each family, and individual living alone, will be furnished transportation to the Reception Center. Private means of transportation will not be utilized. All instructions pertaining to the movement will be obtained at the Civil Control Station.

Go to the Civil Control Station at 1701 Van Ness Avenue, San Francisco, California, between 8:00 a.m. and 5:00 p.m., Thursday, April 2, 1942, or between 8:00 a.m. and 5:00 p.m., Friday, April 3, 1942, to receive further instructions.

J. L. DeWITT
Lieutenant General, U. S. Army
Commanding

THE WHITE HOUSE

WASHINGTON

A monetary sum and words alone cannot restore lost years or erase painful memories; neither can they fully convey our Nation's resolve to rectify injustice and to uphold the rights of individuals. We can never fully right the wrongs of the past. But we can take a clear stand for justice and recognize that serious injustices were done to Japanese Americans during World War II.

In enacting a law calling for restitution and offering a sincere apology, your fellow Americans have, in a very real sense, renewed their traditional commitment to the ideals of freedom, equality, and justice. You and your family have our best wishes for the future.

Sincerely,

[signature: George Bush]

Letter of apology from President George Bush, which Min received with his $20,000 restitution check as authorized by Public Law No. 100–383, passed by Congress in 1988.